The first sequel to the mini-series Kind Hearts and Martinets

introducing

The DaDa Detective Agency Book 1

Road Kill

The Duchess of Frisian Tun

Tread lightly, the darkness is but a breath away...

Pete Adams

An au courant, romantic comedy, crime thriller with scary bits.
A droll and saucy insight into the Middle Class, Haute Monde and, Geography...

Tales of a reclusive England with:
The Journalist, The Professor, The Synchronised Swimming Instructor, The Fish Wife, The Dame, The Actress (really Jack Austin), The Geography Teacher,
The Gossip Columnist, The Spy, The Police Inspector, The Man from the Council,
The Priest, The Knight, The Super-grass (deceased), The Gangster, and,
The Lady Blanche.

"Tectonic plates, fold mountains, earthquakes, volcanoes, hurricanes, tsunamis – it just doesn't

get much better than that, except for maybe ecosystems of the world or, globalisation. Weather and climate, now there's a thing, and then there is water and rivers."
Aedd Murphy speaking to 10 F, St Winifrede's, Roman Catholic School, Portsmouth, England.

AUTHOR BIOGRAPHY

Pete Adams - writing as, and narrated by, Susan Narmee

Pete Adams is an architect with a practice in Portsmouth, UK, and from there he has, over forty years, designed and built buildings across England and Wales. Pete took up writing after listening to a radio interview of the writer Michael Connolly whilst driving home from Leeds. A passionate reader, the notion of writing his own novel was compelling, but he had always been told you must have a *mind map* for the book; Jeez, he could never get that.

Et Voila, Connolly responding to a question, said he never can plan a book and starts with an idea for chapter one and looks forward to seeing where it would lead. Job done, and that evening Pete started writing and the series, Kind Hearts and Martinets, was on the starting blocks. That was some eight years ago and hardly a day has passed where Pete has not worked on his writing, and currently, is halfway through his eleventh book, has a growing number of short stories, one, critically acclaimed and published by Bloodhound, and has written and illustrated a series of historical nonsense stories called, Whopping Tales.

Pete describes himself as an inveterate daydreamer, and escapes into those dreams by writing crime thrillers with a thoughtful dash of social commentary. He has a writing style shaped by his formative years on an estate that re-housed London families after WWII, and his books have been likened to the writing of Tom Sharpe; his most cherished review, "made me laugh, made me cry, and made me think".

Pete lives in Southsea with his partner, and Charlie the star-struck Border terrier, the children having flown the coop, and has 3 beautiful granddaughters who will play with him so long as he promises not to be silly.

Pete Adams on Next Chapter website: https://www.nextchapter.pub/authors/pete-adams

ACKNOWLEDGMENTS

I would like to acknowledge the readers who have reviewed my books and messaged me with comments. I value these observations and they have contributed to the creation of the DaDa Detective Agency. I have written, now, three DaDa books with a fourth on the starting blocks.

I would also like to take this opportunity to thank my Publisher, Next Chapter and in particular, Miika Hannila who took the decision to publish in full the 5 book mini-series, Kind Hearts and Martinets and is now publishing my next four books; watch this space.

Also to A.J. Griffiths, an author I so admire and, if you have not read her, 'Skeletons in the Cupboard' series you are missing a real treat – I thank you for your recommendation of my books to Miika and your continuing support.

I dedicate this book and the sequel to Jackie Lederer and Rod Bacon – not just very good friends but philosophical comrades.

ADD – Copyright notes and paragraph on this is fictional etc...

BOOKS BY PETE ADAMS:

The Kind Hearts and Martinets Series:

Book 1 Cause and Effect – *Vice plagues the City*

Book 2 Irony in the Soul – *Nobody Listens like the Dying*

Book 3 A Barrow Boy's Cadenza – *In Dead Flat Major*

Book 4 Ghost and Ragman Roll – *Spectre or Spook*

Book 5 Merde and Mandarins – *Divine Breath*

The DaDa Detective Agency - Sequel series to Kind Hearts and Martinets:

Book 1 Road Kill – *The Duchess of Frisian Tun*

Book 2 Rite Judgement – *Heads roll - Corpses Dance*

Book 3 Wigs on the Green – *Blood Sport* – (*to be published*)

The Larkin's Barkin' – East End of London, gangster family, a saga:

Book 1 Black Rose – *A Midsummer Night's Chutzpah* - 1966

The Rhubarb Papers:

Book 1 Dead No More – *Rhubarb in the Mammon*

Author's Note:

The DaDa Detective Agency series is proposed as a cosy crime series with amusing notes:

Dadaism was an arts movement that flouted the conventional by producing works marked by incongruity.

The DaDa novels have an idiosyncratic narrative, the intention, to create a DNA spiral of real and surreal narratives, but there is a rational design with a significant and satisfying ending.

Merde and Mandarins, was the fifth and final book in the *Kind Hearts and Martinets* series. The narrative now takes off in two new series: The DaDa Detective Agency and, The Rhubarb Papers.

The two take diverse directions, albeit there are extensions and linking references back to the begetting series and, some of the former secondary characters take on a life of their own. Having said that, the central protagonists, Jack (Jane) Austin and his wife, Amanda, have become very popular, so they continue, starring (Jack insisted I say that) in DaDa.

Road Kill - *The Duchess of Frisian Tun* is a pivotal novel that takes as it driving force, characters and narrative threads conjured in the five books of the *Kind Hearts and Martinets* series. The concluding book, *Merde and Mandarins*, sees the central protagonists, DCI Jack (Jane) Austin and his wife, Detective Superintendent Amanda Bruce (now Austin), retire from the police and MI5 to establish the DaDa Detective Agency.

It is not necessary to have read the previous books as *Road Kill* stands alone as an opening novel that by degrees, introduces the DaDa Detective Agency series. However, the extension of the concluding narrative threads in Kind Hearts and Martinets are the basis for this story. So you may enjoy this and the subsequent books more if you read the originating series.

This novel is light hearted, in as much as it can be, dallying affectionately upon past dastardly deeds with lurid pleasure as real people step innocently into a quagmire of past death and conspiracy. The darkness is but a breath away.

The book is also written, loosely, in the form of a stage play and a tongue firmly in cheek, *Canterbury Tales*, where the pilgrims go nowhere. Various key players tell their stories, informing how the disparate, altruistic *Kind Hearts*, and the sociopathic *Martinets,* played their diversified roles and, how this is not the end. Far from it. The scene is set for the DaDa to impact on the world of deal and double deal, murder and conspiracy, which leads onto the sequel:

Rite Judgement – *Heads roll - Corpses Dance*

Which leads onto:

Wigs on the Green – *Blood Sport*

INTRODUCTION

Road Kill - The Duchess of Frisian Tun, commences with a flashback to the City of Portsmouth, UK, celebrations of the 70th Anniversary of D Day. It was on that day, death and destruction visited, not the beaches in Normandy, but a middle-class Portsmouth Street, Frisian Tun.

The story emerges with a short prologue and a countdown of three brief episodes:

Apocalypse-Idyll:

The Narrator.

The Banana Boys.

Jack and Amanda Austin – DaDa.

The *Play* is a Human Interest Story. An amusing prelude, followed by scenes of a divergent nature where main players tell their story, all the while the *Episodes* dramatically closing in on a final Act; a Machiavellian plot and, as the *play* gathers momentum and the *players act out on the stage of life*, not all is as it seems. There is a shocking ending, but as they say, that is life... or not.

PROLOGUE

APOCALYPSE-IDYLL

DEFINITION: APOCALYPSE – *A PROPHETIC revelation, especially concerning a cataclysm in which the forces of good triumph over the forces of evil.*

It is not, as many believe, a pottie, portable infants toilet that collapses if a fat ugly retired copper sits on it. This is serious and, actually happened, mainly because a fat ugly retired copper got hold of a bazooka. A bazooka used to be bubble gum but, in the wrong mouth, say for instance, a Malacopperism plagued, fat ugly retired copper, the results can be, were, and still are, devastating, fatal even.

Definition: Idyll – *A mental mechanism, operating consciously or unconsciously, in which a person or persons, or a Duchess, overestimates an admired attribute.*

This can be attributed to many British upper middle-class individuals who, in their innate ignorance and air of self-importance, perceive their manor to be better than the average chocolate box picture of an urban or suburban haven. Frisian Tun was such an idyll (prior to the apocalypse). It *was* an idealistic residential, *village* (said with a French accent) and has / had, a picturesque (said with an English accent) cosy appearance. Apart, that is, the house of a cockney barrow boy police inspector, who could not grasp the basics of gardening or decorous conversing. Nor could he comprehend why snooty people didn't laugh at his hilarious jokes? And, "to make an omelette you have to break several things, not just eggs". He would say, so you knew the destruction of an Idyll was not his fault.

Before and After – What follows is before, and then, afterwards, is after. Not afters, as that would be a dessert, say, apple crumble and custard. Suffice to say this is a scary story when you get to the after bits, especially if the custard has gone cold. You, the innocent reader, will be lured into a sense of a secure world of haute-monde and geography and, when you are least aware – Bam!

Warning – What was lovely, could turn ugly. Not Jack Jane Dick Austin, because he was already ugly. However, his wife, Mandy, Duck, Austin, well, she was lovely but, could turn ugly even when Dick had done absolutely nothing wrong, like say, blow up an idyll, kill some gangsters an shit...

The Narrator

'Der Day, 6th Ju... what?'

'Der Day? I think you mean D day, as in Dee?' a megaphone voice from out of the darkness.

'That's what I said Diddli?' ... thinks... 'So, it's not Der then?'

'No - Start again.'

Jack started again, 'Dee Day, 14th June 2014 and it is the 70th anniversary of Operation Lie-in, from the... what now?'

'Sea Lion.'

'Where?' a shared titter.

'It's Operation Sea Lion? Or was that the

planned German invasion of England?' another detached mumbled voice.

A megaphone shout – *'Start again!'*

'What?'

'Did you seriously not hear that?' Mandy asked.

'Hearing aids?'

'Hearing aids.'

'Start again?'

'Start again.'

'Dee Day, 6th June 2014 and it is the 70th anniversary of... what now?'

'We've looked it up and it's Operation Overlord.'

'Start again?'

'Start again.'

'Dee Day, 6th June 2014 and it was the 70th anniversary of Operation Overlord and my brother's birthday, he will be, what, fifty seven, now – shite!'

'What?'

'I forgot to send him a card.'

'Cut!'

'Cut what?'

'He means stop for the time being,' Mandy explained to her Dipstick.

'I could do with a girl grey. Monkey tea for you, sweet'art?' Sweet'art nodded yes, she liked his decision making abilities. 'We'll have a girl grey, no milk or poncy lemon and a monkey tea, please, no sugars – there you go; spit spot.' Pause. 'Nothing seems to be 'appening? Anyfing 'appening?'

'Let's go home. Get your hand off my bum.'

He took his hand off.

'I was joking, dinlo.'

He put it back. She liked the feel of his hands on her bum, although he was most definitely a Dinlo and, when he undressed her, he was like a kid unwrapping a Christmas present. Still, she loved the twerp.

'*Who said that?*'

'Me'

'*Can you do the narration – what's your name?*'

'Susan Narmee... I suppose. Yeah, I can.'

'*Right Sue – let's start again.*'

So Sue started, 'Dee Day, 6th June 2014 and it is the 70th anniversary of Operation Gaylord... what? Was that okay?'

'*Yeah – the editor can pick that bit up,*' resignation.

'It was not a particularly audacious start... what?'

'*Auspicious, it's auspicious – carry on.*'

'Don't you talk to me like that!'

'*Sorry.*'

'Carry on?'

'*Yeah.*'

'Do I detect a note of exasperation?'

'*Yeeeeeeah,*' a distinct sound of air expelling as if squeezed through the neck of a balloon.

'Exasperation, most certainly it was,' Ms Narmee replied, in the manner of Yodel.

'*Yodah!*'

'That's what I said diddli?'

Can you narrate in *italics* please?

Yes.

The Banana Boys.

The week running up to Friday's planned celebrations had been blessed with remarkable weather, or so people remarked. They also remarked upon a marked contrast to the days that ran up to the original D Day, which this Friday's celebrations were to mark. However, if the weather had anything to do with it, this Friday, the day of The *Dee* Day, the seventieth anniversary, would get only four out of ten, which, is not a very good mark.

A dense sea mist shrouded Southsea Common, an expansive grassed tract of land that fronted the ancient fortified seafront of Portsmouth in the UK. The lumps of World War

Two machinery, weapons, materiel and paraphernalia and, the tents accommodating Muppets, who spent their weekends playing toy soldiers in ill fitting *Dad's Army* uniforms, were lined up in a regimented military fashion. The exhibition had been regimentally laid out by Reginald Menthe, Portsmouth City Council's head of setting out lumps. He'd had a lot of experience with lumps. Reg's wife, Mrs Menthe, whom, in their more intimate moments he called "Sugar", was a lump, and in the fog, the result of Reg's regimentation of paraphernalia and, Mrs. Sugar one might add, was, well, grey lumps.

I imagine those who do not know Mrs Sugar Menthe have already conjured a picture, but if you are struggling, bring to mind the vintage saucy seaside picture postcards with the blushing, generously proportioned, battle axe woman. There, got it – well she was like that. If you haven't got it, never mind, because she's not in this book, even though this book, in parts, several actually, is certainly saucy.

Keef Bananas (not his real name as that was Keith) looked on and sighed to his number two, Dave Lillicrap. He was number two because his name was Dave Lillicrap, also known as Shitlegs. Rather apt, those with a modicum of astuteness thought, though he was in actual fact and in reality, really and truly, the second in command of this South London delinquent gang, who up until very recently had been on the Lamb.

This is not a pun on mint saucy, though one might be forgiven for thinking this. On the lamb is an Americanism that roughly translated means, on the run, or in criminal parlance, lying low, hiding from the filf as they had been very naughty boys – see the book: Merde and Mandarins.

Apart from his name, Shitlegs was an unremarkable man and truthfully, not ideal material for command and decision making, on this day of marking and remarking the letter *Dee*. Keef gave him the same mark as the weather, four out of ten, or D out of A to E, which for a second in command was not saying much about the rest of his chums. All things considered, giving this weather of dense fog four out of ten, when it was nigh on impossible to see your hand in front of your face, did not say much for the leader either, though we have to allow, considering it was the intention of Keef and his chums to purloin a Sherman tank, that the cloaking effect of the weather may have been considered a bonus by Mr Bananas.

'Oi, stop there...'

'*What?*'

'I'm not a chum.'

'*What?*'

'A chum. I'm not a chum. We are not chums. Keef may have a Duchess for an aunt but I'm not Uncle Josh.' And Shitlegs looked around and elicited support from his other, for want of a better word at the moment, *chums*, and they enjoined their second in command enthusiastically, as you would expect from *chums*, supporting another *chum*.

'*What are you then?*'

They gathered their heads and discussed a subject that had never arisen before and, after a short while settled on something other than the election of Shitlegs as unofficial spokesman; he was second in command thus his presumed right. Shitlegs turned, because this is what you do in stories, you turn. 'Cronies,' he said, turning back again. They looked at each other in turn, except for Keef who had his head in the mist in exasperation, coincidentally, and also coincidentally, he was tall, straight backed and slim and always held his head high, except when he was ducking. His aunt had told him he was aristocatty and he believed he was.

It was agreed. 'Yeah, we're cronies and Keef is aristo-fingy.'

'*Good, can we get on?*'

The cronies gathered their collective hideous, crony heads, which matched their hideous appearance and discussed the matter. They'd never been asked if they could carry on before, ordinarily by this time they would have been arrested and be on their way to a lovely warm police cell. They were on the lamb until quite recently, as they had only just escaped a capture at a local saw mill and later, a shoot-out beside a Dorset Cottage in the snow. So, you see, the mist was having some beneficial effect in occluding the reappearance of the Banana gang in Southsea, which is likely why Keef gave it four out of ten, this weather being particularly good if you were on the lamb, or intent on stealing some heavy armour.

Having appeared to agree on something, Shitlegs, spokes-thug, replied, 'Yeah – alright then.'

'*Carry on,*' a loudhailer.

'Who said that?' Shitlegs asked nobody, as he could see nobody. He could see nothing, except his hand, which was just in front of his face.

From the edge of the Common, Keef Bananas and his cronies looked on at the labyrinthine, though regimented, collection of murky grey lumps with not their first bewildered look of the morning. To be fair to Keef and his cronies, they were rarely up this early, six am and, were hardly ever down at the seaside, except for Keef who on occasions visited his aunt, the Duchess, in Frisian Tun.

Keef looked at the diagram Reggie Menthe had given him as part of his covert insider dealing, although the Evening News had published it a week or so ago and it was generally available to anyone not of a crony, chum, or even hideous naughty boy persuasion. Keef spun the plan in his hands. Looked this way, then that way, sideways and then decided that this, not that way, was best. 'Oh fuck it, let's just go and find it,' he said, exasperated. This seemed like a plan to the cronies and it is this that marked Keef out as a leader; his ability to make decisions.

This remarkable characteristic was also on his Curriculum Vitae that the London Metropolitan Police force kept up to date for him, to save him worrying about administration. Keef was what they used to call in the olden days, a *Prima-Donna* villain and he had no time for paperwork. Despite Keef's patent leadership qualities, administration was not a particular forte and rarely appeared on his radar. Interestingly, on the top of his Met CV, was a CV he had purloined when he was only seven, when just a lad in Ivver Green...

· · ·

He means Hither Green in south London, but no-way was he going to be Uncle Josh, even if his aunt was a Duchess.

... and that was when he commenced his life of crime. It was in fact, a 2CV, which is twice as good as a CV. A Citroen 2CV was a car that resembled an Anderson shelter on wheels and had the speed of my aged aunt on a bad day, having had a largely ineffective dose of Dio-calm. As a consequence of this remarkable decision of mastermind thievery and, the subsequent shortest ever known car chase in the history of the London Metropolitan Police, Keef's CV had at the very top of the lengthy list, the remark, *Not very bright.* Now at twenty three years of age, and this is only my opinion, we are talking four out of ten on the intellectual scale, a bit like the weather, not at all brilliant and, coincidentally, he was a gangster with a foggy brainbox.

'Oi,' a detached voice sounded from within the mist, threatening, and noticeably not intellectually challenged, more enquiring in a forceful but polite manner that is oft known in Britain as middle class assertive. 'If you wouldn't mind, pretty please.'

'Shut it mush. You shouldn't 'ave put a

fucking tent in such a stupid position.' Keef carried on, blindly leading his stumbling cronies in the fog, here and there, this and that way and, the first part of Keef's master plan, stealth, went well and truly out of the window. Still, what they lacked in creeping, directional, and searching skills, they more than adequately compensated for in aggression and a remarkable grasp of the Queen's Street English that would easily trump middle class assertive, when backed up with brute force.

Eventually they found what they were looking for and Keef stood back before the Sherman tank and allowed himself to be bathed in shrouded crony adulation. He was good, he knew it, and this of course was frequently his downfall. That, and his harebrained ideas like, "Let's nick a Sherman tank and shoot the bollocks off that tart Jack Austin and his missus", both of whom, it transpired, had transgressed the unwritten law, even before you think that as a lady, Mrs Austin, would have no bollocks to be shot off.

I can tell you, as narrator, and as it was obviously not written down anywhere, the unwritten law in this instance was: "Don't go upsetting Keef's aunt, getting Poles in, or digging up his booty or weapons or dead bodies, or there will be fucking trouble, comprendeh". The law, which for the benefit of this book we can confirm, was not written, but was formulated at about the time Keef was watching a number of Clint Eastwood spaghetti westerns, last week. Not that he would have anything to do with any shite Wop stuff, of course. (Wop is a technical literary term for an Italian or any such Italianate shite and, for the sake of middle class balance, shite is sometimes referred to as S H one T. See how the middle class English drop the 'I' and supplant it with the numeral One, and 'E' is dropped altogether as "shite" is Irish; foreign readers take note).

'You got a baby then Keef?' Brains asked.

'What, I don't got no baby, what made you say that?'

'You done said someone half inched (*pinched – stole*) yer booties.'

As narrator I can inform you that it was last week, Wednesday, that Keef mentioned he needed to collect some weaponry and cash from their hidden booty. Now you may begin to comprehend how long it takes for Brains to process information and, why he held the record for the longest interview by the police that involved only two words. I am reliably informed that the two words were "Fuck off". Ordinarily a solicitor would suggest using the words "No Comment" but Brains had just told his solicitor to fuck off, and he had.

Keef flicked his fingers several times and eventually they clicked. 'Shitlegs... the keys.' Keef had moved on and held his hand out, (he'd finished flicking) whilst looking around generally, but in particular up to the turret and the flank of the tank, wondering where the door was.

Shitlegs patted his pockets, but he already knew, he didn't don't 'ave no keys to no tank.

I believe this was how Mr Shitlegs expressed it in his thinking.

'Maybe you don't need no keys?' Brains said by way of amelioration.

'Brains, der, of course you need bloody keys.' Keef replied, waving his arms expansively in the fog, to encompass all of the Banana cronies into his theory, such as it was.

Brains was the intellectual one of the cronies, he had half a GCSE in technical drawing, the actual part he had failed, some would argue the more practically necessary half, was in arse scratching and, he had a Library card. Well, you get the drift? Brains did contemplate asking if he could work with Reggie Menthe in the council, by way of a leg up, so to speak, to better himself, but Reggie, who also hailed from Ivver Green was having none of it. He blamed that bloody Sugar lump of a trouble and strife (wife) of his likely as not, Brains thought, wondering if he should send a saucy postcard home to his mum to let her know he was at the seaside. Then he remembered he was actually on the run from the law; *that was close*. The Banana Boys were, as previously pointed out, on the lamb, because they'd been baaa'd.

'Who are you and what do you want with my tank?' Another polite, but assertively middle class voice from deep in the mist, distant, detached, and slightly effeminate, just the hint of a certain desperation for a trip to the toilet.

Keef turned to a man advancing out of the fog. He was a goofy middle-aged, middle-class, comfortably well off man in Michael Caine, toffee nose twat glasses and pink corduroy trousers. A vision of comfortably well 'orf idiot, emerging from the mist. The man had not changed into his American, Dad's Army uniform yet, probably would do that after he had been to relieve himself, which would likely happen quite soon and directly into his pink trousers, shortly after the Banana Boys had relieved him of his tank.

I'm only guessing, but it is a reasonable assumption I feel.

'This your tank?'

'Yes.'

'Well, give us the fucking keys.'

'It don't need no keys,' the man said, with a vacant expression, seeming to examine grammatically what he had just said, but mostly the manner in which he had said it. He clearly felt uncomfortable and at this stage I would ordinarily recommend *Dio-calm*, it almost did the trick for my Aunt Delores who was at the time running down her stolen 2CV.

'It don't? Well bugger off then,' and Keef nudged the chap in the now soiled pink corduroys and the current representative of middle class England went flying backwards and bumped his head on Shitlegs fist, whereupon, he settled down for a bit of a lie-in, except that was the German plan for the invasion of England, of course. Keef pointed out this very fact, irrelevantly, to the comatose, soon to become, former tank owner and, he and his chums, sorry cronies, were only interested in Der Day stuff, what was Gaylord.

'Right then, where's the door?' Keef asked.

Brains tugged at his partial GCSE, in other

words he scratched his bum in an intellectually ponderous manner as became his status as Brainiac Banana, and suggested they had to go in through the lid at the top. Keef clipped him around the ear.

Blimey, who'd be a baddy? Apart from you get to wear black hats.

'What was that for?'

'For being a bozo. Now, find the door.'

Brains clambered up onto the top of the tank and opened the lid, pointed and said, 'This is the way in.' He was clearly disgruntled.

Unfortunately, Keef and his cronies had quite poor inter-personal skills and were not, in the main, particularly brainy at reading and interpreting the manner and mode of inflection in a person's speech.

'Well, why didn't you say so?' See, Keef did not read Brain's body language or tone of voice, but Brains knew it didn't pay to question Keef.

I suppose you learned things like this early on, when you decide to become a bozo baddie hoping to get a black hat.

However, the way had been indicated and everybody piled in through the lid. Keef, then Shitlegs, as he was second in command, Brains and the two other cronies Gerald and Simon followed.

'Kin 'ell there's no bloody winders (*windows*), turn the lights on,' Keef ordered.

'It's a fucking tank, they don't 'ave no winders...' Brains noticed the circumspect look of his leader in response to his animated reaction and muttered, in a pleading defence, '... it's a fucking tank?' Brains demonstrating not only exasperation, but the cerebral ability that had earned him his half a GCSE and had his teachers scratching their head...

Not their bottoms – teachers don't do this, at least not in the classroom. ...wondering if they should submit him for English Literature; they had of course

spotted his library card, but failed to notice the inscription indicating membership of the children's library and, in particular, the picture book section.

Never let it be said that Keef did not catch on fast. He flicked Brains on the nose with his thumb and forefinger and set about looking for the light switch, some bullets and a steering wheel. 'Brains, you look for the bullets. Gerald, the lights for Christ's sake. Simon, steering wheel please and Shitlegs, you look for the front windscreen. Which way is front? They should 'ave ad bleedin' winders. Put the fucking lights on.'

Brains derred, switched on the lights and pointed. 'This 'andle is for steering, these shells are the bullets and, someone looks out of the lid and shouts down turning instructions to the driver.' He tapped his fingers on the stick that was the steering wheel, and applied a rather risqué grin, which in theory was appropriate as the D day landings were to be in France, where of course, it would be *tres risqué*, as there would have been a lot of Germans not having a lie-in, despite it being their plan.

Keef pondered and, not for the first time, wished he had not decided to rob the local library because Simon thought they would have a load of late return fine money and, it would all be sausage and mash! (*Cash*) It was on that robbery, which incidentally only netted them 75p, they met Brains. Keef should have known that an eighteen year old, spot ridden, beanpole youth, reading *Enid Blyton's, Noddy*, was not necessarily a good sign, even though he could read without following the words with his index finger; quite novel (*not the book*) where Keef came from. However, as it turned out, Brains knew where the Library back door was, had a bike and could give Keef a getaway crossbar. Shitlegs, Simon and Gerald were nicked and would have been in serious trouble if the police had not let them go because they were laughing so much and did not know how to write up the crime of the century.

'Well, sort it then.'

There, you see, Keef commanded

Jack and Amanda Austin – DaDa.

'Oh, Jack'

'Oh, Amanda,' his hand was rummaging around her bottom parts. 'You farted?'

'Oh, Jack, I love it when you talk dirty.' Jack thought for a while, which involved stopping as he was not a famed multitasker. 'What is it? Jack, please, come on. I want to get home and fuck your brains out.' She did titter at her remark, the intimation being he had brains. She wondered if he had no brains left because she liked making love to him and did love him, even if this came with very early morning strolls along the seafront in pea-souper fogs. 'How did you know I'd farted?'

He'd started walking again and the cloud of passion, as thick as the fog and, some might say, uncharitably, as thick as Jack Austin, overcame his enema moment (*he meant enigma, of course*). 'I smelled rose petals.'

'Rose petals?'

Jack may have been in that state of euphoric oblivion he seemed able to summon at a moment's notice, a particularly masculine skill Mandy had commented once, but he was nobody's fool where women were concerned. Of course, most women would see this as his most serious failing but, as I have just mentioned, if confronted by the blindingly obvious, especially by a blindingly attractive woman like Amanda, then Jack could summon up his oblivion - just like that. He knew women. He understood women, to the extent to where he would often remark, even to women, (*see what I mean*) he was blessed. It should be noted that frequently after such discourse with a woman, he would ordinarily adopt a trance like state, which rendered him immune to stares and even the most vitriolic of reposts. It was a master class in denial, the core faith of his C of E (Church of Egypt) faith, De Nile.

He knew women liked a laugh and sometimes he had to filter out the irrelevant stuff and, as far as women farting was concerned, he just knew it smelled of rose petals, even after Amanda had eaten a Brahma of a curry. The reason was, you see, he loved this woman with a passion and he was no fool, of course, he thought, ignoring what anyone else thought.

De-Nile. You see how it works.

It helped that frequently his nose was bogey stuffed and, as he rarely thought of exchanging his filthy handkerchief with a freshly laundered cloth and, Amanda had banned all public displays of a rag that defied all feminine description, it was sadly thus that a handkerchief was seldom employed in the presence of Amanda.

Such was her life and this included that the man she loved beyond all rational reason, as people had tried to reason with her, was not only ugly but also as deaf as a post. He would not wear hearing aids as he thought they would make him look daft and he couldn't see the irony in that either, though he did do the ironing at home. His dad had been a marine and had taught his son to do things like ironing, but most importantly, he cared for and doted on his relatively new wife and, she liked this about him.

Jack loved Amanda. She had lifted him from the depths of sorrow as he mourned the accidental death of his first wife, Kate. After about three years of entrenched grief, Mandy had managed to show him there was a second chance at life and even a sex life that at sixty, he was enjoying probably more than he had ever done. Of course, he knew he brought to the marriage bed, or even out of it, a great deal of skill, experience, and understanding, as ably demonstrated just now with his expert knowledge of the womanly passing of wind, in so much as he could identify clearly the gentle petal like characteristics. He was, he often imagined, the David Attenborough of the famine world.

He may mean feminine.

Amanda, though, thought he was just a lovely man who frequently got his words wrong, known as he had been in the police as Mr Malacopperism, amongst many other quite apt epithets. He was a kind and gentle man and the sex was passionate, if a tad inexpert, improving all the time she thought and had potential, though she frequently wondered if she would live long enough? But, there was no doubt in her mind, this man loved her and, was enthusiastic.

Despite the tip off from the CIA, their walk back from the seafront and Southsea Common was one of barely pent up passion. The sensual stroking that Amanda applied to Jack's intimate regions, to which Jack reciprocated with a fundamentally juvenile groping, all contributed to a joint sexual oblivion, though Mandy, ever practical, guided their route home. The thought their lives could be under threat at anytime that coming day was not paramount, not on their immediate itinerary.

Amanda was Detective Superintendent

Amanda Bruce, now Mrs Austin, because she had married Detective Chief Inspector Jack (nicknamed Jane) Austin, retired? Retired, who knew? It paid not to dwell on matters that affected ordinary people, as Jack was extraordinary and, if you asked him, he would confirm this for you. Jack Austin was generally thought to have retired, though nobody truthfully had the nerve to ask him if this was a permanent state of affairs. He had flounced out of a news conference one day, after a particularly nasty case, saying, "He'd had enough of this shite" and sort of gone off into the sunset. And then, last Christmas, he'd declared he wanted to retire with his wife and sealed this pact with an eternity ring, after which, he announced she would henceforth be known as Duck and he wished to be called Dick, as he had formed the Dick and Duck Austin, Detective Agency; DaDa.

He popped into the police station every now and then and, every now and then, thought about nicking someone in a consultant sort of way, but that was about as far as it went. However, that was now, and, this is then.

This is a flashback of course, and all will become obvious when we reach the, then, bit, or is it the now bit?

Still, the formerly tough and totally in control

Superintendent, known as Mandy Pumps or Mandy Lifeboats, had well and truly succumbed to the juvenile antics of her now husband. As she had become a part of his life and had insisted on knowing everything about him, which apart from being a spy, was pretty much nothing. Therefore, as a consequence of their marriage, she also became a member of MI5 and a part of Jack Austin's discreet group of monkey spanner meat pies (*spies*) that resided in and around the Community Policing department in Portsmouth.

Even if he had retired, not that this is confirming anything officially, as you wouldn't believe the crap I had (so Sue Narmee says it) just because Martin, Jack's dog, got hurt in a fight in book one. And now, Martin had half his front leg amputated in book 5, the finale of Kind Hearts and Martinets, so it's definite schtum on the retirement angle until we understand just how much Jack Austin is loved by his readership and, how the DADA Agency goes down.

I have it on good authority he is resentful of his dog for grabbing all of his limelight. So, it might be reasonable for us to expect some sort of reaction, to redress the balance as he would see it, except he didn't like Lime and asked for some other colour light, maybe lemon, but definitely not orange; he hated orange, it drained the colour from his face.

It is a long story and really and truly, you should read the previous five books of Kind Hearts and Martinets, but MI5 needed a low key, apparently benign police unit, to keep an eye on overt and covert matters in Portsmouth, a strategic Naval and Commercial Port on the south coast of Britain. Jack Austin, however, was not a great meat pie (spy), as he was the ugliest, biggest, clumsiest, cockney barrow boy oaf, you are likely to ever meet, but he did have a redeeming capability that allowed his superiors to go along with his raving mad antics - he was a good analyst. He had never been an action man spook. In fact in the proximity of anything bordering on action, he was a definite liability, to the good and the bad guys.

As a policeman he was often thought to be a "natural". He somehow or other solved crimes almost out of the blue; demonstrating no logical deductive trail. Amanda now knew he had another completely separate group of completely unlikely cowboy sleuths, who did the solving for him. But, and I say again, he was mustard at the piecing together of disparate information, seeing the big picture, lateral thinking, basically cutting *through the crap, most of which was his by the way – so a balance Mandy often thought.*

Following Jack Austin's serious press conference flouncing, everybody in the know, allowed his tantrum to settle and waited for the natural order of things to be re-established, which, after a fashion and, after nearly eighteen months, it did.

Jo Jums, Detective Inspector Josephine Wild, was now running Community Policing, but more importantly, she ran the unit for MI5. Jack and Amanda were not so much disappearing into the sunset as acting in a peripheral role that Jack called an Insultant. He meant consultant, but with Jack not all was always what it seemed. He was known as Mr Malacopperism of course and this, combined with his other multitude of inept bumbling idiocies, contributed to his self-styled persona, an enema, by which he meant an enigma, or did he? He was shite at most things, except for the analysis stuff, as I have already mentioned.

Jack and Amanda bundled in through the front door of their house in Frisian Tun and began stripping each other's clothes off in the hallway. The passion had the potential to become frenzied, except Amanda had to help him with her buttons and finally her bra strap, but that achieved, the release was dynamite.

Despite the humorous banter I touched upon just now, the sex life of this mature couple did have its moments. They called their racy sex, "fizzers", and, in the hallway and just now, this coupling had all the hallmarks, if you get my drift, of becoming a number one fizzer.

'Oh, Jack.' He'd pushed her to the floor, done all the things he had learned and, most importantly, not yet forgotten, she liked. She fizzed and he was there for her. 'Oh, oh, ooooh, er, feck, what the feckin' 'ell?'

'Shit, what?' he said, sensitively responding to an unusual remark from Amanda and checked his bits and pieces for anomalies such as testicular cancer; he liked being tickled but never knew it could give you cancer.

He was also a known hypochondriac.

'I've got my bare arse on a rocket launcher and its lumpy and feckin' freezing.'

He thought she looked gorgeous sitting upon the rather sophisticated weaponry. 'That's a Bazooka, babe,' and he flicked his one eye to the ceiling and back to his bits and pieces.

The unsubtle innuendo was not lost on her, even if she did have a bazooka stuck up her backside. 'Bazooka?' She remarked, not casually.

He could tell she was riled and wondered, not for the first time, where the minds of women went? It was after all, only a bazooka.

As I had mentioned before, Jack had a sense for this sort of thing and this is where he was blessed, of course.'

'Jack what is a fucking rocket launcher doing in the hall?'

'First of all...' he raised his finger to her...

Big mistake, and he was going to need the Papal Blessing they had received in Book 4 - Ghost and Ragman Roll.

'... It's a bazooka and, to be totally honest wiv you, sweet'art, I'm not sure.' And to show he was serious, he did Dib, dib, dib and dob, dob with a *Benny Hill* salute. 'Maybe Jimbo put it there?' But his mind had drifted and in a casual movement, she had shifted her derriere away from the bazooka that she was convinced was a rocket launcher, and the passion rebuilt.

'Jack, should we go upstairs?' But he was way beyond getting up the stairs and she was catching up fast, when the letter box flapped open.

'Jack, Mandy, its Jimbo. I left a rocket launcher in the... oh, sorry.'

Mandy let out a scream that Jack thought a little inconsiderate of his possible heart condition, but knew he had to do something to defuse the situation.

'Jimbo, how nice to see you. Your family they are well?'

It was Jack's, or should we say Jane's, Jane Austen Pride and Prejudice, many quotes of which he was famed for misquoting, (he was known as Jack Jane Austin) but he knew instinctively people loved the classics.

'Tolerably well, Jane, thank you.' Jimbo said through the letter flap, looking like a spook gynaecologist.

From the unborn infant angle, you understand.

. . .

Jimbo knew Jane well, but then he would, as an MI5 minder. 'And, it's a rocket launcher, not a bazooka.'

'Told yer,' Mandy had recovered a little of her pith and poise, gathering the remnants of her clothing and starting to wonder if some of it could be repaired. 'Jimbo, if you could maybe give us a minute, I'll get dressed and put the kettle on.'

'That would be lovely. I'll call Bubba and Abe over. I'll be honest, and I know its June, but we're freezing our bollocks off out here in this fog.'

'Yes, well, I'm about to tear Jack's bollocks off, so you can all be eunuchs together and then I might get some peace and quiet and, maybe a less testosteroned eejit of a husband and his Mossad, MI5 and CIA mates.' She looked at Jack, forlorn, naked, apart from his penguin socks. She melted, she knew she would. 'Get dressed, you eejit, and bring the spy world in from the cold.'

She reflected, that was a catchy rejoinder, when Jack responded in his naturally misguided manner, 'It's a bazooka...' and made a run for it.

. . .

He was no fool and, as we had previously mentioned, he knew women.

CHAPTER 1 - (*the Prologue ends and the story is launched or bazooka'd upon an unsuspecting readership*). The Journalist

Everard Pimple gingerly picked his way along Frisian Tun. He was aware he was walking gingerly and also picking with his feet, but he couldn't help it. He had always walked gingerly, but had rarely picked with his lower limbs; this was new, even for an inveterate gentle man. Delicate would be a kind way of describing Everard and his manner and he accorded this supplementary picking to an increased feeling of apprehension, more so than Everard knew as normal, even for him.

The street had a deserted feel, not barren, as many of the characteristics of this characteristically English middle class street, were still evident, if incongruously battle worn; it did feel alien. The loose debris had been cleared, things tidied away, swept under the English reserved carpet, so to speak. The Frisian Tun Big Society, ably assisted by local serfs, pitching in admirably, the British Spirit, but all knowing their place, which was the British way. The people cajoled and corralled, stiffly and stoically by Lady Francesca Blanche-Teapot, the self-styled Duchess of Frisian Tun.

Even so, to Pimple, in his overly susceptible and Bambiesque way, perceived a shadow, a meta-physical presence, a sensation. It seemed to him that in the street there remained a resonance of warfare, machine gun fire, heavy amour, tank tracks clanking and cranking and urban conflict and, this sense titillated his fear buds that were always close to the surface and even more so adjacent to his nether regions.

Pimple was also aurally sensitive and he detected in the ether of this overly quiet street, as he gingerly picked, an ephemeral haunting of pained shrills that ricocheted off those buildings left standing, and these aching whispers drifted like wraiths through the battle ground ruins. Shrills of pain and fear from people who had lived their lives blissfully unaware they were delicate flowers living in a rarefied environment that should never, ever, have had to witness a rogue planning application, let alone a pitch street battle and a renowned gangster's death throes in this, their little corner of God's earth. This sort of thing never happened in places such as Frisian Tun, the heart and very soul of upper middle class England.

Pimple was the Honourable Viscount Everard Pimple, the fourth degree of rank and dignity in the British peerage, though people ordinarily called him Pimple. He was uncomfortable being called, "My Lord" as would be his entitlement. Generally the famille-Pimple understated their rank. The mother was often referred to as just plain ordinary Dame Pimple.

Pimple was twenty eight and one of life's innocents...

... and it's not often you can say that these days, although I said it just the other day when I referred to myself, though I am considerably older, although you would hardly know it; I wear so well.

Pimple was a delicate plant. A forced stick of rhubarb, or a mushroom cultivated in the dark. People had at various times called him a jolly bean. He, however, suspected this likely referred more to his beanpole like appearance, being narrow in shoulder and beam and all points north and south and, was uncommonly tall for a Pimple; a family that tended to the short, not tall, stout, not lean. The contributory cause of this physical imponderable may be because Everard was starved, predominantly emotionally, but this had a peculiar effect on his desire for nourishment. It would be fair to say that Pimple had led a sheltered life. Sheltered mainly by a devoted and many if not all, would say, behind her back obviously, a controlling mother. Thus Everard Pimple was always sensitive to the vibrations consequent to traumatic events, considering his mother, Dame Pimple, to be a traumatic event all of her own.

Pimple was what was known in the old days, which seemed appropriate picking his way through this formerly picturesque and quaintly English setting, a cub reporter. Not being blessed of the greatest of intellects, or any compensating driving ambition, he had been a cub on the Portsmouth Evening News for nearly ten years. This, after an extended and irksome struggle in boarding school and subsequently a long line of imported tutors, he had achieved straight C's in his A-levels, English and Needlework. He was predicted a knitting B, not achieved and some people unkindly suggested he was the very essence of *dumbed down*, as frequently referred from the government front benches. Pimple's father was firmly planted on the back benches of the Lords, but still, Pimple Senior, resolutely espoused the party line, naturally; he was not a rotter.

Pimple, the reporter, covered mainly court news, ruffians being banged up and so on and, society articles, which made him eminently qualified, or so his mother believed, to do a *Human Interest* story on what had happened in Frisian Tun. The Tun was a cutesy street in Southsea, itself a rather exclusive neck of the Portsmouth woods, thick, in a multitude of ways, outside observers might observe, with Southsea Socialites, many of whom were legends in their own opinions and conspicuous in their self-appointed elevated station within local society.

Today, in this sensitively inactive street environment, Pimple's complex nervousness arose from several additional scores. Probably the most important would be his mother, the formidable Dame Delores Pimple, who had insisted her brother and the proprietor of the Evening News, Sir Wendell Devonshire-Wallop, give his nephew more important journalistic tasks. "Wendy, it is time that Pimple Minor*..."

Everard had an older brother Jocelyn Pimple, something in the city; a brick would be a fair assessment. So he would be Pimple Major

· · ·

"... made his way in journalism", she had said to her brother Sir Wendy, as Wendell was known.

Dame Delores was not a woman to be gain said, a fact Wendy had been well aware of throughout his life. His sister was older than him by some 6 years and carried with her all of the body mass and confidence this differential period might deferentially accumulate. She was a thoroughbred in every sense of the word, even down to her striking and some say patent, equine facial features. It has to be said though, in order to convey a reasonable likeness, there were some, mainly of a Canadian persuasion...

As it is also often said you have to be persuaded to live in the Colonies.

... who could see in the Dame, the look of a moose, and certainly, if you knew what was good for you, you would not want to lock horns with the formidable woman.

Regardless of the debate on physical appearance that was kindly meant when people, ignoring the patent animal likeness depending from whence you hailed, referred to her as stout. Dame Pimple had a temperament and possibly the looks upon reflection, that probably came as a consequence of centuries of inbreeding, and not within the society of Moose and Horse (*a well-known posh society magazine*), but within the Southsea stable of social inbreeds. It was joked around the newsroom, she was cloven hoofed, but even if that was just idle and malicious gossip, her oft evident temper was demonic in every sense and always hovered dangerously close to the surface.

Another cause for Pimple's complex fretfulness, as if his mother was not enough for a gentle soul, was that he had been recommended to do this follow up story by none other than Bernie LeBolt Thompson, the crime reporter of high repute on the Portsmouth Evening News. LeBolt's reporting on this recent incident and many in the past, had been taken up by the Nationals. It was rumoured he had even been offered positions in Fleet Street, though the source of these rumours were suspected to be Bernie himself, being a consummate rumour-monger and proud of it. Bernie's father had been a fish monger of some repute, so it was just a short step to *rumour* monger, logically, and that of course would be proof enough for any reputable journalist, even of repute; not a rumour to be sniffed at in a fishy way, so to speak.

Bernie had though, proudly declined all

offers of alternative positions, saying he preferred this sleepy backwater of Portsmouth that had been anything but sleepy in the recent past. There had been though, until these very recent Frisian Tun events, an almost out-and-out armistice since Detective Chief Inspector Austin had taken, some say irresolutely, retirement from the police service.

And here we have the source of yet another irritant boil on the Pimple mental equilibrium, which struggled for stability at the best of times. Mr and Mrs Austin, he a newly retired (*still to be established*) Detective Chief Inspector, and she a Detective Superintendent, had also been at the centre of this latest effulgent incident in Frisian Tun, the street where they lived. Jack Austin, who was insisting his new name was Dick and not Jane, as he was known in the police and, is apparently in the process of having it changed by dead-pole...

Pimple was sure he meant deed poll – but maybe not.

... had said it was nothing to do with him. He had prefaced this with "Honest injuns", apparently to show he was serious and, further reinforced his immunity from potential prosecution by crossing his fingers and calling out "Vein-lights". Job done, and it is a wonder more of the seriously minded of our criminals did not partake of this form of defence, he, Jack Austin, had often thought and often said, though not to criminals, obviously.

However, not all of the Pimple bodily sensations were malevolent, though all of his internal commotions could be seen as caustic in one sense or another. The bubbles in his belly that had the interestingly additional effect of weakening significantly his lower limbs, causing him to not only pick, but bizarrely, feel weak in the knee joints, risking likely collapse at any time, were not due to nerves so much as sexual tension. Sex and its oft incumbent tension, was the curse of Pimple's life as a virginal sap and, worse still, there was no sign of the status quo changing, which came with its own consequent tensions.

Until the previous morning that was.

Pimple lived, as do most lads half his age, forever in virginal hope, bordering on a particularly quiet form of hysteria. He knew no other form of hysteria, as whatever level of audibility was practically possible or indeed allowable, he always had to bear in mind that any form of exaggerated display of emotional feeling would immediately be out-exaggerated by Dame Pimple, his mother. And, as Jack Austin would say, knowing as he did, Dame Pimple well, it would be served back at Pimple Minor in buckets and spades, and likely with additional brass knobs. So Pimple bottled it up, never knowing when the cork would, if ever, be un-stoppered.

However, yesterday morning, a heavenly early July morning, the sun shone spiritually on Everard Pimple, though this was truly metaphoric as Pimple worked in a cupboard, but that is to not say he did not experience these feelings of wellbeing throughout his body. It would be reasonable to say that Everard Pimple's star had risen, and the cause of that soaring heavenward comet of desire and delight was none other than, Cecelia Crumpet, a celestial being in all respects. Yesterday morning, Ms. Crumpet, the number one Evening News gossip columnist and siren of the news desks, had deliberately and not accidentally, strolled, in her slinky feline manner, which was the stuff of young men's dreams, into Pimple's stationery cupboard that masqueraded as an office. Nobody particularly liked to work with Sir Wendy's nephew and this had nothing to do with his mother. Well, maybe a little bit. Well, a lot really.

Cecelia had made an exaggerated display of sitting herself on Pimple's cheery *Fablon* topped, orange box desk, and leaned over in a revealing way, dressed as she was in a deep cut and billowy, gossamer thin blouse, which permitted Pimple a fleeting glance upon the frilly edge of her brassier; ivory with white lacy trim.

Not that I was looking.

And, breathing huskily, to compound the overall siren effect, she leaned into Pimple's well scrubbed ear, which had the familiar hint of peanut butter, Dame Pimple insisting Pimple minor wear a dab of peanut butter behind his ears each day to keep the floozies away, which clearly had worked up till now. Cecelia said in an asthmatic, though sexy way, 'Take that Frisian Tun assignment Pimple and speak to Aedd Murphy at number 28, flat 2, he will fill you in.'

Ceeley, as Cecelia was sometimes known, considered the message conveyed and looked at the vacant Pimple expression to see if it had been received and, confident the principle if not all of the content had been absorbed, she made then to remove herself from Pimple's orange box. In an overt exaggerating manner, she unfolded her shapely and long legs, permitting Pimple another fleeting and ecstatic pinnacle of sexual reverie; he was blessed with a momentary peek at her suspenders and stocking tops.

As most virginal saps, or just saps in general, know, although I am only guessing as I am writing as a female pseudonym and not I might add from the Isle of Lesbos, such a sight is all that is needed to make a lad's day and night-time dreams.

Now, I hear you say, if you are writing as a female pseudonym, why not allow the readers to partake in a general description of Cecelia, as all we know of her so far is she is sexy, breathes as though she has a cold or smokes sixty a day, has a lacy ivory brassier and wears stockings. Well, ladies, if you ask your male partner, he will likely tell you this is really all you need to know and, perhaps this is early days in the life of a female pseudonym author, but if it helps - Cecelia had shiny black hair like Cathy McGowan had in the sixties, which flicked from her ears to her cheeks. She was tall, probably five ten, pale skin to a long face and dynamite red lipstick that reacted to devastating eyes that flared like an Italian sparkler to azure blue and, strangely, very active shoulders that appeared to move independent of her lacily contained bosoms; wide, and undulating in and out as she talked - not that I was really looking... sigh...

'Go on then.' Ceeley said, and reinforced her assertion with her shoulders, but there was no way Pimple was going to be able to get up from his chair for at least an hour, suffering as he was from a virginal sap that had well and truly risen, similar in fashion to his star. Ceeley broadened her grin, displaying an array of perfectly presented and glinting, white enamel teeth that had the peekaboo hint of a rose bud tongue, conveying her pleasurable appreciation of Pimple's predicament, knowing it was of her causing. And, with an affectionate stroke of his fluffy cheek that had still to display evidence of an inflexible bristle, she pouted a parting kiss and sashayed out of the stationary cupboard, displaying her arse cheeks to great effect; they were not at all stationery.

Make that two hours Pimple thought to himself, as he watched Ms. Crumpet disappear out of his cupboard, her backside curvaceously contained in a pencil skirt and he knew what moved and resided below it, he had seen it in all of his magazines. Make that three hours, which he employed to great effect researching his journalistic commission. This said a lot about Pimple, as many red blooded males would have toddled off to the toilet, hunched maybe, but definitely toddling, to efficaciously deal with an errant difficulty. However, Pimple was a consummate professional and with the aforementioned weak knees, toddling was not really on the cards anyway.

ONE

THE JOURNALIST AND THE
POLICE INSPECTOR

Pimple read through the bonefide background material, by way of preparation, yes, but principally by way of Crumpet distraction. It was, however, a forlorn hope that this cerebral work would even marginally, or temporarily, control his virginal sap. He knew this would be so and resigned himself to having to distract his thoughts all day. So he finished his background material in the evening, just before home time, by reading the concluding Frisian Tun, News article, by Bernie LeBolt. Interestingly, Pimple thought, Bernie had written this sign-off article almost in a prose, which was an unusual departure from this reporter's normal succinct, acerbic style;

. . .

"Frisian Tun, a most decorous Southsea street, had been witness to a pitch gun and heavy armour battle on the Friday morning of the 6th June. The brutal altercation left one, Keith Bananas, the notorious London gangster, dead, his body riddled with bullets and one or two of his limbs, randomly distributed in the formerly beautiful forecourt gardens. Three of Mr Bananas' cronies, not chums, suffered a similar fate, with one other left not at all well and currently being treated in QA Hospital.

The ashlar scribed, stucco facades of the Victorian Villas, as they are known by the Frisian Tun residents, remain pockmarked with bullet holes, so much so it now resembles a street in Beirut, rather than a formerly beautiful and tranquil, picture postcard, quintessential English lane within the desirous enclave of Southsea.

This previously attractive, continuously curvilinear, villa lined streetscape, appeared now irrevocably marred as number 13, the home of the Duchess of Frisian Tun, had been blown up; a rocket launcher, the suspected culprit, though police say they have not found the weapon as yet.

All that remained as evidence of the Duchess's stately pile was a particularly un-stately pile of rubble, the shells of walls sticking up like empty teeth where fillings had long ago departed, the plumbing and cabling exposed as if dead nerves of a deceased body and a first floor bath tub, stubbornly reigned high and mighty, like a large nasal protuberance on a formerly proud face. It was rumoured there was a ring around the rim of the bath, but "This could not possibly be the case", the Duchess had remarked, when asked.

The Duchess, as she is affectionately known, one Lady Francesca Blanche-Teapot, currently temporarily resides and holds court with a neighbour, Florence Frampton-Maxim, wife of General Maxim (retired). The Duchess was, of course, distressed, but as was reported by one of her stoutest lieutenants, Hermione Hooter, local dog breeder and mail order Hush Puppy representative, of number 23, "The local Big Society chappies have stepped in and we can proudly and resolutely report that the Blanche-Teapot stiff upper lip was once again reasserting itself. The Duchess has sounded the clarion and rallied her troops and serfs, to restore a semblance of an ordered Middle Class England to Frisian Tun".

Now, to your average outsider, Pimple may look like an upper class bozo. Truthfully, of course, he was, and privately educated to achieve such a level, to boot, but he did have a minuscule fragment of intelligence lodged within his grey matter and he tugged at this seldom used asset now. He knew Bernie LeBolt, and instinctively knew that if he had written Frisian Tun was *decorous*, then Bernie wrote what he meant. However, Pimple was also aware most people who had read Bernie's article, which had also been syndicated across the country as well to a few American newspapers, always interested in middle class England, understood Bernie's prose to indicate that Frisian Tun was a poetic, leafy, comfortable, warm and welcoming winding street, in a most desirable part of South Portsmouth, which, on the surface, and prior to the recent calamities, it was in actual fact.

Frisian Tun was a street off the beaten track and not often used by traffic or even pedestrians, save for the odd melancholic and musical drunk, winding his way home after a night in the Southsea clubs and pubs and finding the organic zig-zag street a remarkably effortless route to follow. Frisian Tun was contained, almost claustrophobically, by shoulder height, old and weathered brick garden walls that curved naturally with the form of the road that meandered serpentine like. A narrow lane, rather than a street that was manageably overgrown with mature trees that shaded the constricted pavements and cobbled roadway.

It was a beautiful street, or at least had been, except maybe for number five that had a comparatively barren frontage and odd shaped protuberances that may be hailed as exemplary in an architectural magazine, but did not accord with what is generally prescribed as acceptable by the Duchess, or so Mrs Southampton-Meddlesome had said.

Mrs Southampton-Meddlesome was a staunch supporter of the Duchess, even though her grating Northern Irish accent meant she was not allowed to reside in Frisian Tun. She was obliged to set up home, understandably so, instead, in a poorly designed house in a most secondary and tertiary street, a back street truthfully, which did however afford a good view onto the more aristocratic Victorian Villas. Although clearly a secondary citizen, Mrs Southampton-Meddlesome's view over the villas was permitted by the Duchess. However, this woman with the socially unacceptable accent, loftily assumed a status way beyond that which would ordinarily be accorded by the street where she resided and of course, the country from whence she hailed, but all of this, as you would expect, did not deter this woman of diminutive stature and over inflated opinion of herself.

Certainly, Mrs Southampton-Meddlesome knew her place, or at least imagined she did and she asserted it most aggressively, unaware her ignorance was indisputable and only tolerated by the Frisian Tun residents if it were in general support of the Duchess and whatever edict concerned her minions at the time.

However, when Bernie LeBolt reported that Frisian Tun was a decorous street, he was in fact being impishly precise in his meaning; Bernie being a notorious imp of a fellow. You only had to ask DCI Austin (*still retired*) who says that once, in C&A's, the Crown and Anchor local hostelry, he had asked Bernie what he would like to drink and he had replied he desired a "cheese sandwich". There is no need to say any more and imp status was firmly established. Bernie had described Frisian Tun as decorous and, it was indeed a street that behaved politely and in a controlled manner and extraordinarily, it was this uneasy existence of ersatz middle class bonhomie and bravo, well done old chap, hail fellow well met, which eventually was the cause of its current state of disrepair.

Ironic, isn't it?

. . .

Pimple, being a man of inordinate detail, his mind when it worked, worked like that, had done his background research even before he knew he was to do a follow up human interest story, and now he sketched his outline. He padded this out, some say rather naively, with information gathered from a telephone conversation with DCI Austin (*still retired, a bit*), as also breathily suggested, in a suggestive way, by Ceeley and furthermore and impishly, recommended by a grinning Bernie, baring his nicotine stained excuse for tombstone incisors to immense and intimidating effect and if subsequently, Pimple was to toddle off to the men's room, it would likely to have been for an efficacious poo.

Pimple replayed the recording of the telephone interview to himself and Jack Austin's fresh, spiky, cockney manner of conversing, sent relived shivers through the Pimple beanpole body.

"Frisian Tun's an 'istoric street mate, the origins evident in the root of the name, meaning a place of settlement for Frisians see." Pimple was not sure he saw, even hearing the statement for a second time. "Frisians were close neighbours of the Saxons and Jutes, when they were in Europe, of course, before they took up residence in England, obviously, after the Romans had buggered off in 410 AD, about ten past four". The recording of Jack Austin guffawing down the telephone, once again, caused Pimple to retire a little more into his shell, which was oddly coincidental, because Mr Austin had said he was having a word in his "shell-like".

This was the Jack Austin, no less, who was insisting he was now called Dick, and his wife, Amanda, was to be called Duck henceforth, and they lived at number 5 Frisian Tun, the one with the barren front garden as he professed to hate gardening.

An unusual irony, but more of that later.

Pimple was certain he had heard an exasperated sigh of a feminine origin in the background of the conversation, and more than several times. Austin had seemed oddly proud of their name changes, having insisted it was to be their retirement personas mentioning also that they ran, what he called, an "Arty-farty private detective agency. The Dick and Duck Austin Detective Agency, DaDa, and planned to wear nineteen fifties Ooh La Lovelies fashions, but don't tell the bleedin' Council, or the bloody

Duchess for that matter," he'd added, panicking somewhat.

Dick recovered, almost without breaking stride and went on to say, "This was all some time ago of course and there was no sign of the Frisians now, if you exclude the Duchess who was most definitely Friesian". Pimple believed he referred to the bovine and not to any ancient settler, though clearly the Duchess was an aged person.

"The feudal system still remained though," Jack Austin had gone on to say, with more added verve and jollity, explaining the street was a fine example of Upper Middle Class England, with all of its pseudo neighbourliness, faux tranquillity, and hierarchy, preserved in aspic. A transparent jelly used in cold foods, he had unnecessarily explained, as Pimple was posh. "In this case it was quivering cold fish" and the subsequent combined Dick and Duck laughter broke all records.

In the News article, Bernie le Bolt reported The Duchess, who until recently resided at number 13, which now only existed in shell like form, as saying, "It was the natural order of things", and went on to say, "If things had been done as they should. If I had been consulted on the little matter of the Poles, I could have said that such an alien intrusion would not be welcome into Frisian Tun and the surrounding Owenesque boroughs, regardless of what the local council might say. You just cannot tell some people, especially interlopers into a society for which they have precious little understanding and, it is not a ring around the bath, it is dust and dirt from the explosion". She had been most persevering on the latter point, though clearly she had little time for the Poles.

Pimple felt that if Bernie could be syndicated then why not Everard Pimple and, this story had attracted international recognition, read as far afield as the Isle of Wight and Scotland and some of the serious American journals. So, for those persons unfamiliar with the south-coast England City of Portsmouth and its even more precious and some say precocious Southsea, it may be as well he thought, to elucidate at the beginning of his article and, here again, he was ably assisted by Dick, apparently Pimple's mate, although Pimple had not been aware of having had any mates before now.

"Listen, mate", Austin had started and Pimple, being not only a man of inordinate detail, he also possessed a sensitive ear, probably because Dame Pimple had regularly scrubbed it within an inch of its life and still did, before applying the peanut butter. His ear was thus naturally attuned to accents and unless he was very much mistaken, Dick Austin possessed a strapping cockney intonation. Now this was interesting in itself. What was a cockney doing residing in this heartland of upper middle class virtue and values and, some would say and, Mr Austin may have mentioned it in passing, snobby England? Pimple earmarked that for a follow up.

Listening on, Mr Austin shouted, "Oi mush, you listening to me?" Pimple, no longer Dick's mate, but his mush, it would seem, whatever that was, assuming that Mr Austin must perceive him as he would a Husky dog, and Pimple jumped again, even though he knew the rebuke was forthcoming. "Wot yer gotta un'erstan'" Mr Austin continued, unaware of the effect his raised voice had had on Pimple's collywobbles, "is people round 'ere fink they're the dog's bollix and their poxy neighbourhood is so bleedin' poncy precious you have to get permission from the Duchess to 'orse and cart".

Listening, Pimple was embarrassed all over again, as he heard himself enquire of Mr Austin, what a horse and cart was doing in Frisian Tun? Pimple relived his embarrassment and endured Mr Austin's raucous guffawing, which seemed also to be enjoined from the background, which had to be Duck energetically quacking.

"'Orse and cart – fart", and Austin guffawed again. "Mind you, you 'ave to be careful not to follow frew and pony and trap". More energetic hilarity ensued and Pimple noticed he had timidly enjoined the mirth on the recording, clearly not having a clue as to what a pony and trap was either. "Crap son, poo to you. I'm a poet and don't know it", and Pimple could imagine Mr Austin holding out his hands, one clutching the phone, in exasperation at this journalist's lack of understanding.

Pimple heard himself say, "Oh, Mr Austin" again timidly, but it seemed to be of sufficient potency to convince Mr Austin to continue.

"Dick, yer plank", he said, moving on, having made his point. "It's like they see this place as a bleedin' choclit box. Know what I mean?" and there was a pause while Dick waited for Pimple to acknowledge.

"Err, Yes, I think I do Mr, er, Dick," he heard himself say.

Dick continued on in the play back. "Only if you look round 'ere there's only a few of these Thomas Owen choclit box gaffs, though this street, Frisian doobrey, I grant you is a bit bleedin' twee and I don't mean the green fluffy fings what 'ang over the gardin walls". This was apparently very funny indeed and it took a while for Dick and Duck's enjoyment of that particular joke to ebb and, for the very one-sided conversation to continue. "Denial yer see, son".

Pimple didn't, though it was apparently obvious. "Cor blimey, it's all in the imagination, yer see." Still Pimple didn't see, but pretended he did. "Look mate", Pimple noted that he was no longer Dick's mush, but once again his mate, or was he his son and, was that better? "There's more shite stuff than there is the choclit box stuff, but people round 'ere don't see it, see? They fink they live in a perfect idly, don't they love?"

In the background Pimple heard Duck respond to the affirmative, which Pimple was convinced was a quack, and Duck pointed out, he likely meant idyll. "That's what I said Idylly-diddlee?" and that seemed to be the end of the conversation as Dick began ooohing and aaahing and had put the receiver down and, if Pimple was not mistaken, Dick was being fondled by a Duck. Pimple immediately thought of Crumpet and the sap, that had only just begun to subside, arose again to its former status – he may need to go to the loo after all he thought, almost like a red blooded male.

TWO

THE RESIDENTS OF 28
FRISIAN TUN

Trying hard not be too gingerly, inherently aware he could do nothing about the picking of his lower limbs, now so deficient in strength as it were in the knee department, Pimple approached number 28 Frisian Tun, a red brick Victorian pile that sat incongruously in this street of pockmarked stuccoed villas. He was aware from his research that the conversion of this Victorian Manse, into four flats, had also been the source of considerable unrest some four or five years past. Pimple had looked up the newspaper records: "Multi-occupancy in Frisian Tun is insupportable." A quote from Lady Blanche. Having read through the articles, Pimple could recall the furore as the council planning committee had passed the plans and, in response, the Duchess had vowed that she and her serfs would lie down in front of the bulldozers, not fully appreciating that number 28 was to be a conversion and no bulldozers need be employed. However, she was not one to waste time looking at plans. She just knew what was right, or in this case and many others before and subsequent, if confidential sources were to be believed, was wrong.

Still, record pictures showed they had indeed mounted their protest in Frisian Tun. On the day work was due to commence, the Serfs and the self-appointed aristocracy, later to be known as the Big Society, stood tall together, apart from those who had decided to lie down, either to stop the bulldozers that were not coming or, because they were of a frail constitution and would have preferred to stay indoors and watch re-runs of the *Jeremy Kyle* show. All, however, were in possession of neatly embroidered placards proclaiming, "Nasty developer types are not welcome here", in a beautiful needlepoint that had the basic script in a half-cross stitch, reinforced with basket weave with the surround in tent, or, as Mrs Constance Crotchet of number 11 said, disagreeing with Mrs Southampton-Meddlesome of number 17 of a lower status of road and socially unacceptable accent, that it was in fact "Continental Stitch".

She went on to point out that the continuous Motion Needlepoint Stitch was, "A great stitch technique to make your canvas stitch up faster", she said. "It is the Batman and Robin of needlepoint stitches", Mrs Southampton-Meddlesome had added knowledgably, bashfully acknowledging how remarkably up to date she was with new telly programmes and enquiring as to who *Jeremy Kyle* was.

Interestingly, Pimple found himself agreeing with Mrs Southampton-Meddlesome, despite her grating accent and personality and, he had pointed this out in his A level paper, the section on embroidery, not knitting, as he had failed that bit.

Anyway, it turned out that despite the protest on Frisian Tun, the builder had gained access via the back door, which afforded a way in from the parallel back street, and the flats were built and eventually occupied by, of course, unsavoury characters. This was all as expected and predicted by the Duchess, who seemed oddly proud that she could now demonstrate she knew, all along, what would happen and perhaps next time, the planning committee would listen to her before things got totally out of hand. She even suggested all planning applications should be approved by her, before they were formally submitted, as a sort of triaging system, like they did on the railways, she further suggested, amiably. According to the grapevine, Lady Francesca Blanche-Teapot had been a wheel tapper at Hither Green, British Rail, shunting yards, before she married Sir Reginald Teapot and been elevated to the aristocracy and a life of leisure. This latter assertion the Duchess refuted unequivocally, arguing she is in fact a very busy body. But, it could not be argued, it was a role in which she had wholeheartedly immersed herself, often to the patent chagrin of Sir Reggie, who had eventually left Frisian Tun and the Duchess, for a life of gay abandon, one might say and so it is reported, with none other than Cedric Poncenby-Smythe, with whom he had shared a bed at boarding school and lately, a back bench in the House of Lords.

Looking up at the imposing red brick edifice and, screwing up his courage, which as a consequence caused his face to also wrinkle and, preparing to knock on the door whilst still desperately trying to marginalise the mental picture of the Crumpet bosoms and stocking tops, Pimple pictured the socially objectionable residents:

Flat 1, the Pied-a-Terre semi-basement, or garden flat, was occupied by Georgiana Lovebody and she had been proclaimed a woman of dubious character, but in reality, was a synchronised swimming instructor of fine upstanding pedigree, with merely an unfortunate name. Not that this counted for anything; the Duchess had ruled and there was no more to be said on the matter.

Flat 2, had a tenant a tad more acceptable. Aedd Murphy was a geography teacher at the local Roman Catholic secondary school, St Winifrede's. Not much was known of him, except he hailed from the far, far west, and thus would likely speak funny, if ever he was spoken to and, so was of no consequence except he was notably very tall, skinny, with a rabbits bum and, exceptionally wiry, ginger hair and almost certainly was a hermit, which suited everybody. He did however blot his copybook on St Patrick's Day, a day not recognised and subsequently affirmed by Duchess Decree, in Frisian Tun, when he hung the Irish tricolour from his living room window, itself substantial and Georgian paned.

This was only marginally more exacerbated as the Austin's, at number 5, also displayed a crayoned in tricolour in their front window. When interrogated by the Duchess and her very own Spanish inquisition of Big Society sycophants, Dick Austin, as he also reported at the same time he was to be known in the future, believing himself to be a proficient multi-tasker, had displayed the irritant flag as he was an aficionado of the TV series *Father Ted*. "So feck off" he was reported to have said and, was thus recorded in the Minutes, which Dick later denied, but everyone noticed his nose grew significantly.

Flat 3, was on the first floor of the red brick pile and thus was not considered so important, as not many people looked upwards, except for The Duchess who walked with her nose constantly in the air as though she had a bad smell, or indeed peanut butter on her stiff upper lip and as a consequence, could not avoid vision of elevated floors and roofs generally. An elderly lady, Mrs Fish, lived in this first floor flat and she was actually particularly acceptable in pedigree, with her blue rinse and general Margaret Thatcher appearance and demeanour, but alas, she did not measure up aesthetically. In short (which funnily enough she also was) she was ugly, resembling very much the repulsive, big headed fishes one sees on the market stalls in Europe. Therefore, it was recommended that although she was of course welcome to reside in Frisian Tun, heaven forefend, and in Flat 3, even though it should never have been constructed or even given planning permission, she should bear in mind that whenever she felt the need to go out, if absolutely necessary, she should exit number 28 via the back door the builder had so ably used. This was reasonably asserted in a decorous manner, it being explained to Mrs Fish that this was necessary so as not to sully the Constable like, chocolate box, appearance of Frisian Tun.

Finally, Flat 4, the attic flat, housed a University Professor, Thelonius Monkspot. His father, or so rumour suggested, had been a jazz fan, which, it seemed, explained a lot this was assumed, as it was not advisable if one wanted to stay on the good side of the Duchess, to talk to Thelonious in order to confirm the veracity of the rumour. Being a University Professor, Thelonius was considered acceptable, naturally. They were not uncivilised in Frisian Tun and, the Professor would likely have been accepted into street society with open arms, except for the cheerless fact of this middle aged man's proclivity for his young nubile students, generally of a Greek persuasion. All of this would have been tolerable if the windows were kept closed, to mute the sounds of pan pipes and sexual assertions and, if the back door was utilised. However, and here was the nub, the big bushy bearded professor's appetites leaned toward masculine company and that was not even on the radar of tolerance for this Big Society, even though the English aristocracy were oft known to bat off the left foot occasionally themselves, and indeed, unknown to the general Southsea populace, Sir Reggie batted off a similar unorthodox footing that resided firmly on the left side of his body.

However, here in Frisian Tun, it was not acceptable, and the professor seemed not at all interested in a life of monk like abstinence, despite the heritage of his name. So, the street committee had been convened a number of times in order to plot the residential demise of said bushy bearded professor, to date all unsuccessful. Nevertheless, the English Aristocracy were not known as a race likely to give up at the first, second, or even third obstacle, as was ably demonstrated at Agincourt and, especially recently, in response to the Frisian Tun influx of Poles.

The Poles being the subject of this current human interest article by Pimple, or at least, this is what people had said and, even Pimple had thought, in case you had forgotten, or knew, or even cared. But then it gets better, as Pimple knew it must and so he continued with much bravado, to seek entry to Flat 2, number 28 Frisian Tun – and as a consequence, Pimple's life was set to change. For the better? Who is to say, but change it most certainly did.

THREE

THE JOURNALIST AND THE GEOGRAPHY TEACHER

Pimple gingerly picked his way up the stone steps to the imposing oak front portal, its visual importance as a means of entry reinforced as it was encapsulated in a hefty timber porch, the likeness of a cemetery lychgate. Upon reaching the porch, in pretty much the speed of a hoisted coffin containing a fat opera singer, Pimple addressed the panel of entry bells. In his short-sighted fashion, which Pimple said contributed to his buck teeth appearance, since ordinarily his teeth would be viewed as straight and true, he examined the buttons through black rimmed, bottle end glasses, at about a two inch distance. Standing out in a mixture of green and red ink was the name, Aedd Murphy, Flat 2. The Aedd written in red, the Murphy in green. Non-

gingerly, Pimple picked his fingers over the panel, eventually summoned the courage and pressed the buzzer adjacent to the red and green name card.

'Who's on me feckin' bozzer?' Pimple's sensitive aural organs immediately determined an Irish accent, Dublin'ish he guessed, but more likely a little to the north and left a bit. 'Yer, be you talking to me sometime, boyo?' Now this did throw Pimple, the accent had changed to the hymns and arias of the Welsh valleys.

Trying hard not to imitate the Irish or the Welsh accent, and focusing on his more natural mode of speech, 1940's BBC Home service English, Pimple replied with as much assurance as he could muster, picturing in his mind and his trousers, how much he wanted to impress Cecelia Crumpet.

'Er, my name is Everard Pimple from the Evening News? We spoke on the telephone and you agreed to meet with me?' Pimple employed the current vogue of elevating and expressing a questioning inflection at the end of his sentences, he thought this made him appear Antipodean, like someone out of *Neigbours*, and thus he would be taken seriously.

'Ah to be sure, boyo, why not you say in the first place yer feckin' eejit,' and Pimple was startled by a buzzing drone and a repetitive metallic clicking that was the automatic door lock releasing. Unfortunately, the indelible mental picture of said Crumpet was dulling any lightning reflex Pimple could summon to react to the door opening device. The not at the best of times, rapid thinking ability of the Pimple brainbox, had alas only pictorially focused on the Crumpet assets and in particular, the stocking tops, though the lacy brassier featured in there somewhere and so it was that he lost his chance of entry to number 28 on the first opportunity.

Pimple buzzed again. 'Feck me gently, are you still there, isn't it, an all, an all?' Again there was the buzz, followed by the repetitive metallic clicking and Pimple dived for the door handle, this time he made it through.

Rather pleased with himself, he released the door to close behind him and leaning back to recover his heart rate, he surveyed the vast hall and polished timber stair, which he knew would give access to the upper flats of an old trout, and a sexually unacceptable Professor who had Greek leanings. Whilst Pimple considered the living arrangements of this disparate set of unlikely immediate neighbours and working out that the Pied-a-Terre and access to the synchronised swimming coach, must be via an external semi-basement door, the door to Flat 2, opened. Aedd Murphy presented himself and it is fair to say that the occupant of Flat 1, the garden flat, Ms Lovebody, could not have synchronised the gawk of Pimple's mouth with the yawning gape of the Flat 2 portal better, as Pimple took in the look of this geography teacher.

Pimple had of course researched Mr Murphy, but all of that background work could not have prepared him for this physical encounter. Several phone calls to St Winifrede's, Roman Catholic Secondary School, eventually concluded with a telephone conversation with the Deputy Headmaster, which had produced a rough consensus at; "Who?" It was a sad fact that Aedd Murphy was not a memorable sort of man and, despite his obvious height advantages, he had no presence and as a consequence, not very much was known of him, save that he was tall. This fact was undeniable, as Pimple took in the image of the man stood before him who had to be all of six foot six, maybe more; the man soared to the ceiling. Pimple himself was six four, and they shared similar beanpole characteristics, but Mr Murphy seemed taller, narrower.

The Deputy Headmaster, when pushed and assured by Pimple there was a geography teacher working at St Winifrede's called Aedd Murphy, had gone on to say that Mr Murphy was from the west. But how far Pimple thought? Wales, or even further afield, Ireland. "He is, by all accounts, a well-educated man and possibly a hermit", the Deputy Headmaster had said, adding that he taught geography and this was said as though this was all the explanation that was needed, he then hung up the telephone.

Pimple phoned back and the Deputy Headmaster expanded on his previously apparent insightful characterisation, only this time, especially for a dim-witted reporter. "You understand that very often Geography teachers can be assumed to be Hermits, it sort of comes with the territory, a bit like the jumpers and the cardigans with football buttons they wear. If you asked Aedd Murphy and could understand his Bristolian accent..." Bristolian? Pimple had thought, not wishing to interrupt the Deputy Headmaster who seemed to be on a roll. "... he would say he felt very much like a hermit, especially since his wife ran off. It was this traumatic event that had left him decidedly foxed, as, even with his encyclopaedic knowledge of geography, he could not place the Isle of Lesbos. This is where she is reputed to have gone, with Penelope Bloomer, the Hockey teacher from St Winifrede's."

The Deputy Headmaster hung up again, clearly irritated talking to the ignorant press.

Pimple then googled the Isle of Lesbos, which he presumed had to be adjacent to Greece, but he could not find it and however much he tried, he got only pornographic sites that after three or four hours of a fully risen virginal sap, he decided it best to quit as he already wore glasses and had buck teeth.

Well, the teeth appeared buck, but as previously mentioned, they projected down from the upper jaw straight and true, the rest was an illusion borne of Pimple's weedy and short sighted overall appearance.

'Well, are yawl coming or going?' Was that Bristolian Pimple thought, as he gazed upon six foot six inches of skin and bone, topped with an incandescent shock of red hair, the only thing Pimple could visualise, it even blotted out the image of Ms Crumpet's stockings and lacy brassier. This geography teacher had, vivid ginger hair that stuck on his head like a rusty Brillo pad, such were the wire wool characteristics of this unfortunate mop.

'Ginger it is, and like a Brillo pad, isn't it, boyo?' he said.

Now that was Welsh Pimple thought as he

by way of hair distraction, focused on Aedd's cardigan, which he was sure, although a bit blurry, was knitted with a picture of the Norwegian Fjords. It had the appearance of a fjord on the Discovery channel where the telly's horizontal hold had gone a tad haywire, not unlike Aedd's ginger hair.

Aedd decided he'd had enough of being stared at and spun in his Hiawatha moccasins and walked back into his flat, presuming he had left enough smoke signals that Pimple would know to follow him.

Pimple did.

FOUR

THE GEOGRAPHY TEACHER AND THE MAP ROOM

No sooner had Pimple settled his hyper active chops, arranged his cavernous oral cavity into a semblance of stress-free and casual assurance and, fastened all of that into position, than his mouth was fully agape again.

Dutifully, Pimple followed Hiawatha, presumably the last of the Mohicans, his eyes resolutely fixed on the moccasins so as not to excessively stare at the red *Brillo* hair, and upon entering the voluminous living room, Pimple found he was once again awestruck. The room was entirely wallpapered with maps of the world. He noticed immediately Ireland, Wales and England with a blown up section especially for Bristol and its waterways. The ceiling was not omitted in the amazing display, except, as

Pimple craned his neck, for the ceiling was lofty, maybe twelve feet, he saw the pictorial Michael Angeloesque tableau could be viewed, not so much as geographical, but more as an historical display, although it did have a Copper-plate scripted title block, beside a huge compass point, saying *South-West Coast of Spain, just west of Cape Trafalgar*. Most of the ceiling was painted a glorious azure blue, clearly ocean, complete with crested waves, and this sea was populated with authentic appearing, to scale, paper model ships of the line, complete with canon puffs in cotton wool.

Pimple forced his eyes away from the Battle of Trafalgar and back to the moccasins, knowing this was not important, as Nelson was assured of Victory even if he did not survive kissing Hardy, who probably had peanut butter behind his ears, which, and knowing of the prevailing conditions on these old ships, was likely rank. So Nelson had no chance, and neither did that floozy mariner Hardy, if you follow the logic.

Pimple's subsequent visual consciousness, once his courage allowed him to remove his eyes from the Red Skin footwear that appeared well worn, probably from tramping through forests, was titillated further as he absorbed the contrasting colouring, patterns and shapes of the geographical maps from around the world.

These were augmented by geological charts, which had been amalgamated and inserted, presumably relating to the regions beside which they had been carefully placed. The stark diagrammatic, graphic colouring of this and that rock, or geological type or stratum, was beautifully and artistically balanced by the water colour shades of the old fashioned, cartographical, pastel hues.

Aedd Murphy noticed Pimple's state of avid interest and especially the toothy gawk, but ignored it and muttering in Welsh, 'Tea, boyo, isn't it, and whose coat is that jacket?' Casually flailing a hand as he disappeared, indicating as to where Pimple could throw his jacket, or coat, coincidentally, adjacent to the Norwegian Fjords. Pimple discarded his jacket in a Scandinavian direction and began settling into this new environment, unaware he had inadvertently and a tad gingerly, picked his way to an armchair and then he became aware that, although very summery and warm outside, the living room was cool and clearly faced north. Pimple thought this must account for the knitted fjords breasted by Aedd.

If you could ignore the cartography, geological illustrations and the Battle of Trafalgar, the principle feature of this beautifully proportioned, high ceilinged and voluminous living room, was a wide and almost floor to ceiling, Georgian paned, sash window, which afforded an excellent view to the western end of Frisian Tun, now gloriously bathed in late afternoon sunshine. This warm image was bright, compared contrastingly to the gloomy chill air in the living room. The sunlight, he observed, exaggerated the jig and jag shadows of the Duchess's bomb site, which exacerbated further, the alien disparity of violence with the sublimely smooth, though bullet pockmarked, ashlar of the Victorian villas, which had until recently stood proud in semi-detached unison, presenting an image of complete English tranquillity and invulnerability. A peaceful repose, a natural order of things in a way, Pimple supposed.

The cill to the sash window was set just above the deep skirting board and the obvious generous view could be enjoyed whilst taking one's ease in the plump, overly stuffed, 1930's, wide, brown leather armchairs. The form of these armchairs curled and curved generously like the South Downs, almost as though they were respecting the curves of the meandering street, directed as the furniture was to the sash casements, as if the window was the telly, which alien modern appliance Pimple became aware was noticeably absent.

This recumbent sightline was also evidently directed toward the now devastated front garden of number 13, the Duchess's former abode and, if one was minded, a penetrating inspection was apparent through the twisted and singed wisteria and Rose trees, to the previously well-bred villa and presumably, equally aristocratic net curtains.

Aedd, now back with the tea and a beguilingly delicious looking Battenberg cake, the chequered harlequin colourings complimenting the geological cartography delightfully, he seemed to get a degree of pleasure from Pimple's awareness of the visual line to the former patrician villa. He remarked upon this whilst serving the tea, a Darjeeling he said, by way of introduction to the infusion and a segue into a geographical discourse about the Darjeeling region of India. Pimple saw it coming, but could do nothing to stop it. He was feeling unusually comfortable.

'The Darjeeling region...' Aedd started off, '... is cool and wet, tucked into the foothills of the Himalayas, don't you know.' And he pointed with the dripping tea strainer, causing Pimple third degree scalding to the back of his hand, to what was presumably, the Himalayan region of India and source of said Darjeeling leaf. 'The tea is exquisite and delicately flavoured and is considered to be one of the finest teas in the world.' Aedd Mmm'd as Pimple began to nod off, rubbing his hand with no noticeable immediate soothing effect. 'The Darjeeling plantations have 3 distinct harvests and the tea produced from each, "flush", has a unique flavour.'

Pimple had gone. He was all over the place, he was seriously heady and in grave danger of Zizzing. Aedd carried on, oblivious. 'First flush teas are light and aromatic, while the second flush produces tea with a bit more bite. This is a second flush,' he said waving the tea strainer, again scalding Pimple's hand and now alert, Pimple looked at the Darjeeling second flush as it tumbled from the spout like a rusty waterfall and indeed it did look like it had just been flushed. A sort of urine orangey yellow. 'The third, or autumn flush, gives a tea that is lesser in quality,' Aedd continued, shaking his head as if he would have nothing to do with a third flush. Pretty obvious Pimple thought, waving and cooling his hand, trying to alleviate the pain, now fortunately turning into a more tolerable dull ache, beneath the rosy discoloration he thought would likely blister.

Aedd finished spouting, both geographically and with his urinated beverage, and Pimple sighed in relief, a puff of air that was audible from about ten paces and of sufficient force that it served ably to cool the back of his hand. Aedd seemed to remain oblivious, although he did manage a cursory inspection of Pimple's scalded appendage and appeared satisfied. This must be what it means to be a Hermit, Pimple thought. It's as though nobody else existed to Aedd. It was all Pimple could do to stay awake, but he was made of stern stuff and, he had a journalistic mission to execute, not to mention the tenderness in his hand was now more of an irritant than a pain and could be easily soothed by mental distraction of the Crumpet kind.

Satisfied Pimple had only minor scalding, Aedd settled himself into the other armchair and awaited his interrogation, manipulating his jaw in a contemplative manner. Pimple stirred his tea and waited for the two natural cane sugar lumps to dissolve, wondering why he had not been shown the source of the cane?

He already had his opening lines worked out and had rehearsed them yesterday evening, while Dame Pimple washed him in the bath. An uncomfortable wash as bathing goes, as he had to try not to think of Crumpet while mother did his bits and pieces. "Very important" she had said, "for a boy to be spick and span in that department", removing her marigold gloves and departing to get a bath towel she had warming somewhere.

Pimple went to start off, but was interrupted by the geography teacher. 'Aedd is a Welsh name you know, meaning a King of Ireland. My mother, Blodwyn Jones of Swansea, one of a very long line of Jones's you may be aware, married my father Brian Diarmait-Murphy, which in English translates as Dermot-Murphy. My father can trace his line back to Diarmait the 1st, King of Connacht and a King of all Ireland, the last in fact to celebrate the pagan ritual of Feis Tmrach,' Aedd said, whilst applying an authentic manner of conversing and he spat and sprayed some second flush at Pimple's blushing face as he enunciated the old Irish. 'Feis Tmrach... the feast of Tara, which is the ancient home of the great Kings of Ireland, don't you know?' Pimple didn't and was not sure if he cared. 'My mother wanted me to have a Welsh name and Aedd suited, as it meant a King of Ireland for my father and the ancient Irish Kings of Ireland, of course, drank their tea from saucers. I'm not sure why I mention that, but my father thought it had some significance, though dad quite naturally wanted me to be called Dermot and my mother preferred it if I drank my tea from a cup. So technically my name is Aedd Dermot-Murphy, but I'm known generally as Aedd Murphy.

Pimple had definitely dropped off now, a combination of the story and the melodic, up-

and-down Welsh tones, interspersed with a soft Irish brogue, except for the old Irish of course and this had done it for him. But worse, he had allowed his sap to rise with thoughts of Ceeley's bosoms and stocking tops, by way of an efficacious distraction from the irritating soreness on the back of his hand. This distraction was causing the cup in his saucer to rattle. He did wonder if he should drink the tea from the saucer, but he wasn't of regal Irish descent.

Thankfully, none of this was noticed by Aedd, who had now risen from his armchair and walked to another wall and to another map, this being of Ireland and was pointing to and announcing Cashel, a fortified town in Connacht. He moved and pointed to Tara, just up a bit and to the left of Dublin. You see, I have a knack for these things, Pimple thought to himself with a self satisfying smile, pleased he had identified the Irish region to relate to the accent of the time.

'Tara, is the ancient seat of all Irish Great Kings' Aedd continued. And Aedd's dad Pimple presumed, but it was Ceeley's seat that preoccupied the Pimple brain goings-on, that and how much of this diatribe was Blarney, which if Pimple was not mistaken, was a lot further south and resided in the County of

Munster, near Cork, and the Munster people had a completely different accent.

Pimple was unconvinced of the veracity of all he had heard, although the Darjeeling seemed to be spot-on geographically and tasted divine and he was, as previously mentioned, unsure if he cared about all of these shenanigans; pleased with himself that he had begun thinking in Irish. And all of this did enable him a passage of time to reflect upon the Crumpet assets a little more.

In the meantime, Aedd rambled through Ireland and thence to another part of the wall that had a map of Wales and something about Grufydd ap Llewelyn, an illustrious leader and the Welsh rebel's historic relationship with the Swansea Jones's, or something like that.

Pimple now knew how Aedd's pupils must feel in the classroom, as his own pupils disappeared to reside firmly in his forehead and his eyelids became unbearably heavy, but he had to admit to a fact you could not deny, Aedd was enthusiastic, if dubiously knowledgeable.

The room, already previously cool and shady, appeared to have darkened more as Pimple surfaced from his Crumpet trance and realised Aedd was in another part of the room and if Pimple was not very much mistaken, Aedd had moved onto the Scandinavian countries, via

Wales; Pimple aware of this location as his Jacket, that might have been a coat, was adjacent. He knew this also, because his direction of vision was aided by a ceiling mounted, rotating spotlight, which was being remotely controlled by Aedd, who was concurrently explaining that this was where his ginger hair came from, but Pimple couldn't help thinking, if he knew where it came from, he surely could send it back? IKEA had a returns policy and he permitted himself a little titter and Aedd did stop at that.

'Amusing you I am, isn't it?' it was Welsh, when realistically, Pimple expected Swedish or Norwegian, but this required quick thinking if Pimple was to avoid an embarrassing situation. Fortunately for Pimple, Aedd's brain was as ponderous as the Pimple intellect was at quick thinking and, coincidentally, Aedd had also thought of something else to impart and began, but Pimple was before him with his improving wit.

'Know you do, Cecelia Crumpet, isn't it?' Pimple had slipped into Welsh, like a miner bird he thought, rather appropriately, also thinking then of canaries and wondering if they came back up from the bowels of the coal rich earth, to the surface, black, and not yellow. And if they did, did they wash them, then how, and would the miners wear marigolds like Mother's?

Aedd had missed it completely, which was not surprising, and his dialects were all over the place and was beginning to give Pimple a headache, but extraordinarily and in BBC English, Aedd replied. 'I know her because she did a profile of me when I presented a paper to the Portsmouth and Southsea Geological Society, Football Club.' Pimple wondered why Aedd would be giving paper to a football club, but presumed it must have been loo rolls for the supporters. 'I have to say, she is a bit of a corker...' chuckling to himself in a posh dirty old man way that Pimple could identify with, '... and was no respecter of personal space, I can tell you,' and Aedd's ginger eyebrows raised. Pimple didn't need telling, he had lost his personal space yesterday and had hoped it might be a precursor to losing something else as well, virginally speaking. 'Too hot for me and also, I have recently given over my heart to another. I presume you heard my wife left me a year or so ago?'

Pimple confirmed he had and followed this up with an incisive journalistic question, impressing even himself and believing he was finally beginning to get the hang of this reporting lark. 'Who is the current love of your life, Aedd?'

Pimple asked, essential background stuff this and he pictured it now, Isle of Wight syndication, a Pulitzer even, whatever that was? Those awful people in the newsroom had tried to tell him it was Pull-titser, but Cecelia had straightened him out on that one. It did seem to Pimple that Ms Crumpet had a soft spot for Pimple Minor, which he certainly could not attribute to himself, speaking metaphorically, in a bits and pieces way.

Aedd adopted a relaxed, armchair seated pose, crossed his extra long beanpole legs in an exaggerated manner that suggested he was more than pleased to discuss the current love of his life. He brimmed with a self-satisfied grin. It reminded Pimple of the film *When Harry met Sally*, where the girl in the film bangs the table in the cafe for some inexplicable reason. Mother had offered she was likely not satisfied with the service, but to Pimple, it looked as though she was completely satisfied.

'Yes, I will tell you about her,' Aedd said in such a way that Pimple was convinced he would, and then he did and pretty much as the girl in the restaurant, banging on ad infinitum, as they used to say in Roman needlework classes, to describe the blessed woman who had rescued this geography teacher from the Isle of Lesbos doldrums and had even lessened his somewhat vehement aversion of Hockey.

'Her name is Beatrice Flat, and Bea is the music teacher at St Winifrede's. She's a...' and he appeared to settle further into the armchair as he conjured a mental picture, wobbling his head, in a contemplative manner, '... a comely sort of woman. Plump I have heard people say rather rudely, but in the right places. Rubenesque I think, if you get my drift?' Pimple did, and confirmed he did. 'She's a conductor,' and Pimple was immediately confused, why say she was a music teacher if she worked on the buses? But Aedd was once again unmoved by the Pimple musings. 'I have watched her conducting the famous St Winifrede's, Nun's Orchestra, and as she sways with the music, her beautifully rotund buttocks are like shifting tectonic plates and I told her so and, she seemed particularly smitten by my geologically geographic romantic side.'

'Yes, I can see that would be the case.' Pimple had managed to get a word in and appear worldly wise all at the same time. He was, however, a little surprised that following the introduction of his beloved, Aedd was off his seat again and, if Pimple was not mistaken, he was heading due north, for the Midlands, to wit and in particular, Birmingham, which although partially obscured, resided very close to the sideboard.

Shifting a vase and a pile of geography exercise books, Aedd revealed Birmingham. 'I should really move this sideboard, what would Bea think if she came here and Birmingham was concealed, if only partially?'

Pimple could see where Aedd was coming from, sideboard wise, but was more intrigued that Aedd had imparted this recent concern in a Brummy accent, but in the spirit of geographical goodwill, Pimple offered a candid suggestion he thought amply demonstrated also, his maintained attention span and willingness to enter into the spirit of geography. 'It's an awful sideboard, why d'you not kick the dreadful article into touch, and say, replace it with a version of lower height and bulk?' Then thinking even more geographically and geologically, 'This may also afford you the opportunity to insert a chart depicting the geological constructs of this particular area of the Midlands, which may entertain Ms Bea Flat, music teacher from Brum, inordinately, as well as reassuring her that her home city, where presumably the family Flat reside, is well founded.' Pimple then had a double take, which coincided with a swallow of breath in order to resist an attack of the vapours. 'God, I presume

Birmingham does stand on some sort of rock or firm foundation?'

To Pimple, you see, geology was simply a matter of a bunch of rocks, but he had enough savvy to realise not to impart this to Aedd, who was now off his armchair again, having only just regained it and re-established his Bea Flat relaxed and reclining posture, and he headed directly back to Birmingham and the offending sideboard, which partially obscured a Midlands city that sprawled incomprehensibly across the Black Country of England's middle heartlands.

'Yes, Everard. I see completely,' Aedd said rubbing his chin in a thoughtful manner. Then Everard was stunned as the geography teacher began to shift the contents of the sideboard out into the hall. Having redistributed the books, what-nots and nick-knacks, he returned with an axe and after laying out a chart of the geological constructs for Birmingham, so that he might best describe and indicate the sub-strata whilst multitasking with the axe, he lustily attacked the redundant and excessively bulky sideboard, whilst expounding on how Birmingham was secure in its geological supporting stratum.

Pimple became a speechless spectator amidst a shower of splinters, sharp shards and larger chunks of previously attached polished timber and, creating his own form of the Mexican wave, he dodged the larger sideboard portions, occasionally steadying himself in order to best understand the subterranean characteristics of Britain's second city, all of which Aedd described admirably, between grunts, accompanied by accomplished whooshing and swishing axe swipes. Pimple fully expected Aedd to gesture towards the forests of British Columbia and expound upon the economic and sociological structure of the lumber and pulp industry, lumberjacks even, but he didn't, Aedd's multitasking abilities being more or less on a par with Pimple's own.

So Aedd progressed on his Birmingham subject matter. 'In a climate much hotter than the present...' he stopped and looked out of the window, the gloom of dusk did not appear to be alleviating the accumulated heat of the day outside. Although it was cool in the living room, it was about to get cooler, as Aedd raised the lower sash to its full extent and began to discard bits of sideboard, willy-nilly, so to speak. After the initial shock of seeing the sideboard, previously so prominent, exiting the room in random small and large chunks and in a rather dubious manner, Pimple became not unpleasantly aware of an ensuing draft from the open sash, which was particularly noticeable up and around his flappy trousers. Feeling somewhat relaxed, he remarked to himself that the breeze was quite beneficent as it bathed his recently weakened knees and, sooner or later, if it carried on in the equivalent direction and velocity and if ably assisted with some judicial flapping of the Pimple trouser bottoms, it would likely dampen his ardour and newly arisen sap for the delectable Ms. Crumpet.

Aedd continued his geological diatribe and demolition of the sideboard whilst Pimple protected his head with a cushion he'd picked up off a stool, nearby a Mediterranean island, Corsica if he was not much mistaken. Suitably protected and comfortable, Pimple settled down, re-summoning his mental picture of the Crumpet bosoms and stocking tops, by way of passing amusement, knowing his ardour could be cooled at any time he wished with a slightly elevated lower limb, to take advantage of the breeze from the open sash, along with a bit of judicious flapping of the Pimple trouser legs that he now had off pat, so to speak. He did have a casual thought of the receptionist at the evening news, Pat Poultry, a rare bird, not particularly good looking, but her appearance and overtly sexual Mumsey style, did it for Pimple minor, who was now drifting, imagining Ms Poultry bathing him and wondering whether she possessed marigolds.

. . .

It has occurred to me that some people may not have knowledge of Marigolds, other than the flower. The marigolds referred to here are the rubber, orange, washing-up gloves. Right, carry on...

Aedd did carry on in his destructive and informative way, unconscious of the fact that for Pimple, Ms Crumpet and her various scantily clad assets, had been temporarily transposed by a middle-aged woman receptionist, who like B Flat, Pimple supposed, was comely, although no spring chicken. Pimple managed a cackle, chicken like, thinking also he could become a raconteur, or some other sort of dinosaur, with all of these stories.

'Most of the Birmingham area was covered by a vast shallow lake, don't you know...' Aedd was still talking and pointing to the geological chart with his axe, '... which lay below sea level, see.'

Pimple followed Aedd's axe, but couldn't see as he had gone again and only really stirred in a semi-conscious state, in what seemed like several hours later, at the mention of the Midland's stratum, Mercian Mudstone, as this was the name of his mother's best friend; Mercy Mudstone.

Pimple's knee jerk reaction was as a consequence that Miss Mudstone, often encountered at the Pimple residence and a close companion of his mother, liked to join him in his bath and Dame Pimple would wash the both of them, though he had noticed his mother only employed the Marigolds on the Pimple intimate bodily parts. He had to say, that compared to his mental image of Ms Crumpet and even Madame Pat Poultry, Miss Mudstone, who also taught hockey, apparently, and played occasionally with Dame Pimple, or so the story goes, was not a patch on the glorious Cecelia, but each to his own Pimple supposed philosophically, in a *man of the world* manner.

FIVE

THE DAME AND THE SYNCHRONISED SWIMMING TEACHER

Having discarded the remains of the sideboard through the sash window, placated the dear Ms Lovebody, who seemed to take exception to various sized particles and the odd big lump of sideboard, on her terrace, lawn and, occasionally on the Lovebody noggin and, having subsequently blue tacked up the geological chart of Birmingham in the now cleared space, Aedd expressed contentment. He settled in his armchair gazing up to the Battle of Trafalgar and mumbled something about what part of the world dinner should come from, seeming to relish these geographical thoughts more than any prospect of lip-smacking nourishment.

Pimple ventured a non-geographical intervention, his newly acquired irritation with geography enabling him to grow ever so slightly in a spurious confidence. 'Er, you did say you would give me some background to recent events on Frisian Tun, Mr Murphy.'

'Indeed, I did, Pimple old chap, and so I will and a most intriguing story it is too.' Was that a posh Hampshire accent? 'I wager you will be thoroughly engaged. Would you care to stay for some dinner?' He continued, indicating with his hands, one of which was en-route to pick some sawdust and other coincidental detritus from his nose, that no response was required as yet. Pimple wondered why Aedd now pointed to a map of the Hampshire countryside with his spare hand, other than he employed a polished manner of speech. 'I am considering sausages and chips. The sausages I get from an organic farmer in Hampshire,' (*ah, that would be it*) Aedd said nasally and made to rise from the armchair, but stopped mid-air and, as you would expect, assumed a stunned expression as Pimple, rather radically for a normally nervous, reserved, and peaceful chap, asserted himself.

Pimple had indeed reacted not gingerly, in fact quite the opposite, another knee jerk, but this one was bordering on atom bomb, certainly rude to the point of being indelicate, more especially since he had just been invited to dine, geographically speaking. 'I don't give a toss where the fucking sausages come from...' calming a little, '... and yes, I would like sausages and chips, thank you very much.' Smoothing metaphorically his ruffled internal feathers, he continued to address his host in a manner more appropriate to a Pimple. 'Would you mind awfully if I telephoned my mother to let her know I will be dining out and will likely have to skip bath night?'

He explained further to Aedd that his mother did not allow him to have a mobile phone for risk of brain tumours, always assuming there was sufficient brain residing in the Pimple skull for a tumour to attach itself, of course. But, Dame Pimple was notably risk averse where her youngest son was concerned, being aware he had been close to last in line when the brains were being handed out; all perfectly acceptable if you were aristocracy, naturally.

Aedd, nodding to the telephone, seemed completely unaware and thus unimpressed at the prospective bravery of his soon-to-be dinner guest, who was about to ring Dame Pimple and impart seriously bad news. Aedd was in fact more agreeably distracted as he thought primarily about where the sausages came from and channelled his thought processes so that he might better inform his dinner guest in a thoughtful manner when required, probably over dinner.

Pimple was screwing up his courage, which action appeared to be attached to the sinews of the Pimple face...

You may recall a similar reaction when Pimple considered advancing on the entrance to number 28.

... as he headed in the direction of the telephone, which funnily enough was just below British Columbia. However, incongruously, the phone looked like the Khyber Pass, such was the elaborate disguise fashioned in Bakelite; a form of early plastic manufacture if Pimple was not mistaken.

Pimple dialled and waited whilst practicing his pretend brown paper bag breathing in order to stave off a panic attack. Aedd muttered something about lumberjacks and the decline of the pulping mills, but his heart was not in it.

'Oh, hello Mother, it's Everard,' and he listened, for some time. This was normal and for the moment Pimple's emotional equilibrium remained relatively stable. 'Yes mother I do understand...' listened some more, '... I am sorry your hockey match has been postponed.' He listened even more and gave the appearance of being a glutton for punishment, as did Aedd, as the volume of Dame Pimple had reached its zenith and Aedd was aware, as were probably half of the residents of Frisian Tun, since the bottom Georgian paned sash remained open, that, "Those darn groundsmen had messed up the pitch bookings and Mercy will not get sweaty and may not need a bath this evening". This, to Aedd, seemed to be the very nub of Dame Pimple's ire, so adequately and forthrightly thrust down the telephone and, ironically, out through Pimple's very own Khyber Pass.

Khyber Pass – Arse, in cockney rhyming slang, bottom department if you are posh.

'Mother, I am sure Mercy will want a bath this evening, unfortunately Uncle Wendy has asked me to do a story for the paper and I will be late home...' Pimple instinctively halted mid sentence, also normal, and waited in dread. Aedd heard no response and even felt a degree of empathetic trepidation. 'Mother, you've gone awfully quiet,' but this was only a temporary state of affairs as Pimple and even Aedd knew to be a racing certainty; it was. The Dame issued forth in a baritone foghorn blast that Aedd thought resembled Lady thingy in the Oscar Wilde play, thingy, the one where she cries "A handbag!" Being a geography teacher and a man with a confused national identity, this consequently resulted in Aedd not having any particular interest in English Literature, other than he was aware Stratford upon Avon was a tad up and just to the right of Bristol, which was...

Lady Pimple detonated and Pimple held the phone at arm's length, so as to protect his rather sensitive aural organs, all as we have previously mentioned are unusually wired to his similarly sensitive nether regions (*not Holland, that would be Netherlands*), from being assailed by a vocal barrage, potentially more damaging than a blow from any handbag or indeed microwaves from a mobile telephone.

'Everard, I shall be speaking to your Uncle Wendy, he knows very well when your bedtime is and that Mercy visits for a bath on Wednesday evenings, following our hockey match. I will not tolerate my domestic arrangements being trifled with because of a damn newspaper article.' She seemed to mellow, just a little, 'You have lights on your bike I presume, your reflector bicycle clips and fluorescent yellow jacket?'

'Yes, mother'

'You have a vest on?'

'Yes mother, although it is darn hot.'

'Everard, do not swear at your mother. I laid that vest out for you this morning just so you would not get double pneumonia and this is the thanks I get?' She mewed, fully mellowed in a sickly wretched way and Pimple figured this was an appropriate time to mention he will not be requiring dinner as he was due to have sausages and chips with a geography teacher.

'Where are the sausages from?' Dame Pimple immediately enquired.

Knowing his mother would require an informative answer and in a light bulb moment of divine inspiration, Pimple looked up to Aedd and gesturing with the phone, 'My mother would like to know where the sausages are from? If you could tell her while I avail myself of your facilities, I would be most excessively obliged.'

You would have thought it was Christmas, as Aedd lunged and snatched the phone whilst directing Pimple to the bathroom, unconcerned, even in any geographical sense, if the directions had been conveyed correctly or indeed received and understood, as he lunged verbally to inform

Lady Pimple of the source of said Hampshire free range bangers.

Feeling both relieved he no longer had to speak with Mummy and, excited at the prospect of an exploration adventure as he had not understood at all where he might ablute, Pimple left the living room on his quest to flush out some second flush Darjeeling.

He closed the living room door behind him and leaned back against it, taking pleasure in the relative peace of the hallway, recognising and savouring the familiar ebbing of tension he always felt whenever he completed, or dodged, a conversation with his mother. He decided, rather expansively for Pimple, another puff of air might be afforded as a reward, with the additional beneficial effect of cooling the back of his hand, which still nagged at the pain synapses of the limited Pimple brainbox, which for its limited size, was abnormally attuned to pain.

In the event, the bathroom was not particularly difficult to find and Pimple was successful on his third try. However, such is the way with a man's urinary tract, if combined with a limited brain capacity, that once the mind is settled upon relieving the bladder, if it is indeed not physically relieved immediately, pronto-tonto, one could find oneself in dire trouble and in not inconsiderable discomfort, causing blindness and all forms of involuntary body contortions. Unfortunately, Pimple had allowed himself to ponder too long at the door where possessed of thoughts of a pleasurable wee, resulted in just such contortions, combined with blind panic.

Entering the bathroom in a speedy way and, in a temporarily blinded and contorted condition, the WC presented itself to Pimple, and Pimple immediately presented his modest equipment to the WC and released his first flush of second flush Darjeeling, appreciating coincidentally, the cooling breeze from the open sash window that drifted across his bits and pieces throughout the duration. A most pleasant experience, he remarked to himself. As his sensibilities slowly returned, Pimple considered the benefits of this window breeze in his control of those indefatigable thoughts of the Crumpet assets, this soothing zephyr having lost none of its meter, having to pass via trouser legs, however ably assisted with judicial flapping. Such was the sublime nature of the cooling effect from the window behind the lavatory that Pimple allowed himself to drift off into a transcendental sense of wellbeing and thus was completely knocked for six when his member was bonked, so to speak, with a lump of sideboard thrust through the open sash.

'Take that, you fucking loony.'

Shocked and in pain, in a very sensitive part of his anatomy, Pimple had to acknowledge the intended efficacious rubbing of his member, in order to offer a soothing respite to the sudden soreness, had the opposite effect he expected and produced the now familiar Crumpet virginal rising sap. This sap showed no sign of dissipation either as he was coincidentally presented with the face, then the shoulders and a goodly proportion of the upper lady bits, of Georgiana Lovebody, expertly easing herself, cat burglar like, through the window, so efficiently and speedily that she could not avoid what can only be described as an inadvertent kiss of Pimple's principle part of his bits and pieces department. Pimple knew not what to do, but clearly all of such bodily functions do not necessarily require the conscious prompting of the brain, as Pimple's virginal sap rose even further and the aristocratic idiot felt nailed to the spot, rigid, so to speak.

'I think you may have a splinter in that.' Ms Lovebody said, halfway through the window and simultaneously taking a hold of Pimple's principle component part, 'Yes, I can see it, hold still now, there's a dear.'

Pimple had no life experience upon which to draw and so stood still as ordered, a little like his reaction to his mother's assertions. Well, that was some sort of life experience he supposed. 'Stubborn little bugger isn't it, I may have to see if I can draw it out with my mouth. Now be a love and help me through the window, please.'

Pimple did, managing an accompanying 'Er, er...' several octaves above his normal speaking register, which naturally modulated closer to soprano than tenor anyway.

Ms Lovebody was through and she straightened her flimsy summer dress, lowered the toilet seat, flushed, at the same time admonishing Pimple with a look his mother would be proud of, enquiring if Pimple's mother had not taught him to flush the toilet after him. She dropped to the seat and grabbing the principle member, she pulled that particular intimate part of Pimple to her face.

Pimple followed rapidly behind and felt like he was going to have an out of body experience, which was one way of putting he supposed, as Ms Lovebody expertly addressed the splinter with her mouth. Pimple could only moan and groan and eventually the inevitable happened, which to Pimple's amazement and consternation, did not seem to surprise Georgiana Lovebody at all.

'There now, that's got it, do you feel better?'

Pimple did and he also remarked he was now also most ardently in love with her, asking if he might take up synchronised swimming at her earliest convenience.

'Well, you seem to have the build, but I may have to give you personal lessons. How does that sound?' She said licking her lips rather salaciously, though also in a practical manner.

Such is the multitasking way of women you see, and I would know, I am writing as a female pseudonym.

'Oh dear, dear Georgiana, may I call you Georgiana? That sounds simply divine, when can I start?' he replied breathily.

'Call me Georgie and, yes, we can commence the basics shortly after I have kicked that Welsh, Irish tart up his Khyber Pass and told him what for. I see no reason why we cannot get you off with the starter course straight away,' and she flicked her glorious and shimmering blond eyebrows, which had all kinds of effects on the Pimple brain and sensory organs that before he had only experienced when the blousy Ms Crumpet had alighted so recently on his orange box desk.

Nervously, Pimple immediately saw before him all of the drawbacks and instinctively felt it would be the correct and gentlemanly thing to do, to mention them. 'But, I do not have a swimming costume with me?' He ignored the rest, like, what would his mother say, as he had observed Ms Lovebody's gaze was directed, again, to his bits and pieces; probably noticed another splinter he thought, only slightly worried medically. However, he was confident that dear, dear Georgiana knew what to do when confronted by a troublesome splinter and so he tried very hard to deport himself casually, as she spoke to him with overly animated lips and energised eyes (or so it appeared to Pimple).

'Oh, I don't think trunks will be necessary, do you?' She stated, now enthusiastically fondling his bits and pieces that had begun to respond and in a not particularly gentlemanly or courteous way, although if she were to leave the room at any time in the near future, he was already standing up. Georgie correspondingly stood and tippy toed, as Pimple was a six foot four inch beanpole and although he was still curved in latent ecstasy, Georgiana was petit by comparison.

Pimple and Georgie stayed looking at each other for a little time, as lovers do he imagined, having had no personal experience other than the stories in his magazines. Pimple certainly appreciated the massaging of his splintered member and he could not disguise his disappointment when Georgie began to fold things away and raised his zipper, saying, 'Okay, let's put this away for the time being shall we. Follow me, I think I shall call you Everhard.' And, stepping over a mountain of clumsily distributed lumps of sideboard that Pimple, in his blind urinary passion, had not noticed, very much as he had missed she knew his name, Georgie daintily trod her way to the door, looking back to Pimple as she disengaged the lock, and flicked her eyebrows for him to follow. This very act of feminine wile and direction, resulted in major ructions in the Pimple trouser department, at the same time causing him to fold his body, not unlike he had recently done in response to a build-up of Darjeeling in his urinary tract, only more pleasurable he reflected, trying to get rid of the grin he had plastered all over his face, evident he noticed, looking in the mirror as he passed gingerly by.

Pimple followed the delectable Georgie through the hallway toward the living room, fixated on her hindmost regions, which he noticed gyrated and in such a way he understood exactly what Aedd meant when he referred to the conducting Ms Bea Flat's, tectonic plates. At the living room door Georgie turned back to Pimple, presumably to be sure he had followed dutifully and she acknowledged he had whilst making an inordinate fuss of fondling the orb-like door knob. Combined with the previously established success of the flicked eyebrows, Georgie encouraged Pimple, the now hunchback of Southsea, to follow. He did, completely trapped in this woman's tractor beam.

In the living room, that Pimple was now want to call the map room, Aedd was still on the phone describing the various benefits of a variety of grazing options on a northern slope, compared with a south facing incline, whether this be pig, for pork sausages, or whether your bent be for the formidable British beef banger. Georgie went up to Aedd and took the phone from him and passed it to Pimple who noticed immediately, as his senses were heightened, that Aedd had been talking to the dialling tone. This meant either, Lady Pimple had gotten fed up with the origin of said sausages or, Mercy had arrived expressing a desire to bathe. Either way, Pimple was relieved not to have to explain to his mother he had had a portion of sideboard in the principle member of his bits and pieces and she was not to worry, as Georgie had said she could sort this and kiss it better. He assumed dear Georgiana had *Marigolds*; a boy can only hope.

Pimple replaced the telephone into its cradle, looked, and he had not been mistaken, there was a *Dynotape* sign that said, "This telephone is an authentic replication of the Khyber Pass" and was dated 1938. He could see it now as he remembered the geographical features distinctly from the *Carry-On up the Khyber* film mother had banned him from watching as it had rude references and double entendres.

It was quiet he noticed, as previously mentioned, Pimple's senses were on red alert. He saw that he was being observed questionably by Aedd and lovingly by his adorable and outstandingly voluptuous, though as also as previously mentioned, petite, Georgie, who was positively miniscule beside the overly elongated Irish Welsh twat, who also seemed unaware he was about to get "what for".

Satisfied the phone was up the Khyber, so to speak, Georgie directed Pimple to stand beside the Horn of Africa, out of the way, while she dealt with the errant geography teacher. Pimple did as instructed and couldn't help noticing that as he took his ease against the wall, his bum settling upon Table Top Mountain, the view from the front Georgie would likely observe, was anything but a flat mountain top. She smiled and the African topography changed yet again, all missed by Aedd of course, who was summoning up the courage of his Irish warring ancestors, his very long line of Welsh Swansea Jones's and Grufydd ap Llewelyn, Pimple presumed, in order to face down the patent ire of a synchronised swimming instructor, who bore an uncanny resemblance to the young Hollywood starlet, *Shirley Temple*.

Aedd was therefore somewhat disconcerted, having focused his mind on controlling his watery bowels, when Georgie playfully slapped him on his face and said, 'Next time you decide to drop a sideboard, in part or whole on my head, rest assured you Welsh Irish dinlo, I will ram it up your arse, in whole or in part, so far they will have to pick the splinters out through your mouth. Do I make myself clear, Aedd?' Aedd nodded. 'Now, I am taking my Pimple downstairs for a jolly good seeing to and I will present him to you tomorrow morning, duly scrubbed and ready to interview you for whatever cockamamie story he needs and, you will oblige. Is that clear?'

Aedd nodded again.

She seemed satisfied with that and swung her gaze to the Horn of Africa, said nothing, she did everything with her eyes and eyebrows, which as previously mentioned, could elicit the most sensual responses from the Pimple body, which was further geographically announced by his trousers. She offered up a sideways glance, a slightly elevated right eye that could have been a wink or may have been a quick glance to British Columbia? Pimple guessed it likely was a wink and allowed his jaw to drop, which permitted, uncontrolled as his nervous system now was, his tongue to loll and slobber onto his chin – she smiled. It must be attractive Pimple thought and stored that up for the next time he wanted to appear attractive to a woman. He still had not put together any reasoning as to how this woman knew his name, knew also he was a journalist and, was here in Frisian Tun to get a story from an Irish Welsh dinlo.

Georgie gestured again with her eyebrows, which Pimple interpreted as a questioning look, saying possibly and rather hopefully, do you want a seeing to? He presumed so, and controlling his gag reflex, he managed a stuttering "Mm mmmm", followed shortly after with "rather, yes please", as he had been brought up properly and ordinarily he would flush the toilet, but thought he could mention that another time, maybe when they got downstairs, if he needed to break the ice.

Pimple was beginning to note a little frustration creeping onto the beautiful Georgie visage with the subsequent two looks, which were soon accompanied by a crooked finger, which either meant she suffered from arthritis or that Pimple should leave Africa to follow this Goddess across the globe to the map room exit and, thence to submit himself to her will. Yes, that would be it, and Georgie at last seemed to convey satisfaction he had understandingly, if not yet so enthusiastically, done as she expected. He set off feeling a lot like a crooked David Attenborough about to nestle with a female gorilla, not in a hairy sense you understand, but in a predatory sense, though he had noticed in passing, a blurring under his dearest love's armpits.

'Everhard, please do not talk to yourself. Are you mincing?'

Unsure of himself and speaking certainly with more confidence than he felt, Pimple responded to Georgie, 'Er, I suppose I am...' and he instinctively lolled his tongue onto his chin with a hint of slobbering, to compensate for likely appearing stupid in front of the woman he loved with a passion. He explained, 'When I am nervous it seems to go to my legs, which ordinarily behave gingerly, though today have assumed an additional picking disposition, but now I am unsure and definitely unable to control my mode of perambulation, which has been added to by an action that is certainly mincing in manner.' Pimple was mildly encouraged by Georgie's sensitive kitten viewing face, so he added further, some additional facts by way of amelioration. 'The picking seems to have cleared up, so that's good isn't it, Georgie, my voluptuous and wondrous Goddess?'

She looked back to him and extended a gentle smile. For him? He was unsure as it may have been because she was fondling the door knob, this time from inside the living room; an activity not missed by Pimple and clearly conveyed to Georgie by unsubtle movement within his trousers, in particular the Table Top Mountain department. 'Come along Pimple, and try not to mince, please, it is not particularly stimulating for a woman.' Pimple put his tongue on his chin on impulse again, instinctively knowing he needed to compensate for the mincing.

Aedd watched Pimple mince out, following Ms Lovebody, and resolved to give Bea Flat a call and invite her over to see Birmingham and, as he approached the Kaiber Pass, he heard Pimple and Georgie leave through the front door.

'Please, don't mince, there's a love.'

'I'm sorry gorgeous, but my brain is saying do not mince Pimple, but the Pimple legs are not responding.'

'Well, I will just have to attend to that as well won't I? I think you will find the brain is connected to more than just your legs, Everhard.'

'It is?'

'Yes, my love, it is.'

Everard was grateful Georgiana was so knowledgeable about the human anatomy and resolved that he would allow her to lead on that one, knowing he could, by way of informative balance, put her in the picture regarding embroidery if the occasion should arise.

SIX

THE DAME, THE JOURNALIST, THE SYNCHRONISED SWIMMING INSTRUCTOR

PIMPLE STIRRED AND LOOKED AROUND HIM. Yesterday evening, having minced his way down to the garden flat, consumed in the perfume saturated trail of the fragrant Georgie, he had sensed a feminine aura within the Lovebody boudoir, but not until first light of the morning had he the wit or indeed the conscious presence, to notice how fluffy and pink it all was. This also, he thought, could appertain to the heavenly delights of Georgie's bosoms, although these were fluffless, as he watched them rise and fall in time with her gentle breathing. He took advantage of Georgie's snoozing, a rare event in what had to have been, Pimple reflected, the best night ever in the life of Pimple minor. Georgie's breasts were fuller than he imagined the

Crumpet bosoms to be, but then he had only had a fleeting glimpse of those and a lot of that time his gaze had been distracted by the lacy trim of the brassier, which he considered to be extraordinarily alluring.

'Do you like what you see, Everhard?'

Only now did he venture a glance at Georgie's face which, although radiantly beautiful and certainly worth a gaze or two, Pimple believed he thought practically; her face was something he could presumably see anytime, the breasts however required urgent attention this morning, lest this be the last he sees of them which would be to summarise the Pimple luck so far in his life of reluctant innocence, emotional and sexual deprivation. Such was boarding school, he thought also to himself philosophically, recalling the cold baths, flogging and buggery that he had been assured would stand him in good stead in becoming a shining example of an upright English gentleman.

'Everard, look at my face, please, you can examine my breasts both visually and physically at any time you wish,' and Georgie turned ever so slightly toward him, causing a gentle and rhythmic movement in the sumptuous appendages that, despite his desire to obey the facial command, this erotic mammary samba required all of his attention lest he miss the subtleties. As Georgie's breasts settled into their natural angle of repose, Pimple considered they indeed did have an appellation characteristic, which was both as warming as it was attractive and also served to be in context geographically, being both a mountain range and a location where the grapes that make wine are grown; the nectar of the Gods, and who could argue with this. He was sure Aedd would agree and certainly these glorious protuberances were akin, as far as Pimple was concerned, to a wine from the Bacchus, not that he would know as his mother had advised him off the demon drink, though he did have the occasional orange squash when she was not looking and, as a consequence, oranges held a certain frisson quality; a forbidden fruit and, if presented with orange marigolds, well...

'Everard.'

Pimple thought how much he loved the way dear Georgiana spoke to him. She used a more earthy vocabulary than he had ever been used to, apart from some of the people at work, who were, according to his mother, "pig ignorant". The Georgie natural earthiness had however acquired a downright filthy intonation and vocabulary he had noticed and, been thrilled by, throughout the night. A thought passed momentarily by, of the fleeting kind that ordinarily could be dismissed, but in this instance raised in Pimple a degree of importance. He considered it was lucky he was recumbent beside Georgie in her pink fluffy bed, or he most certainly would be mincing.

'I'm sorry my Goddess, but I do so adore your breasts,' and he ventured a grazing touch to the left nipple.

Georgie moaned and covered his hand lest his natural timidity cause him to remove it. She had been aware during the night it was this very coyness that likely was the foundation of his tenderness, which she appreciated, but right now she wished he would just fuck her. She let out a subconscious sigh, a mixture of sexual longing and a base animal desire to bash Pimple. However, she reflected she was a teacher and probably needed to teach. Pimple was unaware of the sigh or its subliminal message, or indeed his summon to duty, but he did respond to Georgie's ministrations. Though still unpracticed in the art of making love to a woman, he allowed Georgie to take the initiative, which she seemed more than ready to do as she embarked on whatever it was she did that made Pimple feel sensations he had only ever read about and, as a result, he felt truly as though he could bang the table in any cafe with an accomplished aplomb, regardless of the quality of service or fayre.

Interestingly, whilst Pimple and Georgie were putting the finishing touches to their moment of sexual oblivion, Georgie noting it was only a moment, but realising also in her practiced manner, Pimple had time to become skilled and she was after all a teacher of synchronicity and knew also, only too well, this required patience and tolerance, at this same time, the bozzer to Flat 2 bozzed and, in authentic Dublin fashion, Aedd had in an Irish response to the patent bovine officious demands, deflected Dame Pimple to the front entrance of the garden flat.

Ecstatically unaware of what lay in store for him, Georgie coaxed the wobbly legged and fulfilled Pimple, out of bed, suggesting they shower together and she will ensure she cleaned off all the residue peanut butter, including the crunchy bits, from behind his ears. Pimple had already noted the ever present earole peanut butter had not stopped Georgie's desire for him, so Pimple, with incontrovertible masculine logic, had presumed Georgie was not a Floozy and would be met with wholehearted approval by his mother whenever she is introduced, unaware this was imminent.

Georgie asserted that after the peanut butter

is removed she would personally attend to his bits and pieces, 'A man must always ensure his bits and pieces are well and truly clean,' she remarked, as she steered him to her wet room with a firm hand on his rabbit bum. Now where had he heard that before Pimple thought, as the door bell ding-donged, accompanied soon after by a handbag shout reminiscent of *Lady Constance.* Pimple had remembered the play, to wit, Aedd had eluded as he had taken the telephone call yesterday evening and was thus alerted to a heightened conscience and acuity of mind that could only be put down to the recent intimate nurturing of the dazzling Georgiana Lovebody.

It may be opportune to mention that the above is an interesting fact many men may want to remember when negotiating sex with their wives or girlfriends, who may, by unfortunate error, consider them to be somewhat temporarily dim-witted. A man should sensibly point out that if their current view is one of dim wittedness, then it is well known that sexual favours could be a recommended remedy – I mention this in passing, as I think it is relevant in many men's lives, speaking as I do, as a female pseudonym, but more of that anon.

. . .

The all too recognisable, to Pimple, bellow, was moose-like and thus conveyed an atmosphere akin to a mist draped dawning in the Canadian tundra territories, as it shattered the morning peace in Frisian Tun, as well as the peace of mind and sexual serenity Pimple minor had had the benefit of up until this very moment, along with, of course, its benefits of increased mental dexterity.

'What on earth is that?' Georgie enquired of Pimple, sensing he already knew, as he had stopped mincing his way to the shower room and commenced prancing gingerly and, with a definite pick to his gangly gait, towards the closet adjacent to the doorway.

'My mother', she heard his muffled call, having nestled himself within the various pink anoraks, pink coats and, pink wellington boots with fluffy faux fur tops, that must be the prerequisite, Pimple presumed, of any synchronised swimming teacher, after a pink bathing costume and pink swim hat with pink flowers on.

Accepting that Pimple needed more than synchronised swimming and sex lessons, Georgie allowed him his sanctuary whilst opening the door fully, in the buff and in the pink, so to speak, to receive a full on blast from what she presumed logically to be Dame Pimple. The blast however, slowly diminished in strength and eventually muted, via a whimpering bellow, to a kittenish mew, when the full picture of the naked body that only some twelve hours or so more ago, her son had so avidly fallen in love with, became the full on focus of Dame Pimple's infatuated, doe like, moose eyes.

Georgie was immediately struck by the equine, or was it moose-like features and though wide and shortish, in a *Sponge Bob* way, the intimidating bulk of Dame Pimple was indeed monstrous. It would have been kinder to refer to the matronly Pimple as stout, but Georgie did not feel her kindness genes surfacing just at the moment and so summoned her feminine cunning chromosomes to the situation. She allowed observation to become the precursor of any pre-emptive strike, as she allowed Dame Pimple a moment of study whilst observing she could see nothing of any similarity between mother and son. Looking directly at Pimple's mother, noting the corresponding gaze was directed to her own bosoms and exposed lady's bottom, Georgiana accepted the Dame was looking for entry and so she beckoned, suggesting she might like to trot her way into the living room, thinking coincidentally, do moose trot and recalling she had Canadian friends and Georgie resolved to ask them when next they spoke?

Dame Pimple did indeed trot to the living room, remarkably light on her feet, unaware of the equine or moose references, assuming, in her naturally haughty manner, this must be the way lower class people spoke and behaved these days. Georgie noticed the trot held a remarkable similarity to Everhard's gingerly way of walking. Maybe he is not walking gingerly but performing some sort of dressage manoeuvre, Georgie considered, determined to discuss this with Everhard at some point, maybe after she had telephoned Canada.

Georgie allowed the dame to brush past and gently closing the door, she followed, calling back softly and with a strong hint of womanly affection to the cupboard, 'Are you alright in there, Everhard?'

'Mm Mmmm.' A muted and definitely timid response emitted from the closet, which did not go unnoticed by the acute hearing all horses have.

We have to rely on this for the time being, as the aural capabilities of moose are unknown to the author, although one suspects, Aedd would know, perhaps in a later chapter Georgie will enquire or maybe telephone Canada sooner?

Dame Pimple however, refrained from a neigh, summoning a bovine snort as she planted her substantial hind quarters into an armchair, fortuitously capacious with designedly reinforced legs and here she waited upon Ms Lovebody's attendance in the living room.

'I was just going to wash your son,' Georgie said, having returned wearing the flimsiest of frilly pink negligees, which had an overreaction on the part, or more accurately should we say, parts, of Pimple minor who was venturing a look from the crack in the closet doors, having regained a sense of the adventurous self he had found whilst seeking the bathroom the previous evening. Although, in that instance, he was driven by Darjeeling, whereas this morning's bravado was more instinct for preservation.

'You know, you really should refrain from the peanut butter behind Everhard's ear, or at the very least from using the crunchy variety,' Georgie said, as she sat on the edge of the armchair and draped her arm around the shoulders of Pimple's mother, fingering, as she spoke, the huge lobe that dangled and, tantalisingly, Georgie allowed her breast to gently brush the moose shoulder. Pimple's mother began showing all the signs of distinct edginess that told Georgie she had her man, or moose, so to speak, in a Mountie sort of way. 'Now, you make yourself comfortable and Everard and I will attend to you directly...' Georgie paused and thought for a while, '... unless you would like to join us in the shower, there's plenty of room?'

For a fleeting moment it appeared Dame Pimple seriously considered the offer, but regained her composure and was set to launch into a full frontal attack, however, before she could lower her antlers, Georgie kissed the stocky woman full on the moose lips. This dampened the blast to a stuttered, 'I say, what... what?' and Georgie stroked Dame Pimple's face and fondled her muzzle, where she was sure, a bit, harness and reigns, should be attached and was quite titillated by the thought. 'We'll be back in a moment. Make yourself comfortable,' Georgie said, in an asthmatic way. 'I do not have *Horse and Hound* but there is a copy of *Hello* magazine on the coffee table,' gesturing with her head, causing the Georgie curls to bounce in a similar fashion as Dame Pimple's generously proportioned, matronly, ear lobe.

Dame Pimple, unable to disguise her disappointment that this Floozy had not only surpassed the peanut butter barrier, but also, did not subscribe to *Horse and Hound* magazine, allowed her eyes to follow Georgie's sashaying synchronised tectonic plates, as the beauty glided to the closet, collected her son, who, in his birthday suit, and evidently aroused, dutifully followed this sensuously striking woman, whom she also wanted to follow into the shower room, being likewise aroused, only in a lady way.

'I say Georgie, you have a way with mother I have only ever seen Mercy Mudstone achieve.'

Georgie smiled, 'Everhard, you are such a sweet boy, are you not aware your mother bats off the left foot?'

'Bats of the left foot?' and Pimple chuckled. 'My mother plays hockey not cricket.' This was a nervous observation, as not only had he stepped under the shower with Georgie, but she had chosen that moment to soap his bits and pieces, coincidentally mentioning that they needed a thorough cleaning, before going on to talk about the Isle of Lesbos, which both Aedd and himself had yet to locate. Pimple thought about asking Georgie where said Isle might be geographically, when without warning, he lost the drift of his thinking and may even have called out something, as he heard his mother's responding holler as to his welfare; least that is what the baying sounded like.

Pimple had to admit to feeling astonishingly invigorated, to the extent he remarked upon it to Georgie. 'Dearest Georgiana, I feel simply marvellous,' and she smiled up at him, as she helped him on with his pants that were still a little damp after she had rinsed them through the night before. Boys she thought, flicking her head up, tutting and tittering to herself. 'Everard, I think you can dress yourself and after you have managed that and, without my aid, I am going to give you your first synchronising lesson, featuring the bra coupling or principally, the uncoupling.'

Pimple was amazed at the efficient way Georgie donned the brassier and buckled the wondrous garment behind her. Georgie then took Pimple's hands and directed them to slide behind her back, where she dextrously guided his fingers so he might readily release the catch. 'Everard, you're not paying attention,' and she gave up, rather enjoying the clear pleasure he was getting from gazing at the frilly pink trim to her encased bosoms. 'I think we should go and give your mother mouth to mouth, and then, up to see Aedd and get your serious journalistic career underway, don't you?'

Everard could not disguise his disappointment.

SEVEN

THE JOURNALIST, THE FISH WIFE, THE PROFESSOR

'I SAY AEDD, COULDN'T RUSTLE UP A SECOND flush of jolly Darjeeling, old man? A beverage has not passed my lips all morning and I am seriously parched, how about you Georgie, my dearest, darling love?'

Georgie nodded agreement, noting a novel command in Pimple's voice; a man emerging she ventured to hope, wanting secretly for Pimple to command her to undress and ravish her; she sensed an involuntary shudder.

Aedd noted also Pimple's confident directive, masquerading as a posh request and, swinging his gaze around the rest of his guests, he indicated to the base of the Himalayas, asking if they all would like to partake of a leafy infusion of Darjeeling origin, a second flush.

Simultaneously, and almost carelessly, he flung his redundant hand in the direction of France and conveyed to the company he had croissants and pain au chocolat, if the fancy took them.

'Rather,' Pimple called out, 'I could mange a chevaux...' and he looked instinctively at his mother.

What is the French for Moose?

And the Dame indeed looked like she could manage a nose bag or two, appearing also as if she was considering consuming more than her oats, as she cast a lascivious glance toward Georgie; champing at the bit, with no sign of delicate reigning-in.

'Right you all are then, my old china's,' Aedd said, passing the East End of London on the way to the kitchen and calling back, 'Georgie, Boyo, the honours you would do and introduce our most intimate neighbours, isn't it,' he then modulated his cadence, 'an all, an all,' and disappeared into a door beside the Mont Blanc tunnel. Pimple was left wondering if that was Welsh, Irish or Yodel out of Star Wars, or would that be Swiss?

· · ·

Of course; Mont Blanc.

Georgie stood and smoothed her sheer, flowery print, cotton, summer dress. Although Pimple was yet to be matched in the masculine embroidery classifications, he was not particularly versed in fabrics and colours or, identifying flowers for that matter, although, if pushed, he would say they were roses. Georgie stepped over to a bent woman of an indeterminate age, Pimple thought, never having acquired that skill that some possess, of being able to pinpoint the age of someone. However, this woman had to be circa one hundred and fifty he considered, rubbing his chin that may have developed a bristle overnight. He wondered further that if he wished to acquire a fashionable stubble and sooner rather than later, maybe he should nip back down with Georgie and partake of more rumpy-pumpy, since this current whisker, which was proving to be moderately robust, had appeared shortly after a night of energetic coupling. He noticed Georgie was fixing him a stare, which did not synchronise with his own carnal way of thinking? Maybe he would sit and be quiet.

The aged woman was sitting on an upright chair upon an absorbent pad. Pimple was aware of such things as his father, who is considerably older than his mother and when he is allowed out from the House of Lords, had a similar pad on his favourite armchair. He presumed the red leather of the government benches in the House are similarly protected, but with Noble absorbent pads. So, let us say for the sake of good form, the woman was elderly and had the look of a Cod that had been deprived of water for some considerable amount of time and was most definitely floundering to remain swimming in mortal waters, most of which it is hoped was being absorbed and chemically deodorised.

'Mrs Fish,' Georgie said with a flourish, suggesting to the practiced eye that she was passing by quickly whilst fanning and dissipating rogue uric fumes, more than being beautifully eccentric, Pimple suspected. There was a distinct pong, reminiscent of an aging haddock he had once and completely accidentally, left out on the kitchen work surface the fortnight mother had been away with Mercy Mudstone on a hockey tour; it had to have been 2005 or it may have been 2006. It doesn't really matter, as the whiff was uniquely identifiable as a rotting fish and so Pimple dismissed the date thing as a quirk of his mental makeup, very similar to his inability to assess the age of a person or his knowledge of fabrics, type of thing. Whilst reflecting, he reflected also and by way of a reassuring remedy, it is good for a man to have a few quirks, it is what makes them interesting to women, that, and lolling tongues, which he had recently learned, whether necessary to accompany this with slobbering or not, he had still to determine.

Mrs Fish lifted her gnarled hands, by way of acknowledgment and Pimple noted they had the look of crooked discoloured fish fingers, dressed in a papery thin gauze, which he presumed to be her aging, liver spotted skin.

Georgie had moved on and Pimple fast forwarded in order to catch up with her bouncy bottom cheeks. 'Professor Thelonious Monkspot,' she called out as she scratched at the bushy, salt and pepper hedge that covered completely the lower visage of this bulky academic man, save for a pair of overly pink and rosy lips, which protruded rather like haemorrhoids on the anus of an extraordinarily hairy bottom. This astonishing beard grew rather untidily, but without doubt, academically, down to his bow tie, which had been screwed into an inexpertly tied knot. The Professor of Flat 4, Pimple acknowledged to himself, knowing also this man batted off the left foot and he made a mental note to ask, discreetly of course, if he could direct him as to the whereabouts of the Isle of Lesbos. The man looked all knowledgeable, which, compared to Pimple, was not what one could call *no mean achievement*, however, he did look like a man of the world, Pimple thought, amusingly, sitting as they were in the map room.

Aedd returned with the beverages and French pastries and placed them neatly and squarely on a Canadian Lake that resided below glass, on a particularly sixties looking, spindly legged, coffee table. Pimple couldn't help noticing, prior to the arrival of the Darjeeling and confections, there were ducks or more likely Canadian Geese, flying in an exact opposite direction and the picture had a peculiar and quite disarming, positive and negative symmetry. Could it be the picture had been opened up, as if unfolded and the left half was the mirror image of the right? Too late, just as Pimple was getting to the nub of the photographic conundrum so he may partake in the rest of the morning's discussion with a good and balanced humour, so the Darjeeling and croissants were deposited by Aedd in a form of silver service that could only be described as cast iron, obscuring the water fowl. Pimple had not even sought the depths of the background to see if there were any lurking moose.

Aedd, satisfied the tray was sufficiently well placed on the distinctly unsteady coffee table, an act Pimple mistook for covering up the unnatural balance of the lake, moose and water fowl, opened up by way of explaining the reasoning behind the attendance of the multifarious peculiar people, namely the Professor and the most unsavoury and aging Fish. Interestingly, he did this in a pinched nasally voice of indistinct accent, as whilst out in the kitchen preparing the brew and collecting the pastries, the assembly had, and without open and balanced discussion, allocated Aedd the chair beside Mrs Fish. Aedd did not mention the presence of Georgie, recognising in the look of both Pimple and Georgie that they were, at least for the time being, joined at the hip or more accurately, the loins.

Dame Pimple required no introduction as her presence had been announced, rather noisily, just prior to being directed to the garden flat a little earlier. More is to the point, mother Pimple had her noisy chops actively involved in devouring her third pain au chocolat with resultant and ensuing neighing sounds that the collective company took for equine Mmmm's, and patent enjoyment of the French delicacies.

Aedd continued in Irish, his nose having presumably acquired a natural, or at the very least, a temporary resistance to uric acid. He explained that Mrs Fish had been present when Cardinal Teapot and her Spanish Inquisition had visited the Austins. He proposed we hear her story first as this was the origination of the recent Frisian Tun difficulties, as they had been recently described in a typically English understatement, just prior to the appearance of the World War Two armour, machine guns of various vintage and, subsequent bazooka fire. 'A little like the Irish civil war or insurrection, was always described as, "the Irish Difficulties" or "the troubles", in news bulletins.' Aedd went on to say, by way of explanation that was not necessary, as everyone, with the exception of Aedd, of course, who was of indeterminate origin, Welsh, Irish or Swedish or even Bristolian, was English, and thus, quite as you would expect, appreciated an understatement of any event of such gargantuan importance, as normal.

Aedd, with his non-nose hand, pointed to the facial hedge. 'The Professor was present when the man from the council came calling...' for some reason this was in a Welsh accent, '... and I was present, so I was, when the Catholic priest, Father Mike O'Brien visited,' he'd switched back to Irish when he mentioned the Priest and Pimple thought the company would have been exceedingly disappointed and felt it quite going against the grain, if it had been in any other intonation. He went on to mention he had expected, at any time, for a chap called Weasel to be joining them, explaining he could have related what happened when the police arrived, but more of that anon. It was noted with a communal quizzical look that Weasel was referred to in the past tense and that Aedd had a marked sadness to his countenance, which miraculously disappeared as he directed his gaze and conversation to Georgie.

'Georgie, you were attendant at the first visit of the gangster, Keith Bananas, I believe?'

'I was Aedd,' and Georgie said this whilst looking as though the recollection of the moment filled her with utter abhorrence and, not a little fear. Fear it was and, as if by way of comfort, she grabbed Pimple's hand and thrust it between her thighs and we are not talking adjacent to the knee department either. The shock was only patent on Dame Pimple, who allowed her tongue to droop to her chin Georgie noticed, very much in the style of her son, though she masked her drooling and slobbering remarkably well as her massive, moose-like tongue, collected residual croissant crumbs distributed about the perimeter of her muzzle and redistributed them into her mouth with much savouring delight, if the accompanying neigh was to be interpreted correctly by the assembly of horse, or was it moose, whisperers.

Pimple put his spare hand up and gestured with his head to Aedd. He had a question. Aedd nodded. 'Er, you mentioned a person called Weasel and, if I am not mistaken, in the past tense?'

There was a collective intake of breath from everybody except both Pimples, as Everard was asking the question and, Dame Pimple was on her fifth French pastry and looking like she had her eye on the remaining two, the lingering crumbs and possibly the plate as well, Georgie thought, squashing her thighs together and eliciting a squeal from Pimple minor. Whether this high pitched Pimple exclamation was in sexual delight or pain, bearing in mind the back of his hand was still recovering from third degree scalding, was uncertain and not of any consequence to Georgie who sought only her own comfort and gratification.

Aedd adopted a posture of deep reflective thought and regret. 'Weasel, one Sidney Stoat, unfortunately died this morning in hospital of his wounds. We were hopeful he would make a full recovery, but it would seem, according to the police and my latest information from Dick and Duck, he had been "Polished orf". I quote again Jack Austin, sorry, Dick, who said to me, "He was done-in because he was an oily bit of work and a duck's arse", by which he meant a squealin' feckin' tow rag or, in other words, he told on people. Weasel was a local lad and incongruously, an old and close friend of Keith Bananas. It transpires that he had, rather inadvisably as it transpired, told on him to people of an authoritive employ, namely, and I quote Dick Austin once again, "the Filf". He was a grass.'

Pimple instinctively looked towards Georgie's lawn, completely clear of sideboard detritus, all of which now resided, albeit in a haphazard manner and bearing no resemblance to an item of furniture, within Aedd's bathroom.

'However,' Aedd continued, unabashed, although Georgie looked threatening and might bash him anytime soon, 'he did impart to me one or two snippets of events as they had come to light, when I visited him in his, upon reflection, ill advised, unguarded hospital bed. I will be able to pass on those morsels of background information at the appropriate juncture.'

Aedd seemed to allow that piece of distressing news to sink in. Weasel had been a popular local villain although of no exacting social stature, obviously, which would ordinarily allow him to come within a country mile of Frisian Tun, except on burglary missions, he had indeed been a childhood chum of Keith Bananas when, as a juvenile delinquent, Keith visited his maternal aunt in Southsea. It was a naturally obvious friendship since Mr Bananas had resided in the Hither Green part of London where, as he grew into a strapping young thug, he had developed and honed his gangster skills to an extraordinarily moderate level, if Aedd was not blarneying. However, any intake of breath to accompany astonishment was put on hold as Mrs Fish passed audible wind.

It had long been suspected by Pimple that this was a regularly occurring phenomenon from the Fish bottom, however, this was the first audible evidence. Pimple also considered it was just as well the Fish wife part of the tale was to be at the beginning, so Mrs Fish could afterwards retire to her sea-bed and, presumably a clean pad, for it was beyond any comprehension of Pimple, not that he had any expert geriatric experience as his father was generally kept well out of the way, ensconced as he was in Whitehall and other seriously important geriatric wards, that the pad could remain unblemished, and may even have already reached its design capacity. Then, coincidentally, he noticed a Boots the Chemist bag beside the Canadian Lake and presumed it contained the very likely soon to be urgently required, replacements.

EIGHT

THE JOURNALIST, THE DAME, THE FISH WIFE

AEDD EXPRESSED THE CORPORATE THOUGHT and pressed Mrs Fish. 'If you could impart your tale now, Mrs Fish, you may then retire to your flat and rest up?' He said this with an antipodean inflection, which Pimple thought he may have inadvertently copied from him, as clearly Aedd was standing nowhere near Australasia. Pimple felt, unusually for him, inexplicably offended, but discarded that thought as frivolous and focused his mind elsewhere as Georgie seemed to have rather pressing business and it involved his hand, currently well and truly trapped in and around Georgie's erogenous zone and, we are not referring to the climate in sub-tropical Africa. As a consequence of Georgie's consistently strong squeezing, the Pimple limb was displaying all the signs of developing an ache in the humorous bone, coincidentally manifesting uncomfortable signs of impending pins and needles in his metacarpus, (*not the fish*).

This presented Pimple with an additional quandary. He currently considered his quandaries were twofold, the maximum he felt capable of taking on board at any one time. How was he going to take notes if his hand was otherwise employed and, how would he convey to Georgie, that of course he revelled in the delight of his hand between her thighs but, he needed to maybe wave it around a bit in order to stave off a major attack of pointed embroidery implements? The quandary multiplied. Georgie appeared to be getting excited and, if he was brutally honest with himself and were it not for the aforementioned dilemmas, Pimple had to admit, so was he. He considered he could readily stand in front of Table Top Mountain and completely change the topography of that part of the Horn of Africa; so to speak.

Then he had it and never let it be said the Pimple brainbox is completely devoid of exceedingly interesting and diverting plans. He was, relatively speaking, the *Mr Kipling of exceedingly good ideas*. 'Mother, I need to get my notepad and pencil so that I may take notes for my article, would you be a dear (*or moose*) and do me the kindness of taking my place between Georgie's thighs, just for a moment please?'

Georgie, interestingly, appeared not to be quite as offended as Pimple's speedily assumed mental risk assessment had predicted, and he put that down to the fact his actions and fleet of thought, had not only saved him from an aching humorous and pins and needles, but also saved the two remaining pain au chocolat from imminent consumption. The Georgie thighs were out of reach, geographically, if you know what I mean, as the erogenous zones were closer to sub-continental Darkest Africa than the Canadian Territories of the coffee table.

Dame Pimple knocked her son over in her indecent haste to assume her much desired station, so much so, the recently saved pain au chocolat bit the dust along with a number of symmetrical wild fowl and, God knows how many, to date, undiscovered moose.

Picking himself up off the floor, Pimple looked over to his mother and thought he had never seen her smile so sweetly before, except when she bathed Mercy of course, but if he was honest and recalled the memory picture, the Mercy related smile seemed to have a pinch to it and generally quivered.

Having regained his feet and equilibrium, Pimple headed to collect his school satchel, which he recalled leaving in the hall yesterday evening. Approaching the hallway he fixated on the orb like doorknob and recalled, delightfully, the manner and mode, yesterday evening, by which Georgie had used this knob to not only to open the door, but to elicit such amazing sensations in his, at that time, innocent body. Innocent that is if you excluded the sideboard projectile in the bathroom, which, all things considered, could likely be seen as the precursor to Pimple's slide into a life of debauchery (*not embroidery, he's already done that*). He crossed his fingers and hoped and, this positive thought was only tarnished when he recalled that he embarrassingly had not flushed the toilet.

In the hall he picked out his satchel amongst a scattered array of geography text books, moccasins and hiking boots, the bag easily identifiable as it had his name written on it in thick black felt tip. A tad over the top and this had often been the butt of office humour amongst his fellow reporters, but his mother had insisted nobody would steel it now; as if anybody would want to steal a school satchel.

I may have forgotten to mention that in the Scandinavian countries, it is normal for visitors to remove their shoes upon entry to a home and

Aedd, having ginger hair that hailed from IKEA, insisted shoes be removed and, if you had them, slippers donned, or moccasins, if your bent ran to Indian attire, sans feathers of course. Interestingly, Aedd had said this not in a Swedish accent but Bristolian and Pimple wondered if Aedd had yet to master the Scandinavian accent. He made a mental note to suggest he visit an IKEA store as soon as may be.

You may also recall that yesterday evening, or to a reader, several chapters ago, I mentioned an interesting fact that most men would recognise, but for the benefit of my female readership I will expound again. This is that a man, having decided in his mind to have a wee, will thence find himself powerless to stop an imminent stream and thus will need to seek out, as soon as may be, a loo, or in the case of a dire emergency any receptacle or bush, though not an academic beard I hasten to add, even if this may not be overly unwelcome by Thelonius. If you recall this or can understand that, then you will understand also, likely even more so, whether you are male or female, that when stimulated sexually beyond any tolerable level, a man, or woman I have to presume, may have similar directional tendencies, and here I feel I should digress.

Though my chosen pseudonym suggests I might be female, I can assure you I am a man, although I may admit to timid tendencies when dealing with females of the line, which is how I can so readily describe how Pimple feels. So, if in a state of sexual frenzy, a man and presumably, for the sake of a politically correct balance, a woman, must find a loo pronto tonto, so to speak.

And as this very thought passed rapidly through the miniscule Pimple brainbox, so he recalled the location of the bathroom and sped, almost in gay abandon, except that would refer to the professor and clearly not Pimple, into the bathroom, multitasking to the effect of opening his fly and removing his principle member with the immediate predisposition to efficaciously relieving his excited self, so to speak.

Imagine the shock to Pimple, have you got that, well then imagine the even greater shock to the people in living room, or map room if you prefer, with the exception of Mrs Fish who not only stunk to high heaven, she was also profoundly deaf, to the piercing scream that emanated from the bathroom and more importantly from Pimple. For Pimple, in his carnal haste, had tripped on portions of sideboard that remained recumbent, willy-nilly, if you get my drift, on the bathroom floor. He received a splinter in his right foot, big toe, but also, as he fell full frontal onto a, for the most part, jagged exposed element of what he later recalled to be a sideboard cupboard door, he acquired a particularly nasty splinter that took up again, willy-nilly, and hopefully he thought, temporary residence, in the principle member of his bits and pieces.

Georgie launched herself in a vertical direction and in recognition of the origin of the scream, she virtually dragged Dame Pimple with her to the bathroom. The moose was reluctant to release the undergarments. Georgie stopped, looked back at Mother Pimple with what can only be called in polite circles as an admonishing look and, expertly she detached Dame Pimple, by removing the article of clothing to which the moose woman had become so fixated emotionally and physically.

Dame Pimple, unfazed, placed the flimsy undergarment, securely in a pocket of her bell tent dress, thus enabling Georgie to continue on unimpeded, if more scantily and draftily attired, to the rescue of her Pimple.

'Oh, my darling what have you done to yourself?' Georgie asked, as she entered the cluttered bathroom.

'I've got a fucking splinter in me toe and knob you dozy cow.'

Georgie was made startlingly aware, for the

second time that morning, of the transformation of a shy and easily startled, weak and innocent boy, into the semblance of a commanding presence of a man, albeit he was disabled, standing on one foot and thus presumably, would not be able to manhandle her to her garden flat to have his manly way with her, and, if she was not mistaken, his principle member actually did have a splinter this time.

Whilst taking up the most important wounded part of his body for examination, she was mildly encouraged at firm evidence of engorgement, which conveniently displayed the splinter to good effect. Georgie carefully examined the member and was then of the opinion it would most certainly need immediate attention and, definitely before any further use could be employed for more recreational or procreational uses. 'Come along sweet-pie, let me get you downstairs and I will see to this for you,' she said as she tenderly folded his privates away, very much as Miss Nightingale had likely done for her Crimean patients who had suffered similar splintering, and Pimple hopped alongside her to the door and down the outside stairs to the garden flat.

'At least you are not mincing,' she remarked amusingly.

Pimple did not object to her frivolous

comment and smiled, breaking into an equally frolicsome hopping chuckle.

Encouraging signs indeed, she thought.

With a little careful, caring and judicious use of her pink tweezers, Georgie had secured both splinters and rubbed and kissed his principle member better. She desisted from such ministrations to the big toe, aware that even though Pimple had shared a shower with her only a short while ago and even though she was partial to a smidgeon or two of *Pont L'Eveque*, the toe gave off that distinct aroma that whilst not unpleasant to her when emitted from cheesy comestibles, the cheese was indeed delicious to one who considered herself a part of the fromage cognoscenti, however, such a whiff off a toe it can be said in no uncertain terms, is disagreeable.

Georgie immediately resolved that in future, following the washing of the bits and pieces, she would direct Pimple to ensure his pedal department and especially the crevices, be cleaned out and rinsed thoroughly, not unlike she did with the crevices in his underpants the previous night.

NINE

THE FISH WIFE, THE SYNCHRONISED SWIMMING INSTRUCTOR, A CANADIAN LAKE AND A VOLCANO

Promising Pimple that at lunchtime they would return downstairs to provide a test run for his principle member, in the interest of ascertaining it functioned and with minimal pain, the odd couple returned to the map room.

Pimple collected his school satchel, notepad and pencil en-route and they entered with Georgie making an overtly teasing play with the door knob, just for her Pimple. The assembled company settled themselves and after a few mild titters at the thought of what had just happened to their esteemed reporter and, Dame Pimple looking mildly disconcerted at being marginalised in the Georgie erogenous department, they called upon Mrs Fish to give up her part of the story. She could then get the hell out, so they might all breathe more casually.

Mrs Fish, who Pimple noticed had now been moved to beside the open sash window, did not respond to Aedd's request. He asked again, 'Mrs Fish,' Aedd called out rather loudly, 'CAN... YOU... TELL... US... YOUR... STORY... PLEASE?' ... said slowly, loudly, and distinctly; BBC English? Georgie picked up an old snooker cue that Pimple thought must be used for pointing to cartographical detail whenever Aedd could not be bothered getting up from his chair or the ambient light did not permit the spotlight to operate functionally, and she poked Mrs Fish in the side, several times.

Mrs Fish responded to the pressure on one side of her body with a release elsewhere, parping audibly, but seeming to get the message, as did everyone else, the not so absorbent pad began to fill with a not particularly aromatic liquid. Aedd commented, the smell and viscosity was not unlike the essence of the open tar lakes of Canada and, rather aggressively pinching the snooker cue from Georgie, he pointed to Canada and presumably the province that contained tar lakes. Aedd sniffed some more and shuffled and pointed to Iceland, mentioning the sulphurous geysers, coincidentally swinging the cue to the East End of London and mentioning that geezer is a cockney expression, a term used colloquially for a man, although patently this acrid aroma currently emanated from a woman.

Everyone got the drift in both geographic and colloquial parlance and, most certainly with the wafting malodorous pong that drifted cloyingly around their nostrils. Then, a strange thing happened. In a gentle kindness and softness, hitherto only witnessed by Mercy Mudstone and recently, Georgie's intimate lady parts, and in an animated moose like manner, Dame Pimple stepped toward the foul smelling Fish and suggested she would take her to the bathroom and, "Attend to her botty".

Nobody was more shocked than the son of Dame Pimple, who could never recall such softness or baby cooing expressions from his mother, even when attending to his own botty, which she still did, but not so often these days. He remarked upon this to Georgie, at the same time expounding his view that Marigold gloves, whilst seen in a prudential light in washing up terms, could also be regarded in a rubbery erotic way, and he for one, would never dismiss out of hand, so to speak, their stimulating quality. He did add a provisional note of caution, suggesting proper care should be taken to avoid over excitement and the consequent risk of chafing. Georgie nodded her understanding, mentioning she had used her washing up gloves before, in extreme cases of sexual arousal, but this was mentioned conspiratorially and in a squeaky voice, whilst pinching tightly her nostrils as Fish and Moose passed by.

Pimple had completely forgotten to pinch his nose as he tried to convey his Marigold excitement to Georgie and thus gagged his response, but she did get the message to him, in a subliminal way, since conversation now proved impractical, that they may be able to partake of some Marigold delight tonight. Pimple looked completely perked as his mother returned, gathering up the *Boots* bag beside the disarranged Canadian lakes and, multitasking as only women can, collecting simultaneously one of the two remaining pain au chocolat. One had to admire the cast iron constitution of this stout, posh moose, that she could not only ably assist a decomposing fish with a runny bottom, but could also partake of a sweet and crumbly French delicacy at the same time, seeming incongruously, to savour both.

Throwing open the top sash, to join the bottom one, and opening the kitchen door beside Mont Blanc, Aedd allowed a beneficial through draft to disperse the noxious fumes and shared a passing and amusing thought, enjoyed by Georgie and Thelonious, in that the waft would be in the direction of the former abode of the Duchess, on Frisian Tun and, the socially unacceptable residents, quite liked that notion.

'I think, until we are rejoined by Mrs Fish, I could perhaps provide Everard with a little background information on the Austin's since they are central characters in recent events, this being an article of human interest, if I understood you correctly, Mr Pimple?' Pimple nodded yes, and Aedd continued, 'Although I should point out for the sake of a sense of balance that Mr Austin would very likely deny he was central and most likely vehemently, adding also that he was, in point of fact, left wing, not central and most certainly not left footed.'

Pimple shocked Georgie from her Marigold daydream, as he withdrew his hand from her below stairs intimate clutches, to get his pencil and pad from his school satchel, managing a judicial pins and needles hand wave, whilst the opportunity presented itself. Georgie displayed a hitherto unseen by Pimple, face of irritation and followed this up with a pointed remark, since the air had cleared sufficiently to permit normal conversation, as Aedd had just ably demonstrated.

'Pimple, can you not record the conversation? Do you have to take notes? And take that disgusting pencil out of your mouth that I was looking forward to kissing. I have no desire to get lead poisoning.'

Pimple was devastated and again on many fronts, only two of which he could countenance because, as previously mentioned, Pimple's brain could only handle two dilemmas at a time. 'But, but...' all previous evidence of a developing manly stature had deserted him. '... but, Georgie darling, Bernie LeBolt takes traditional notes and I am sure I have seen him lick the end of his pencil... er...' He stopped as it appeared to Pimple's simple and inexperienced mind Georgie had mellowed.

'Everhard, dear,' he noticed she had used his affectionate epithet and thus allowed himself to relax a little, a gesture that did not go unnoticed by Georgie. 'Sweetest, get your recorder out, place it on that moose in the background of the Canadian Lake and then, put your hand back where it belongs. There's a good boy.'

Pimple urgently scrabbled to get the recorder out of his satchel, at the same time desperately scanning Canada for a moose. He did, however, note that Georgie had omitted to say please and thus he was alerted. 'Are you unhappy with me, sweetness?' he asked.

There was a definite mellowing now as he applied his shy and easily startled, kitten look, which was a naturally occurring simpering countenance for Pimple, but just to make sure, he lolled his tongue on his chin. She giggled and said, 'Okay Everhard, but consider yourself in for some serious chafing tonight,' chuckling and fondling at the same time. Pimple was thinking, women are so accomplished at fondling, as he fumbled to switch the recorder on, unable to disguise his excitement at the thought of the nocturnal Marigolds. And then, with flustered excitement, he spotted a moose. It was behind a bush and a big tree, a Maple if he was not mistaken, and he put his recorder on it, then it was gone.

'Yes, well, Marigolds aside, the Austin's,' Aedd continued, somewhat embarrassed, adopting a posture suggesting curvature of the spine, having found himself mildly excited about the washing-up gloves. He resolved to invite Bea Flat over that night, not only to show her Birmingham, geologically speaking, but to also suggest a bit of washing up in the bedroom department. Having made his decision, Aedd continued with a fixed grin that fooled only Pimple. 'Jack Austin, whom we understand is known in the constabulary as Jane, was a Detective Chief Inspector in the Community Policing Department, run by his wife, Detective Superintendent Amanda Bruce, now Mrs.

Austin, obviously.' He tittered involuntarily, which enabled him to pause naturally and within a conversational flow to allow Pimple to replace the batteries of his recorder that had given up the ghost as he had gotten to "constabulary".

Aedd paused his discourse, having immediately picked up Pimple's request to put the old batteries in the oven. Aedd's response was simply a glance that Georgie and Pimple's mother would have been proud of. Looks, which Pimple presumed hailed from his Irish father and likely all the way back to King Diarmuid the 1st and he gathered also that any prospect of getting a bit more juice out the dying batteries was a forlorn hope. Georgie leaned over and whispered in the Pimple ear, now noticeably more agreeably fragrant without the peanut butter, and she suggested he could have the batteries from her vibrator since she did not anticipate using it for a little while.

Pimple's cheeks turned scarlet, mainly because Georgie had winked and tittered when he, by way of an enquiring reply and in a correspondingly hushed tone, revealed that he did not know what a vibrator was, other than he presumed it vibrated. The blush turned to beetroot when she conveyed in a reciprocating undertone that it was a familiar implement on the Isle of Lesbos and much favoured by hockey players, or so she was lead to believe. 'I'm sure you get my drift, darling'. Pimple didn't, but pretended he did as she had called him darling and he accompanied this with a knowledgeable nod that would likely convince any man on a bar stool, but it didn't fool Georgie.

Aedd was getting irritated at the continual interruptions to the flow of his presentation and, as if to labour the point, he pointed with the snooker cue to Scapa Flow, emphasising, "Flow".

Pimple presumed this was some woman called Florence that Aedd knew and was of Scottish descent, or more particularly the Orkney Isles and, coincidentally wondered if the Isle of Lesbos was a part of the Orkneys, which unfortunately, because of his distracted and latent Marigold excitement, he had managed to speak out loud.

Undeterred by Pimple's uttered ignorance, Aedd continued. 'Yes, well, it would be underestimating things to say that the Austins' were singularly successful as police officers and, I have heard it suggested they were a little more than that,' and he tapped his nose in a knowing way.

There was a communal intake of breath, but it was Georgie who said what everyone else was thinking. 'How so, Aedd? More than what?'

Aedd fluttered his hand underneath his armpit and wafted a dodgy masculine scent, which was fortunately carried away on the breeze in the general direction of the Duchess's bomb site. Pimple turned to Georgie, who momentarily opened her legs as she leaned forward to participate in the conversation, enabling him to wave his hand around to defend against pins and needles, before getting it back in place avoiding any serious rebuke. He did remark, however, about how difficult it was to record a wobble of the hand under an armpit and that generally this is the sort of thing he would note in his journalist notepad, by way of informative characterisation. Georgie said nothing, but her look indicated plainly that she considered Pimple was being a dipstick. She nodded to Aedd that he may continue, his point had been ably made with his judicious hand fluttering and nose tapping that need not appear in Pimple's article.

However, despite his resolve, Aedd had to wait as just then a limping moose entered the map room conveying a wriggling, marginally more fragrant Fish, under one armpit. Dame Pimple sprayed the seat of the Fish chair with an atomised disinfectant, laid out a fresh absorbent pad and, in a practiced way, deposited Mrs Fish, giving her a gentle and reassuringly playful slap on the cheek. 'There you go old girl, hopefully that cork I have shoved up your bottom will do the trick until you can get back to your commode,' and having satisfied herself the Fish was stably seated and, more importantly, stably contained in an intercontinental manner, Dame Pimple made her way back to her own seat, moaning like a Stag, or more likely a moose at bay.

'Delores darling have you hurt yourself?' Georgie remarked, removing Pimple's hand with less courteousness than he felt appropriately due an ardent lover.

Pimple's discomfort was even more exacerbated as his mater expounded in a vehement manner, which of course Pimple was familiar with, but it was the language he found so disconcerting. 'No, I'm not fucking alright. I've got a bleedin' splinter in me fucking toe from some sort of sideboard debris in the mother-fucking bathroom.'

That seemed to be it, but the tears that seemed to be forming in the corners of her moose like, doleful eyes, dried and shone as Georgie kissed them, at the same time encouraging Dame Pimple to sit back down into the armchair. She assisted the Moose to settle, as though accommodating her into her natural Canadian habitat, whereupon Georgie lifted the wounded cloven hoof into her squatting lap and commenced soothing the throbbing big toe and, unlike she was prepared to do with Everhard's pedal digit, she sucked Delores's toe to soften the hardened skin, which apparently many hockey players get, from the shoes presumably. Suitably softened, Georgie took a hairpin from her beautiful blond, Shirley Temple curls and deftly removed the black splinter, after which, she kissed the hoof better.

Not even on the banks of a picture postcard Canadian lake are you likely to see a more radiantly happy moose as the throbbing toe was allowed to recover in the folds of the Georgie upper lap region. Pimple had to admit to a momentary green eyed feeling, coincidentally sensing the Marigolds becoming a distant and forlorn dream. Maybe Georgie needed to go to *Specsavers*, he thought to himself, but rapidly discarded that thought as it made his own countenance, in the eyes of Georgie, diminish, and his ego so recently puffed, deflated more than slightly and was manifestly audible.

Georgie, tiring from squatting on her haunches, although patently delighting in the moose toe massaging ministrations, decided, ironically, she would sit on a moose. By this of course I meant only metaphorically and, you had to wonder if Georgie in fact played hockey, maybe in her spare time Pimple mused. Georgie lifted herself up and sat back down on the already destabilised Canadian Lake coffee table, which promptly collapsed, causing Georgie to roll backwards throwing her legs into the air and, as a consequence, she displayed her recently undressed ladies bottom; the pink lacy underwear's, of course, were currently residing in the pocket of the moose bell tent dress.

Dame Pimple could not disguise her delight as she bellowed and, if the squeals of mirth emanating from Georgie were anything to go by, she was equally pleased with the gymnastics and resultant moose effects, though patently not synchronised, and Pimple wondered if he should mention this.

Aedd, however, expressed his indignation at his now destroyed Canadian lake table, as well as the sad fact that the final pain au chocolat had been well and truly squashed into the rug that depicted a cross-section through a volcano, with several thrusts of flame captured erupting from the top and one from the side. Curiously, and if you were in a certain position in the room, as Pimple was, these erupting flames appeared as an ignited bottom discharge from the exceedingly attractive and bared behind of his dearest, lovely, Georgiana. Pimple listened, there was no according parping noise, so it must have been his overactive imagination, which like his senses, had been on red alert since recently losing his virginity in a most exceptional way.

Before Aedd's righteous anger over his destroyed Canadian lake and the pain au chocolat encrusted volcano could be vented in full force, volcanically speaking, he himself having a similar view of Georgie's lady bottom, though from another direction, Georgie, still putting on a show, winked at him. Now Pimple could testify as to what effect that can have on a man, or indeed a feeble boy in his case. As a consequence, Aedd's intended verbal repost fizzled. He managed only a gibbering retort, which if Pimple was any judge, and he was beginning to assume an air of superior expertise in the matter of accents, was definitely Irish, maybe Gaelic he reflected and not gibberish at all, giving Aedd the benefit of the doubt, as he had a fondness for the geography hermit.

TEN

THE GEOGRAPHY TEACHER

'Oh, for Christ's sake get on with it, this cork will not last forever,' said Mrs Fish, with hitherto unknown clout for a trout.

Pimple assumed, being one whose mind often turned to such thoughts, that this outburst from Mrs Fish was to prevent another sort of outburst, as he considered the Fish malodorous gasses were likely building internally and could well be close to reaching red on the pressure gauge, the evacuation route below having been bunged by his mother, and he knew how that felt.

There was little point in apologising to Mrs Fish for any incommodious delay as she was as deaf as a post and so Aedd continued on his way, grateful her expulsion was oral and not, well...

'Anyway, as I was saying...' Aedd continued energetically, imagining his excitement more than adequately concealed his embarrassment, '... there may be more than meets the eye with the Austin's.' He touched his eye, and it hurt. 'But most important in understanding our chalk and cheese neighbours...' he continued rubbing his now sore eyeball, '... is that they are just that, chalk and cheese and I would know, as for instance in magnetism, opposites attract.' He halted, aware as he espied through his fingers, a reproving glance from Georgie and, instinctively, for he knew Georgie well enough even for a Hermit, he considered there may have been enough geography this morning, if that was possible.

'Jack Austin...' he said, carrying on, '...would likely call himself an aging rough diamond. Indeed he does call himself, "A jewel amongst men", which may amount to the same thing, although his eccentricities incite one to call into question the gem references, but rough around the edges would indeed be apposite. However, Amanda Austin, the mature cheese to Jack's dry, powdery chalk, well, she is the most fragrant of fromages...' Aedd flung his hand in the direction of France and, if Pimple was any guesser, it was likely directed to one of the more fragrant areas, possibly the Bois de Boulogne in Paris.

The professor jumped at the mention of boys in Boulogne and Pimple cursed he had spoken out loud.

Aedd continued, nodding to Pimple as an aside, that he may have a point. 'Jack Austin used to call his wife Mandy Lifeboats or Mandy Pumps, but now insists she be known as Duck and, I have to say, she is the total and complete opposite of Jack, or should I say Dick, as he now wishes to be known. Dick is a whale of a chap in shape, size and behaviour, assuming whales behave in a juvenile frolicking manner and who is to gain say me,' he said flinging his hand to encompass the Seven Seas, where presumably, whales frolicked in a juvenile manner.

Maybe when they are not in a school? Pod knows, but Georgie is insisting Aedd gets on with it...

'Get on with it Aedd,' Georgie said, and it wasn't her sexy kitten voice.

Told you...

· · ·

Aedd took the verbal prod in the spirit it was meant and looked scared for his life. He continued. 'Amanda, though not the last in line when the height genes were being handed out, is womanly and handsome in every respect. She is beautifully proportioned, a fine body in a full, sensual way and, she would be a jewel any man would be happy to have adorning his arm. In summary...' Aedd noticed a hush in the room and sensed he may, with the intention of conveying both the character and appearance of Mr and Mrs Austin, have dwelled a tad too long and, patently delighted in, the embellished description of Mrs Austin, but he decided that where women were concerned, there never were enough superlatives. So he continued, 'Whereas Dick, was most certainly running to fat and at a rate Usain Bolt may consider heady. He is also and, unfortunately for the chap, ugly. Amanda in striking contrast has a beautiful face.' He gazed, as if in a dream, to the Battle of Trafalgar ceiling, 'She has... a certain *Sophia Loren* countenance. Hmmm, light olive skin, though Dick calls it ivory as he doesn't like olives, and ivory sounded nicer, though I understand he has never tasted ivory either and, although Amanda Austin would argue her nose was too big and, if I had to be frank, it is, and so much so, she is likely to hail from Nose City...' he made to point to a city and giggled as he realised his mistake. 'She is, especially for her age, a most handsome woman, though clearly defective as far as her choice of husband that is, in the eyeball and brains departments.'

He took a natural pause to drink in some of the cleaner air, glancing towards Mrs Fish, aware it could become foul at any point, then following on from another barbed comment from Georgie, to the effect, "Is that BBC English you're speaking?" he continued on his way. 'I have been asked to do a programme for BBC South, *Rocks around the Docks* and they appear happy with the prospect, but have suggested I refrain from the variety of accents – so there.' A mature response he considered and, all things considered, it was.

Aedd continued, unabashed, although Georgie looked like she considered bashing him, all things considered.

'Now, you may note, I said Dick Austin was ugly, but...' and here Aedd put his finger in the air as if to pick his nose, considered it, but moved on, he could always pick it later and he needed to practice not picking for the BBC, '... to be fair to Dick, he assures me, without laughing and giving the game away I might add, that he actually has a disarming smile or would have, if he were not frightened to go to the dentist. However, his ugliness for the most part stems from a brutal and gross disfigurement, to wit, no right eye, that he exhibits, sans patch...' a quick flick to France, '... and to all and sundry, he proudly displays, inter alia...' a point that Pimple presumed was to Rome, '... the puckered wrinkly skin that sinks into the vacant eye socket and, as if by way of enhanced distraction and additional curiosity, there is a vertical raised scar running from his forehead and onto his cheek. A police wound by all accounts and all of which he views as a minor blemish to his otherwise faultless features. But, and this is a big but, what gets up the nose of the self appointed aristocracy of Frisian Tun and especially the Duchess, as if Jack Austin being as broad a cockney you are likely to find south of the Bow Bells, is that Jack Austin is a GM, CBE and something or other that is the Queen's gallantry thing for coppers?

I understand also that Mrs Austin is not far behind her husband in decorations, though Mr Austin insists that when it comes to decoration, it is Mrs Austin who will pick up the paintbrush. He, claiming to be the brains of the outfit, therefore took on the most important part of decorating, which was all about the preparation and that involved principally, sitting down and thinking about it, an art form at which, he assures me, he is consommé. He is the self declared thinker in the partnership he insists; mainly when Amanda is not around it is as well to be aware.'

As a narrator of consommé female pseudo characteristics, having sat down myself in a comfortable armchair by way of preparation, I feel I should say you could go no farther, and not be accused of dwelling in the realms of fantasy or fiction, (which this book is of course) than be aware that no man would walk the streets thus disfigured, without a pirate's eye patch that, of course, is irresistible to the ladies. No, take my word for it, as someone who has walked the aisles of Sainsbury's and other supermarkets, thus attired in the eyeball department, by way of experimentation of course. It is akin to winking at ladies without the effort or the risk.

Sorry, I occasionally like to digress, especially after a meal and, in an armchair.

Anyway, I can tell you, as clearly Aedd is not likely to get around to it as he is picking his nose at the moment, Mr and Mrs Austin were married in the Roman Catholic Cathedral of Portsmouth, no less, and the Austin's later received a Papal Blessing. This is true as Jack Austin has told me himself (although the character is fictional of course, as am I, at least as a female pseudonym that is) and, as if to confirm the veracity of the statement, Jack added "honest injuns" and his nose remained exactly the same size. Though he did say he was confused that the Holy Father would offer his blessings as he hadn't religiously sneezed.

Then to rub salt into the patrician wounds of Lady Blanche-Teapot, it is known also he will soon be knighted and Amanda will become a Dame, presumably shortly after this Frisian Tun, little "to do", as Dick calls it, has settled, one has to assume – I will undress now, which is the opposite to digress, which is Welsh for having a sit down after dinner.

Aedd took a breath and flicked a nasal boulder at Mrs Fish; she wasn't paying attention. Mrs Fish made to start, but Aedd shut her up with a prudent bounce on her head with the snooker cue and went to recommence but was interrupted by Georgie, who was clearly not a candidate for a bounce to the head with anything. She even took particular exception to the odd portion of sideboard. No, she was a different kettle of fish, if you forgive the amusing pun, and so the cue remained firmly at Aedd's side.

'You said Austin was an eccentric and since

our ace reporter, here...' and Georgie gave Pimple an old fashioned look, '... has not followed up on this...' But this response was to be delayed for Georgie gave the impression to be currently less enamoured of Pimple. Pimple observed and was saddened, naturally, but put Georgie's demeanour and lack of amour-dalliance, down to his mother's foot that resided where, by rights, his hand should be, although he felt blessed relief the pins and needles had passed, although his humorous bone still ached when it should be laughing. Georgie was though a sensitive soul and registered Pimple's malaise-amour, and so, removed the moose foot and returned to sit with her Everhard and, as she took his hand she whispered it was the Marigolds for him tonight and nobody else. To Dame Pimple, Georgie said, by way of ameliorating the cheerless look on the Moose face, 'Delores, I think your toe is on the mend but I can look at it another time if you feel the need, so to speak.'

Pimple was sure he saw Georgie wink, but had to logically assume it was for him, or she may have developed an affliction of course, it can happen. He'd seen that look before, though mainly directed at Mercy Mudstone at bath time. He worried, trying to think if such an affliction would preclude carnal relations, with or without Marigolds, but reassured himself it wouldn't, unless it distracted him and made him laugh? He was worried now, could he make love to a woman whilst laughing?

Mollified, Pimple's hand was again at severe risk of pins and needles, back within the heavenly folds, causing contented sighs from Georgie and the odd squeal and oooh, whether of delight or pain was unclear, to Pimple.

Aedd continued in response, having been on hold for a reflective moment or two, considering the nature of Dick. 'He is eccentric, Georgie, and that would likely be an understatement, as truly the full extent of his eccentricity would only be borne out by an extended period in his company. By way of an example, if you were to visit right now,' and Aedd stepped over to the window, peered around the marginally more fragrant Fish, so he could see into the equally large front Georgian sash window of number 5. He had his answer and continued to convey this to all. 'Yes, if you were to call right now, you would find Jack, sorry Dick Austin, lying in a foetal, Walrus fashion, with his not insubstantial bottom in the air and head flat on the carpet and only inches from the glorious front window. Now, I have been there and witnessed this myself and I have to take Mrs Austin's, sorry, Duck's word that this is a regular occurrence and, by way of testament, I have just looked and it is so, right now. When I enquired of him, he said it was his Alexander the Great technique and nothing to do with elephants going over mountains, although there is a patent similarity. He argues also this is a most comfortable position upon which to muse the problems of the day. I understand from Amanda that in Dick's last police activity he did damage to his back when he carried her for some distance as she had been injured, to wit, two broken legs and, he now has to do regular back stretching exercises.'

I interrupt Aedd here at a convenient time, as he has just located a particularly stubborn BBC bogy. I also say, as those who have followed the travails of Mr and Mrs. Austin will have read in 'Merde and Mandarins', and so could vouch for the veracity of the fact that, Jack Austin did indeed carry his wife some considerable distance, as she had broken both her legs and he struggled all of the way, being as he was, of a fairy like constitution, albeit physically he defied that description.

Jack Austin, for the sake of balance, always denies this, insisting he was seriously wounded at the time and that may have given the impression of him struggling to carry his wife to safety, when, in point of fact, he quite easily carried his wife to the ambulance, no sweat. However, Mandy has since told me it was this effort that put his back out and not playing shuttlecock, which Jack Austin says is a little bit like sex over a net, but with feathers.

'Aedd, stop tapping your foot – please continue.'

'What tune was it that I was tapping?' Aedd asked his assembled socially unacceptable guests.

'Fucking Doctor Who – get on with it,' Georgie's famed impatience would always out.

And isn't this just like women, and I should know being a pseudo one, for this book only, but I am starting to get a true insight – Ho ho, hang onto yer girdle Gertie.

'Yes, well, Jack Austin argues that in this foetal arrangement, he calls his Lotus Walrus position, he can see very well out of the window and be aware if the Spanish Inquisition were to come calling. And, if the Duchess was intending to make a personal visit, he could pretend to be dead with very little effort on his part, confident his well-known consommé acting skills would carry off the role to great effect. He was, he tells me, a major proponent of the school of method acting and had learned at the knee of Sir Larry. I have since discovered this was not *Sir Laurence Olivier*, but *Larry the Lamb*, a stuffed toy he had as a boy. At this juncture, I have also to note that Mrs Austin has said she would settle for that, the dead thing that is, and not the acting, which she was able to verify he did a lot and further confirmed, he is a consommé actress. But the other thing Dick assured me of, was this position enabled his requisite faculties to be so aligned as to present a prime farting arrangement, with the facility to accommodate multi directions, apparently paramount in his mind, although I have tried this and it requires, I suppose, experience and long practiced control.'

Aedd began to lower himself to all fours to demonstrate but was halted by a piecing glance from Georgie. 'That will not be necessary, Aedd,' and indeed it was not.

So, Aedd continued, standing. 'The Lotus Walrus position is also, Dick expounds, good for the grand children, just growing to the toddling stage, a little girl called Meesh who Jack, sorry Dick, rescued from a paedophile gang, and his dog Martin, a border terrier who now lives with Meesh it seems, who also has a brood of puppies that often visit. So the walrus that Mandy insists is a whale, provides a cracking play area he would say and he just loves it and reports proudly, he is Number One Grandfevvers and that this is also, apparently, due to be recognised by the Queen, just as soon as she gets her sword out from the cupboard.'

There was a stunned aura of disbelief, had Aedd made a joke?

'It would appear,' and Aedd began to convey the Dick explanation, 'the Queen has two swords, one for knighting and that sort of stuff, running through Tories and the other, a more ceremonial sword, is for number one granddads. I had to take his word on that as he has met the Queen several times. One incident...' and here Aedd chuckled, '... of which you can see played often on TV Blooper programmes, is the time he got his George Medal wearing Prince Philip's morning suit, although it was nearly the afternoon he says and he had a touch of diarrhoea, by way of explanation of the way he walked approaching the Monarch. The Queen can be seen quite clearly on the telly, hardly able to restrain a regal titter, the Duke of Edinburgh having lost it a long time since, so to speak.

However, Amanda, the eminently sensible and long suffering one of the partnership, although I have to say she is most definitely totally and completely in love with her eejit, as she calls him, and he clearly reciprocates the feelings, she says he likes to lie on the floor and call out to her about things that are happening outside. He does this, apparently, so she has to look out of the window and he can then look up her skirt. She rarely wears trousers. She tells me, quite unabashedly, she gets as much pleasure from the experience as her dirty old man.

So you see, we are talking about an elderly couple, he must be sixty odd? And she has to be late fifties? And if you met them, what you will see is a delightfully in love elderly couple, full of patent carnal emanations, goodwill to all men and with a remarkably successful track record behind them in the police, if a little dubious, I am told and, decorated by the establishment almost to the point of embarrassment, literally.'

Aedd furrowed his brow, pointed to the furrowed arable parts of Great Britain and, looking through his ginger eyebrows, said, 'Nevertheless.' His tone and manner was grave, 'This couple are, to the Duchess, of such ill repute that they most definitely do not fit in with how the old cow...' he swung his hand to the pastoral farming areas, coincidentally pointing to where the Hampshire free range beef sausages came from, Pimple noticed, '... sees things within her manor,' and swung the cue to a London

Underground map, in particular to Manor House Station.

They knew it was coming and felt powerless to stop it, and even Dame Moose let out an exasperated sigh, or she may have been otherwise, more agreeably diverted, it is difficult to say without a more intimate knowledge of Moose generally.

...is the plural of moose, meese?

Aedd was undeterred, though he did give the Dame a circumspect look, before going onto mention, 'Manor House is a station on the Piccadilly Line of the London Underground, and, interestingly...' he said, '... straddles the border between the London Boroughs of Hackney and Haringay, three of the entrances being in the former borough, and other entrance in the latter.'

'Aedd, get on with it, you tosspot. You were talking about the fucking Duchess, so skip the diatribe on the London Transport system please.'

Aedd could not be sure if Georgie was serious, knowing that a discourse on Tube stations can be fascinating, but a toe poke from the synchronised swimmer cleared that little matter up for him and so he continued. 'It is a sad case, Dick and the Duchess and, there is not much more to be said and, whenever Jack, sorry Dick, meets the Teapot Duchess, skin and hair flies. It is a sight to behold and no wonder it ended so tragically.'

Aedd had finished and it was with a stunned silence he was greeted by both Pimples, Everard and the Dame, with their mouths agape and tongues lolling in a most seductive manner. 'Close your mouth, there's a good boy Everard,' Georgie said, pushing the tongue with a notable indelible pencil stain upon it, back in, and closing Pimple's mouth manually, accompanied with a gentle uppercut with a clenched fist Mohammed Ali would be pleased with.

'But, I thought you found this look attractive,' Pimple responded, opening his mouth only slightly, and she laughed heartily. He had his answer and squirreled the knowledge away for future seductive forays with the opposite sex, but resolved, for the time being, to keep his mouth firmly closed. He almost opened his mouth as Mrs Fish stood and with hitherto unknown spry limbs, made her way across the room to command the attention of all and sundry, grabbing the snooker cue from Aedd and poking him in his privates, several times for good measure, as she moved to assume an authoritative position, dangerously close, for Aedd's liking, to the Volcano.

Everybody could see, except for Aedd, who was doubled up in what appeared to be the lotus walrus position, in considerable pain and squeaking in a high pitched shrill that was likely an Irish banshee accent, that this woman was of a strong constitution, which, as men of experience know with women of the elderly kind, will always out at times of great import. Very much like bodily fluids, solids and gasses will, eventually, but not yet, as everybody hoped, if all of the crossed fingers amounted to anything, that the bung would remain secure as other indescribable things wobbled.

ELEVEN

THE FISH WIFE, CARDINAL TEAPOT, THE FRISIAN INQUISITION

Mrs Fish adjusted her stance, unsteadily at first, her legs appearing to be closely held together. This was likely due in part to arthritic fusion of the hips, but her pelvis was seeming to give out a tell-tale creak, so it was more likely a desire to retain in place the Dame Pimple patented bung. There were some uncomfortable noises emanating from the Fish posterior, which might be more easily described and attributed by a mechanical engineer, as similar to rasping noises made by balloons when clowns made funny animals. The informing reek though was obvious. It was hoped that the mechanical device would hold true, or at least long enough for Mrs Fish to recount the visit of

Cardinal Teapot and her Frisian Inquisition to the Austins.

What was concerning Aedd though, was that Mrs Fish had chosen to impart her monologue, whilst making it clear she would brook no interruption or exchange of conversation that could constitute a dialogue, as she stood over the volcano rug, which already was preoccupying the mind of Aedd in just how to get a pain au chocolat out from what is technically known as the throat of the volcano. A compounded anxiety, as he worried that any accumulation and ultimate expulsion of Fish magma may cause irrevocable damage to what was, in Aedd's view, a unique rug. Aedd did take some comfort in that the Fish posterior volcano had no side vents, as they were known technically and, the principle Fish crater had been sufficiently stoppered. Dame Pimple appeared to be the sort of moose accomplished in just about anything she chose to take on and, clearly knew how to insert a plug when required to do so, as apparently Ms Mercy Mudstone, centre half hockey player, could attest. Aedd sat back, relaxed and allowed Mrs Fish to speak.

She did start and, in what can only be described as a Margret Thatcher tone of voice, which complimented her mode of attire, which Aedd knew would cause Jack Austin, a committed socialist, to flip his walrus state and shake as a convulsed sea mammal might if faced with a killer whale on the starboard bow. Mrs Fish authoritively set about her allotted task, regardless of the proximity or resultant effect it may have on nearby or passing walruses or indeed volcanoes.

'I can mainly speak of Amanda Austin, as I refuse to get down onto the carpet to converse with her idiot husband. I refuse also to call him Dick, although his behaviour suggests this may be an appropriate epithet,' she said. This aside elicited a Fish giggle, and it was possible in that briefest of moments to imagine this old and unsightly fish as a school girl. She straightened her face and it was possible to see how she might have, as Prime Minister, scared the whole male populace of this blessed Sceptred Isle. 'If you can imagine yourself as Amanda Austin,' she went on to say, having adjusted her bottom with her gnarled fish fingers that revolted Pimple as he was aware she had, through her tweed skirt, lifted the rim of her incontinence pants. He knew this of course as Lord Pimple, Papa, wore similar pants and not just to the parties he frequented at the House of Lords. And so, Pimple immediately expected a gushing to dampen down the volcanic ash cloud, which in truth, was just a crushed pain au chocolat, for heaven's sake.

Now, I did mention before that Pimple had limited intellectual power and this could, coincidentally, be correspondingly attributed in a similar fashion to his memory capacity, as he had completely forgotten about the Fish bung, as if the pained stance and manner of walking had not been sufficient to dislodge that bit of information from the inadequate Pimple memory bank. So, his diving for cover under the Georgie skirts, to avoid a gush of tsunami proportions, was misinterpreted as pent up sexual desire by all, except for Dame Moose, who knew her son well, and Georgie, who just knew, but decided to take the opportunity to push Pimple's face into her recently unclothed lady parts, and with a strength that belied her petite stature; just sayin'; 'Ooh err…'.

Pimple, after a minute or two, reappeared with a gargantuan grin, salaciously licking his lips, pretty much as Georgie had done when she first met Pimple in Aedd's bathroom, over a water closet and dismembered sideboard. Pimple made a mental note to share this as an amusing story with Georgie later, in an anecdotal manner, aware most couples ordinarily get to know one another over dinner, not the toilet or a dismembered sideboard, or both. His intuition never failed him, he knew she would enjoy that joke excessively and felt he was getting to know women uncommonly well. He thus was more confident in himself as he returned to his seat.

Mrs Fish continued, as if unaware of the goings on, which in fact was her general manner. Her ponderous way. Pimple noticed the unaltered Fish mode, her ability not to allow herself to be distracted or sidetracked, marking this in his limited brain capacity, which coincidentally bumped out the bathroom and sideboard anecdote as there simply was not enough room for both, and thus he hoped the Fish story was short. The nocturnal activities of the previous night had left Pimple desperately short of somnolence, having been more agreeably engaged in well and truly losing his virginal standing, and thus, he felt he was likely, at any time, to fall into a deep slumber, which he had no doubt would produce giveaway Zzzzing.

'Yes, well,' she said, looking at Pimple in a disapproving way that chilled the Pimple spine as it had the definite look and sound of the bogeywoman, Margaret Thatcher. Pimple's mother used to quote and show pictures of the

Iron lady if she wished to scare the bajeezers out of her youngest son. With most children, he had learned from others at boarding school, it had been the bogeyman. For Pimple however, the bogeyman sounded a relative baby doll in comparison to the Battleaxe Prime Minister, who apparently, in her youth, played a mean game of hockey his mother would say, but the very picture and sound of Margaret Thatcher in Pimple's immature brainbox, resulted in a watery sensation in his bowels. A signal sign his mother had singularly succeeded.

'Pimple darling, you are distracted and Mrs Fish wishes to get underway again, be a love and focus, please,' and Georgie smiled, which made Pimple quiver, in a nice way.

'As I was saying, if you were Amanda Austin and had to live with Mr Austin, you would be regularly occupied in mind, dreaming up various activities to keep your idiot otherwise engaged. I know this to be so, because I have discussed this with the long suffering, over a short period of time, Mrs Austin, and she, or I say in truth, we, have come up with many such activities and diversions and more so since he took, on an apparent whim, accompanied by most consummate flouncing, retirement. For example, and this was one of our earlier suggestions and not particularly successful I have to admit, going to the gym. Jack Austin was immediately engaged with his typical over enthusiasm and predictable unaccomplished relish, as he did most novel things, having, as is evident in most men, a brain that had not matured beyond early childhood. So he took up the gymnasium, as I said, with verve...' she stopped because Pimple had his hand up, 'yes, Mr Pimple?'

'You said relish, not verve. I am most particular in these matters being a journalist.'

Georgie clipped Pimple around his peanut butterless ear and Mrs Fish continued, she'd not heard anyway, but allowed Georgie her moment of fun and assertion of female dominance, which was, as Lady Francesca would say, "The natural order of things."

At this juncture, I make haste to inform my male readers that I do not believe this for one minute, but as I write this novelette, (note I use the female form of novel or would that be novelless, no, that would suggest there was no novel at all, or at least precious little), under a female pseudonym, I feel almost obliged to add something of female suffrage, although when I discussed this addition, my female partner corrected me by saying, "it is female suffering".

Who am I but a figment in the firmament of

my imagination, such burdens willingly taken on for the sake of my pseudonym and such knowledge and insight gained from my female partner as someone, who is first and foremost female, and would know these things, and I know this because she said she did and that is good enough for me - you recall I mentioned I had bouts of timidity?

However, I reflect that my thoughts, though pseudonymical and feminine, are akin to masculine blue sky thinking, as they say, or so I am told they say, as I often have my male head in the clouds and I am apt to miss the odd thing or two.

In the meantime, Mrs Fish was ploughing on, in an arable and agricultural manner, which suggested she might be manuring at any minute.

'As I was saying, Mr Austin took to the gym like a brick to water. Had he been able to concentrate and not be continually ogling the Lycra clad young women who frequented the establishment we enrolled him in, he would likely have been able to stay on the running machine and not fall off with such boring regularity and thus benefit a little from the exercise. He had, however, made adequate progress in the free weight department, moving from children's weights up through five years old, and was on, when by general consensus the gym management agreed he should leave, girls weights of between eight and ten years. Mr Austin considered this momentous progress was of such import that he boasted about it in C&A's, the Crown and Anchor pub, the Austin local hostelry he called his rubbadub, being of a cockney persuasion, and much to the amusement of the locals and, embarrassment, naturally, of Amanda, who loved her spindly armed, tub of lard husband, though God only knows why?'

Mrs Fish seemed to take a deep breath, she had lost her sense of smell in her old age, which all agreed was probably just as well.

'Of course, there were many more activities, all equally unsuccessful...' she was off again, '... for the man's only natural gift was that of being a gifted copper and thus, I have to agree, a fish out of water when challenged in pastimes most consider as passably easy, in a day to day manner. However, the latest thing, and here one might argue in actual fact, the fatal one, was gardening, which prior to our enthusing him of, he ranked well and truly alongside his interest in decorating, which as I have already mentioned, principally revolved around a philosophical contemplation of the task, rather than anything of any practical import.'

Mrs Fish allowed a brief time for a fit of the giggles, which she could see but not hear, to die down, and continued, relishing her task with verve she mentioned, for the benefit of the very particular Pimple journalist. 'As is the way with those familiar with feminine guile, both Amanda and I managed to elicit in Jack Austin, a modicum of enthusiasm by suggesting this and that, but it was principally the book by *Diarmait Gavin*, the well known sculptural garden designer off the telly that did the proverbial trick. So, and here is where the plan, which at first seemed to have wheels as they say, crashed and in such a way, it was like a runaway train hurtling toward old buffers that can only be described as Duchess like. This railway track was littered with obstacles that so enthused Jack Austin, it was as an inevitable consequence that the green-fingered activity and not inappropriately, was guaranteed to get up the snotty nose of the Duchess, who I can additionally inform, was once a nurse in the Hither Green, British rail infirmary, shortly after she gave up wheel tapping in the shunting yards as a career. Thus the train wreck reference and snotty green-fingers was not without fortuitous merit.'

Her point made, Mrs Fish allowed that little bit of information to be digested while she scratched her bottom and such was the stunned silence at the story, as well as the overt gestures the fish fingers were making in order to relieve the posterior itch, that the ensuing noise of fingernails, long overdue clipping, made on the rough texture of her Margret Thatcher tweed skirt with coordinated twin set and pearls, was such that it broke into the Marigold reverie of the journalist, Pimple minor.

Pimple felt the need to assert his Pultitzer acuity, principally to impress Georgie, but also for the benefit of the tape recording, should it at some time be listened to by Uncle Wendy. 'Mrs Fish, are you saying it is *Diarmait Gavin* who is to blame for the carnage and wanton destruction of Frisian Tun?'

Georgie clipped him around the ear. 'That's for the benefit of the tape, you plank,' she said, for the benefit of the tape.

Mrs Fish caused consternation for everybody as she went on to answer. 'Yes, this is exactly what Jack Austin would say and, I understand Mr Gavin was arrested by the Metropolitan Police who questioned the celebrity gardener for some hours, before being released on police bail. Apparently, he was denying all knowledge, not only of Frisian Tun, but of Jack Austin. It was this statement that made the police suspicious as Jack Austin was more famous than Diarmuid, what's his name, thingy Bob, the greengrocer. Furthermore, Thingy Bob, did not own a rocket launcher, which of course is a regular asset for most landscape gardeners if they were not in possession of an Exocet missile and, he gave himself away, by all accounts, calling it a bazooka.'

Pimple's reflex reaction was to stick his tongue out to Georgie, the problem was she noticed and worse, it still had the mark on it from where he had licked his journalist pencil, in the mode of Bernie LeBolt. She flicked his ear with thumb and forefinger and Pimple, in his mind, called it a draw and, he would of course know these things as he was now quite au fait as to the ways of Irish women called O'Fay.

'You see...' and Mrs Fish pondered again with a pained expression on her face as she looked at Dame Moose. 'Delores dear, I do believe the stopper may be unstoppering, would you be a dear and oblige me?'

Dame Pimple was up, like a moose up a drain pipe and took a hold of Mrs Fish as would a ruby player securing a the ball under arm as she tore out the living room in a way any English winger would be proud. Following a number of door noises and the obvious shifting aside of sideboard debris, there was an "aaah fuck" expletive as Dame Pimple managed to get Mrs

Fish into the bathroom for a touchdown, but the try was not converted in the normal sense of the word, as Dame Pimple had omitted to remove the incontinence pants and the Margret Thatcher tweed skirt. It would be understating matters if we were to say it would take the video ref some time to sort that lot out, and so Aedd suggested they adjourn for lunch and at that announcement Georgie grabbed Pimple, saying it was time for a splinter test run.

Pimple needed no second urging and as they passed the bathroom, which Pimple knew now how to get to with his eyes closed, well at least in a blind semen...al fashion, Georgie and he could hear, "You fucking daft old cow, why did you let that happen? There's shit everywhere".

Georgie remarked, 'I've never heard Mrs Fish speak like that before, it is so like Margaret Thatcher,' and at the mention of Pimple's bogeywoman, Pimple's appendage momentarily shrunk, so much so he thought Shirley Temple may need her hair grip again.

Thankfully everything was okay for Pimple, if just a tad frustrating for Georgie, reconciling to herself that with Pimple it may be an uphill struggle in the synchronised sperm swimming stakes.

TWELVE

THE FISH WIFE, THE POLICE SUPERINTENDENT

Lunch consisted of cold Hampshire, free range sausage sandwiches for Aedd's guests, and a kind of carnal sustenance for Georgie and Pimple. They resumed the gathering after what for Georgie was too short a break, which left her wondering if Pimple would ever master the art of sustained synchronisation.

Mrs Fish was now incongruously dressed and seeming oblivious of the fact, in Aedd's grey nylon track suit bottoms, prudently clipped at the bottom with Pimple's reflector cycle clips. The amended ensemble simply did not co-ordinate...

· · ·

My God, I have embraced my female pseudonym...

... the shiny artificial fabric of the shell-suit trousers, clashed inordinately with the Fish silk blouse, the buttoned cardigan of the twin set and pearls ensemble. Her tweed skirt discarded presumably and likely residing amongst the sideboard debris.

Mrs Fish was, as they say, unfashionably attired in an and uncoordinated Jam and Jerusalem, Women's Institute manner, the silk blouse having the most gigantic bow, reminiscent of Valentine's Day, except in Tory blue. Atmospherically, it was noticeable that Dame Pimple, having made a sterling effort in the cleaning up stakes, had also made judicial use of the atomised disinfectant spray. The previously malodorous air and furniture was now suffused with the essence of mountain lilies, including amongst the pot-pouri of nosegays, the ashes of violets perfume Mrs Fish had liberally splashed on just before she set out for the meeting this morning. Those with a sensitive olfactory organ seemingly preferred the Violets and *Dettol* to the eau-de-toilet of the Fish bottom.

'I am sorry Georgie, sweetie, I packaged the tweed skirt and soiled drawers in a Waitrose bag and lobbed it out of the window onto your lawn. Still, with any luck the foxes will have carried it off before we have to dispose of it later,' Dame Pimple said.

Georgie smiled in an understanding way, still a tad frustrated, but also wondering if the bathroom alpine atmosphere was of sufficient potency, as she felt a judicious dash to the loo may be required, for herself and, Pimple can whistle if he thinks he will get the batteries from her vibrator.

Pimple saw the mind machinations on the face of the woman he so passionately adored and beamed his newly acquired and confidently applied, manly grin. However, he was surprised at the contorted grimace he received back and so, falling back on what one knows has been successful in the past, as is the trait of all men, he lolled his tongue by way of a pleasant and stimulating interlude for his woman and, to his delight, Georgie laughed almost uncontrollably. This said more about Georgie's frustration than to the superiority of the seductive modus operandi, which Pimple thought he now had off pat, allowing himself a fleeting and warming thought of the Poultry receptionist. But alas, such subtleties of womanly wile and guile and even unsubtle mannerisms, were sadly missed by Pimple, who continued on in ignorant bliss.

. . .

And who can say he is not the better for it, apart from maybe Georgie that is? For Pimple, as it is for most men, it was again reaffirmation of his theory regarding the seduction of women and it took pride of place in his limited memory banks, where it had of course been this morning but had to step aside for another important matter, now also forgotten, as it had to make way for something else. You see how it works, and I know this for a fact, as I had previously met a man in the pub who, not long time in passing, had taken of a drink with a brain doctor in a different pub and he had been assured of the fact.

Looking like an elderly lady footballer for the House of Commons, Tory party, geriatric eleven, Mrs Fish, standing precariously over the volcano, the principle throat of which remained bunged by a pain-au-chocolat, the side vents remaining open and potent, she recommenced her diatribe.

'Thank you for sorting my botty Delores, now, where was I?'

'YOU... WERE... TALKING... ABOUT... JACK... AUSTIN'S... GARDENING' Aedd said, with no realistic hope of being understood, but it seemed Mrs Fish remembered without his guidance, spelling, and animated sign language.

'So, you see...' Nobody did, as Mrs Fish pondered on the Austin gardening, everybody desperate to get this bit over with. Even Dame Pimple tapped her hoof...

And, as any Canadian frontiersman will tell you, a tapping hoof on a moose is a sure sign to get up and get out - hold up – she's started again.

'... Jack Austin had as a consequence, spent many hours in contemplation of the *Gavin* manual which, although lacking in a certain amount of the Austin magic, he had thought and informed others of the fact, including *Alan Titchmarsh* apparently, he found the size and weight of the tome remarkably easy to read whilst in the yogic *lotus walrus* bodily arrangement. The basic perambulations of reading, which mainly consisted of looking at the pictures and the big writing whilst sitting down, or walrusing and so it was, the philosophising suitably disposed with, it was now down to the practicalities, a talent Jack Austin believed he had in abundance, no matter how many times women, who know about these things, informed him to the contrary.'

Mrs Fish waited while the women in the room nodded sagely.

'And here I have to take my hat off to Amanda Austin, who seemed quite content to let her husband expend his creative juices and inexpert impractical skills, on a project doomed to failure, in the sure and certain knowledge that in some form or other, she would be involved in the clearing up process. She did say to me however, she enjoyed watching him fail as he did it with such enthusiasm.'

This remark received more tittering from the ladies and the professor and, dim-witted looks from Aedd and Pimple.

'And so, in the Austin rear garden, he set to with much pacing and sizing-up mentally. Jack Austin had no need for tape measures or the like, which were for "Nancy-boy designers who put gel in their hair", apparently, and in a similar vein, he felt no need to sketch or to write things down. He was a natural and thus did not stoop so low as to commit his thoughts to paper. "It's all in the bonce, babes" he had said to Amanda once, and in my hearing and so concluded, I was included in the comment, tapping said bonce several times with his index finger, and adopting his intelligent *Diarmait Gavin* pose, that in truth didn't really come off. But, he was happy and that was all that mattered, or so it seemed, although I did have to point out to him that I haven't been a "babe" for quite some time, but appreciated the compliment nevertheless.

So you see, in so many ways and ironically, he was very much like the Duchess, in their shared arrogance and confidence in what they were doing, except he would argue in his own particular, intelligently reasoned way, "She was a stuck up old cow. A Friesian, which are okay for milking but that's about it, unless the black and white dapple effect was your bent". Whereas, and in contrast, he considered himself a man of "flavoured status" with the common man... and woman, he had hastened to point out looking fearfully at his wife and it has to be said, he had an uncommon belief he was right and, erroneously as it transpired, he believed in a pathetic childlike way he had the mental capacity to imagine what things would look like and more is to the point, that it all would fit. All of this you must comprehend, he understood and firmly believed, before setting out to implement the grand design that he fully expected to be transferred to next season's Chelsea Flower Show and, "Knock the feckin spots off that Irish twat, Gavin's bonkers design". '

She took a breath, then continued. 'So, even if the Duchess had not been there in a railroading capacity, things were predestined for catastrophe that even the combined minds of the best women in the street, namely myself and Amanda Austin, could not conspire to divert...' She paused, 'Please accept my apologies for your omission Georgie, and you of course, Professor.' Georgie smiled acknowledgement with a genteel sideways tilt of her face that seemed to suggest, to those who knew genteel sideways glances from a woman, that Mrs Fish was wrong in her assessment, but she was going to allow the old trout to get on without showing she was offended.

The professor pursed his revolting hairy anus lips, blew some bubbles and continued to gaze into the middle distance. He could have been thinking anything, but likely his thoughts were on his Greek male students, or looking at Birmingham's geological foundations and the Mercian Mudstone.

My guess was the former but both would be wrong – see later.

'So, the materials had been ordered and one day, it would have been early spring as the birds were up early and singing, whereas Jack Austin, also up at the same time coincidentally, whistled, not particularly tunefully and clearly upset more than just the local sparrows. He was not a great whistler considering how often he partook of this musical amusement, which he put down to a slight tug of the skin where his scar reached the corner of his lips and so, his former particularly expert whistle pucker, was restricted. He had contemplated suing the doctors for a bad job, but wiser heads prevailed and a calming influence was accomplished by some of the women, current in his life at the time, saying, "What a lovely whistle he had, so tuneful" or words to that effect and that was all that was needed.'

Except this came with consequences almost too awful and ear splitting to go into, in what is meant to be a rather light-hearted and happy ending, though violent, and saucy, crime thriller novel.

'By and by, a lorry with obscure, obscured markings, loaded with telegraph poles, arrived at the rear street behind the garage and their back garden. The crane on the rear of the lorry looked as though it had seen better days and, it had of course, but under another's ownership that was likely still current. Eventually, things were offloaded, accompanied by a lot of cursing that Jack Austin argued colourfully, saying the swearing was, "All part of the building industry darlin's." I did point out to him that whilst I appreciated the warm and touching address, I had not been a babe or a darlin' for quite some time...'

Pimple looked to Georgie, ducked, but on the whole the point was agreed.

'And, numerous lengthy telegraph poles were hoisted over the garage and placed in the rear garden, awaiting direction by Capability Austin, as Mr Austin was now calling himself. He had tired of using *Diarmait Gavin's* name, which all in all, he considered beneath his skill level, even though he liked the Irish, *Father Ted* in particular. To Jack Austin, Mr Gavin appeared to be a decidedly dodgy character, a fact I might also add, he reminded me of when the Metropolitan Police apparently arrested the Irish gardener at a later date. So, under his inexpert guidance, the team of monkey spanner builders waited for expert guidance as to where the poles should be placed.'

Mrs Fish paused to take a breath and reinforce her internal resolve before continuing. 'Now, those of you familiar with the grapevine governance of Frisian Tun, or similar middle class streets across Britain, which is a lot like the

Civil Service in Whitehall, don't you know...'
they didn't, just wanted her to continue, so
nodded, '... you would realise that by now the
jungle drums would be beating at an energetic
pace, matched only by war dances, which Austin
was convinced was the reason why it rained
shortly after the poles arrived and thus caused
the crane to slip and drop one of the poles across
next door's greenhouse. Jack Austin was not
overly worried about that, as the next door
neighbours', "Don't 'ave green fingers like what I
do", he said confidently. But mainly he was angry
that the Duchess and her Inquisition could not
tell the difference between a war dance and a
rain dance, "For heaven's sake" he said, gazing
skyward and expecting the Lord to intervene, as
one more post needed to be dropped, so to speak,
over the garage and saying if a papal blessing was
worth anything, then this was it, obviously.

He derred at God, but behind his hand, in
case an unpredicted thunder storm was conjured
by the celestial being with the odd thunder bolt
being tossed willy nilly, aimed at the Duchess of
course, but everybody knew God was a hopeless
shot and many innocents died in natural
disasters that were, naturally, aimed at naughty
people.

Amanda Austin reminded me of how many
other times he had invoked the Holy Father's

blessing, which her husband treated as small change in his pocket. A pocket that interestingly had holes that he argued defined them as officially holy, so there.

So, the moment a lorry with a crane, albeit of dubious origin, along with the poles themselves, had parked up with a builderly intent, the Inquisition lookout posts, which had been established at various strategic points around the Owenesque neighbourhood, including the shite street behind Frisian Tun that had shite-box houses with shite people in, began their corresponding, tittle tattling with the Inquisition.

Mr Austin pointed out some time later that these neighbourhood pill boxes were completely out of chocolate box character, but it was reciprocally pointed out to him that these lookout posts had planning consent from the Duchess. "Oh forgive me for feckin' breeving" I think was Jack Austin's response, that and two fingers up at the Duchess as she passed by to rally her lookout troops.' Mrs Fish giggled like a child and for some duration. 'If you will excuse my French...' Mrs Fish said, but people were more impressed by her cockney accent. 'Mr Austin's response to this rallying was, and I recall it vividly as I do the resultant look of Big Society shock on the faces of those pioneer Inquisition members who turned up as an initial foray, to scout the territory, so to speak. "That's total bollix you raspberry tart faced menials of a Friesian cow"', and Mrs Fish tittered again, thoroughly enjoying herself and, despite her gainsaying, it appeared she quite liked the ugly cockney walrus.

'Once again the demarcation lines had been set and here is the interesting part, without a pole having been placed, unless you count the one sticking out of next door's greenhouse, which Austin didn't, counting not being one of his strong suits. He would say, to whomever would listen, as he considered this pearl of wisdom suitable for general broadcast, "You can't make fings wivout breaking somefing," said in an all knowing fashion by way of reinforcing his argument, which irritated everybody except Amanda and me. We found it all rather amusing and felt just a tad cuddly and maternally protective to the man-child as he dug an even bigger hole for himself. Ironic when you think about it as the holes for the poles still needed to be dug and hadn't even been set out.'

Pimple failed to see the irony. However, Georgie was able to point out in the nick of time that Pimple had a feeble mind and a feeble inability to stay the course sexually, by way of multitasking, as is the way of most women, but, as is the way of most men, he was sublimely unaware of the barbed comment and lolled his tongue, which amazingly again, Georgie found irresistible, he thought. Pimple was beginning to think that after many years of post-pubescent abstinence, due in the main to peanut butter behind his earoles, he was in actual fact, God's gift, so to speak.

Georgie clipped him around the aforementioned ear thinking she might put peanut butter on his ears herself, and not the smooth kind either, but the stuff with great big crunchy lumps and afterwards she would shove the jar up his arse.

It would be reasonable to say that Georgie was still a little irritated you see, as is also the want of women, hence the term wanton women. It's all to do with peanut butter, simple when you have it explained to you and who better to explain this than a pseudonymical woman? I'm sure you agree I have an unusually adroit insight into women – so much so, I am thinking of writing a book, "Men are from Mars and women are from somewhere else, but definitely not Mars, and may be they are allergic to peanut butter".

I am still not sure if I should write this as Susan Narmee or Pete Adams?

THIRTEEN

THE DUCHESS, THE BARROW BOY SPY, THE LADY SUPERINTENDENT

Mrs Fish, following an amusing interlude, was back up and running, the cycle clips holding up well, held in place and securely fixed with additional string, as she had sparrow's ankles and the clips rotated in position and thus were considered unreliable. Pimple had mentioned earlier that if the proverbial was discharged at pace from the anklets of the shell-suit trousers, she would likely take off and this would make her a flying fish and oddly, nobody had laughed, but it did illicit a flick of his ear and a frown from Georgie.

'Now we come to the nub, as they say in France.'

This confused everybody except Aedd, who

pointed to Paris with his snooker cue, the Bois de Boulogne again, unless I am much mistaken, and said, 'N'ube', as if this made things crystal. Georgie clipped Pimple around the ear, nothing to do with Nub or N'ube, just because she remained a smidgen fed-up, which manifested itself in a mild form of Tourette's, which worried her for the long term, but for the moment she thought the condition came in handy.

Madame Poisson continued, so to parle, as they parled en N'ube en France. 'Mr Austin had several marking out sessions whilst Mrs Austin and I looked on. We offered encouragement, but mainly pointed critical comment, as is the want of women when employed in an undisguised supervisory capacity. When it looked like the poles were to be erected, the Duchess mobilised the Inquisition. A time and date was set for the inquisitioning, or a triage planning pre-application meeting as they say at Hither Green, British Rail Infirmary.

By the due date and time for the arrival of Cardinal Teapot and her Spanish Inquisition, several of the poles had been erected by a chap called Paddy, a friend of Kipper, a notorious villain from North Portsmouth, who was ironically a fast friend of DCI Jack Austin, still retired, but thinking about it. Jack was reconsidering his retirement plans, you see, as he started to have a sneaking respect for Gavin and this "Gardening lark", Jack commented, "might not be as simple as it looked at first sight, or the pictures in the book might suggest and maybe he needed to sit down and think about it a bit more"; we wished.'

By way of elucidation, Jack Austin saw Kipper, coincidentally, as a clip 'em around the ear type of friendly rogue, although he was, in point of fact, a notorious villain. But such were the policing skills of DCI Austin that he didn't see, or at least chose to ignore this fact, as he was not in Portsmouth for these skills as anybody who had read my (in my masculine persona) earlier books would know. And earlier on, Aedd had hinted at these nefarious other connections and, if that was still not enough, I wrote it on the frontispiece, so stop whinging for heaven's sake. It's not like any of you had a papal blessing, although it is not beyond the realms of possibility the Holy Father himself would read this book and presumably he would bless himself every morning after going to the toilet and, this story has definitely got some catholic bits in it. The sequel, brilliantly, has a story that revolves around St Winifrede and has loads of catholic bits, guilt and everything – so there. And, as Jack Austin would say, "Stick that in your papal pipe with brass knobs", or something like that; I think you have to light it, then Holy Smoke it.

Mrs Fish continued, following the rant of the author, who in the context of this story, apart from his insightful insights into women, writing as a woman, may be irrelevant.

'This mate of Kipper, Paddy, apart from securing the lorry of shady origin, had also been able to get the telegraph poles cheap, as these poles had coincidentally fallen off the back of another lorry, if you knew what he meant by, "nudge, nudge" and apparently a wink being as good as a nod to a blind bat, which to Jack seemed logical,' Mrs Fish said knowingly, and trying to imitate the flutter of the hand under her armpit that had recently, thank the Lord, been sprayed with atomised *Dettol*. 'I should say that it was reported not soon after in the News that a number of telegraph poles had gone missing from the Paulsgrove Estate and telephone communications were down.'

Pimple nodded knowledgably in a newshound way, about nudged bats and recalled verbally the story of the missing poles. He giggled and ducked before Georgie could strike, going on to say to Georgie, he was quite enjoying the clipping game, as he called it, then Georgie hit him with a Brahma, which sent him reeling very close in proximity to the volcano and worse, the rapidly filling track suit trousers secured only by reflective bicycle clips and string.

'Mother, did you not bung Mrs Fish this time?' he asked from the floor, adjacent to a volcano side vent, worried for the vents in the Fish track suit bottoms.

'No, Everard, I'd run out of bungs. I am utilising your cycle clips and string and, if you would shut up and let Mrs Fish finish, we may just be in time, but...' and she looked to Aedd by way of reassurance, a look which was quite amusing on the face of a moose, '... I am afraid I may have to pass the trousers on to the foxes later, sorry Mr Murphy.'

Aedd said he was not bothered. He had given up running as the Duchess had advised he looked silly and completely out of place when jogging, even when he left via the back door. "This is a Thomas Owen zone" she'd said, "and, unattractive joggers are banned by Duchess Decree."

'See what I mean about the Duchess,' Mrs Fish said. 'It is no wonder Mr Austin stitched the old cow up a treat, to use his cockney parlance,' and she tittered again.

Aedd quickly flung the snooker cue to point to London, but got it wrong, as he had panicked and pointed once again to Paris, but covered his tracks by saying, 'Oui...' which ironically the doubly incontinent Mrs Fish was doing as he said it. 'Je N'ube' he added, as if to suggest he was aware of this and all continence of the world, as he was a consommé geographer and as such, knew also of double incontinence, as most men will know when having had one too many at C&A's, or other fine hostelries or rubbadubs.

'What happened then?' Pimple asked, lifting himself from the floor, ducking and experimentally sniffing the uric acid enriched air.

'The inquisition turned up of course. I was there being invited by Amanda to join them around the dining table.'

'Who was in the Inquisition?' It was Georgie, showing interest that was soon forgotten, as Pimple thought it was his turn to clip Georgie around the ear. 'Pimple, what do you think you are doing?'

Nervously, already suspecting he may have misinterpreted the rules of the clip-em round the ear game, stuttered, 'Clip-em around the ear game?'

'Clip-em around the ear game?' she

responded, mimicking his panicky tone, 'what on earth are you talking about?'

I would like to interject here as a female writer, though in pseudonym form of course and those that know me, will testify that I am a roughty toughty type of fellow, who rarely minces, but, you see, this is where men can go completely wrong. Not consulting a woman before they act, you see, as invariably they get it wrong, which amusingly, as it turns out, the judge of what is right and wrong is of course, the woman.

Now, here is the irony. This is exactly what the Duchess said to Mr Austin at the commencement of the Inquisition, only she meant instead of woman, read "The aristocracy", and went onto refer to sub-section 77 of the Middle Classes Act. "In the event an aristocrat is not available, consult a middle class woman" blah, blah, and the Act goes on to refer to their God given birthright to rule and, speak loudly in restaurants and posh shops. As she said that, so the Duchess received a clip around the ear from Amanda Austin. Amanda was not aware there was a clip-em around the ear game and, I think we have established conclusively that from a woman's stand point there isn't, she cleverly passed this off as an accident. She shouted duck, which she also mentioned, was her new name and prospective retirement persona, proving almost irrefutably women can multitask, regardless of social status.

Mrs Fish carried on, saying more or less what I have just said above, but noting the Duchess was oblivious of the remarks, or the bat around the ear by Amanda and, Mrs Fish said she put that down to being as thick as two short telegraph poles as a consequence of inbreeding in the Hither Green area of South London, as is the wont of many British Rail wheel tappers.

'Anyway...' Mrs Fish continued, '... the Duchess was accompanied by the Pioneer corps of the Inquisition, namely deputy Duchess, General Maxim, retired of the Coldstream Guards, who was not amused when Jack Austin suggested, "He should carry a handkerchief with him then, and summer colds can be a nightmare"...

See how Jack Austin's jokes founder on middle-class stony ground.

Mrs Fish continued to inform the complement of the Inquisition, a Mrs Southampton-

Meddlesome, needle bearer and, Mrs Constance Crotchet, defluffer. The first a scratchy diminutive Northern Irish bird, the other a substantially built bovine Friesian, both women being Ladies in Waiting to the Duchess and they were accompanied by a new girl on the block namely, Marigold Glover, young and vivacious in a beanpole *Joyce Grenfell*, jolly hockey stick, sort of way.'

This mention of Marigold gloves did get the attention of Pimple and, as a consequence, he was diverted in thought making him dead meat in the clip-em around the ear game that wasn't a game.

'So, the Duchess started off the meeting, being minuted by General Maxim, by rubbing her ear lobe and saying they had come about the poles. Mr Austin said he wasn't using Poles, it was Paddy whom he believed had scrupulous Irish ancestry and liked *Father Ted*. Unless you counted Frank Podleski, he added, who was doing some work in the second bathroom that had Mr Austin's mobile phone stuck down the water closet. He had to speak like this as the Duchess, being uncle josh, would not know what a bog was,' and Mrs Fish tittered; the track suit bottoms wobbled ominously.

'Jack Austin, and those who know him will attest to this, had gotten fed up with the phone and decided to flush it away on the basis, out of sight out of mind, a fast Austin aphorism he pointed out to the General, expecting him to minute this. You see, Jack is not one for modern technology and although his son, lovely boy and hard to believe he was the fruit of Jack Austin's loins, always programmes the phones to make them eejit proof, as Mrs. Austin and *Father Ted* would say, but nobody could make a phone Jack Austin proof. I understand *Nokia* and *Apple* have been trying for some time, but alas... So, Mr Austin said to the Duchess, so as to avoid an issue with using Polish labour that he was using Irish labour to erect his *Diarmait Gavin* design, which was really his own, for the very reason they could "Feck" to their hearts content and share banter in a blarney sort of way. Further explaining, "The Polish were known to not understand *Father Ted* or indeed blarney, but were very good at sausage talk", by which, I believe he referred to them speaking a load Boloney.'

Aedd nodded that this was so and it was also well known as he pointed to Warsaw with the snooker cue.

'But, of course, the Duchess didn't see and even if it made sense to anyone else, the Duchess was determined. Her mind was set and this was backed up by a feeble minded councillor...'

. . .

Who I forgot to mention, as he was almost so feeble he nearly didn't get into the book, though he is mentioned on the front cover or maybe just inside.

'... who had accompanied the Pioneer squad that Austin had renamed the Pie and Mash brigade, being from the East End of London and this councillor, although masquerading as a Liberal Democrat, hauntingly harboured fetish like desires to become a Tory. Sadly he was in awe of the Southsea aristocracy, which ensured he was voted into office regularly, not through any innate ability to manage local governmental affairs, but precisely because of an inability to do so and, because he had an ingrained ability to kowtow. "A Friesian expression a lot of us in the dairy business use", Jack Austin said rather cheesily to the Duchess and the Councillor, who it had to be said, did as a rule, respond positively to her every whim.

There you go, and as you would imagine, the Duchess, in her overly polite manner, demanded Mr Austin reveal the plans of "His monstrosity, so out of context in this Owenesque delight of a situation; Frisian Tun and its environs".'

Mrs Fish scanned her audience and sought a reassurance she had conveyed her story. 'I am sure you have a pretty clear picture of Jack Austin by now and the manner and tone of the Duchess was enough to rub him up the wrong way, even before the erroneous content of the aristocratic argument was made evident. Austin did point out she was ill-informed, as he had not erected anything yet, if you excluded the two poles already put up and the one in next door's greenhouse. But, he reasonably explained, these needed, in a designedly way, to be tweaked and, the one in the greenhouse, which although interesting in a Mondrian manner and would be of interest to the Tate Modern, he was sure and fully expected the hear from them shortly, but in the event the Tate forgoes the greenhouse pole, he said, it would of course be removed and likely toute suite, apparently quoting *Mary Poppins* although we thought it was *Truly Scrumptious?* He did mention he had personally assured the neighbour he would replace the cucumbers with straight ones and stressed vehemently to the Duchess she should not judge what she has not seen.

He pointed out also that even with her all Seeing Eye in the centre of her noble forehead, she could not have seen the drawings as he still had to do them, explaining his granddaughter had hidden the crayons, possibly down the toilet with his telephone. Frank might find them, he suggested and if he did, he could start when they dried out and so, how could she determine it was a monstrosity? He also said in passing, but the strength with which he used to make these passing comments would suggest to any dispassionate onlooker, they were more than passing, he would be mentioning the philistine attitude that prevails in Frisian Tun to the *Chelsea Flower Show* committee when he is next up there.

He had of course not been up there yet, but knew it was only a matter of time, as with the Tate Modern and he would then let them know how the "The Pie and Mash brigade in Southsea do not give a tinkers cuss for the struggling garden designer". So, employing all of the tact he is known not to possess, he told the Duchess to "Foxtrot Oscar" as she had clearly already made up her mind and, whilst pointing to the side of his head, he indicated all the plans were up there, he said he "still had to finalise a few bits and bobs and the design for the polished stainless steel summer house pod that will go up and down the poles, will be remotely controlled" by what Jack Austin called a conch, similar to the one he has to control the telly, which Amanda had broken.

All of this I add in passing,' Mrs Fish said, 'seemed to be news to Amanda, but also she seemed to be not at all astonished. Amanda did point out she generally looked after the conch as Jack was want to break them, another occurrence of which she had just learned. Jack Austin considered this a juvenile comment from his trouble and strife, who up until then, he had viewed as mature and sensible. This was however, a technical issue, and thus of little consequence to a prima-donna garden designer, he was sure, saying, "*Diarmait Gavin* did not have to put up with such stuff from Mrs Gavin". He pondered, unsure if Diarmait was married or indeed batted off the left foot? Not that this bothered him as he had gone off cricket since England had lost to South Africa.'

Pimple had his hand up, ducked, but was clipped around the ear on the way back up. There was no doubting Georgie was good at this game that wasn't a game. He was a mite confused at feminine logic.

I am only just beginning to get an insight myself, as a relatively new pseudonym.

'Yes, Mr Pimple?' Mrs Fish asked.

'Er...' Pimple said rubbing the side of his head, 'what is a conch?'

'Were you not listening? You daft 'appeth,' Georgie said, emphasising her point with a swipe that missed. 'It's a telly remote control and I presume it has something to do with the book, The *Lord of the Flies*?' She said, looking questioningly to Mrs Fish, knowing she was as deaf as a post and so answered her own question in a multitasking sort of way. 'He who has the conch shell has control, I believe,' she said with a superior smirk, directed at Pimple. Pimple felt the smirk hurt more than the clip around the ear, but had to stop as Mrs Fish seemed to be finishing off and, not before time, as the runny poo meter was indicating the track suit bottoms may be getting close to capacity, as was attested by Aedd as he poked them in the side with his snooker cue. They wobbled and squelched like silvery grey blancmange.

The Fish did continue, 'It was a forlorn hope and, Cardinal Teapot with her Inquisition left, threatening all kinds of authoritive retribution as the Austin's' were transgressing the unwritten law. Superintendent Amanda, as you would expect, would not leave a law reference unchallenged and, bringing to bear all of her police stature, she disputed this preposterous notion of an unwritten law. And, as you would well expect, this had little effect on the snooty cow, know-it-all demeanour of the Duchess, who simply pointed out that this country of ours does not have a written constitution and all of the laws are established by precedent and, the precedent here, in Frisian Tun, was by decree on her own authority. Although, and after some deliberation, she confirmed she thought some of her laws may have been written down in biro, in an exercise book and put in a drawer. She was sure, but for the life of her and just at that moment, she could not remember which drawer, but felt able to assure everyone they could rely on her good word.

This seemed good enough for the Pioneering sycophants and Tory wannabee Councillor, attending in the guise of the Spanish Inquisition and looking forward to the pie and mash lunch they felt sure must be coming, having recalled it mentioned somewhere. General Maxim, who was of Prussian origin, confirmed in a Cossack way, it was all in the minutes and tapped them, ironically, with a biro, blue and of *Bic* origin; a town in Prussia presumably? He pointed in a military fashion, clicking his heels, which Jack Austin said reminded him more of the Gestapo, but conceded that Prussians had a proclivity to tap their heels and he knew this because he like jellied heels.

Of course, Jack told the Duchess to "Foxtrot Oscar" once again, and to "take her toadying disciples" with her. A sentiment, I must add, Amanda shared but reiterated in a more polite and acceptable way as became a Superintendent in the Filf, and that was it. The Inquisition left to lick their metaphorical wounds, determined to do all in their weaselly powers to bring this arrogant man and unfortunately, his wife, down. They knew instinctively Mrs Austin would ordinarily be accepted into Frisian Tun as a well spoken Superintendent of the local Constabulary, but as she seemed stuck on the gigantic cockney oaf, she would have to accept whatever was coming her way. "It was the natural order of things", the Duchess could be heard saying to the Pioneer Corps as they left through the gate in the wall and she followed up knowingly with, "you can't make fings wivout breaking somefing." She did look a tad taken aback at that statement, wondering if she had actually said it, I seem to recall...' Mrs Fish pondered, but not for long, and everyone was relieved about that.

'The lines had been drawn, not only as a challenge, but also for the setting out of the poles and, with only a few poles erected, Paddy and his chaps sat around having a cup of Monkey tea, I think Jack Austin said it was, certainly not a second flush of Darjeeling, Mr Murphy. And they fecked and blinded as builders are want to do whilst awaiting detailed instructions from "Mr Capability, Sor",' she said, adopting an Irish conversational mode, which was appreciated by Aedd with a quick point to the Emerald Isle, just to the left of Wicklow.

Mrs Fish had finished and it was late afternoon, almost twenty four hours since Pimple had arrived at number 28 Frisian Tun, Flat 2. So much had happened and yet he felt he had only scratched the surface, as Mrs Fish was coincidentally doing with the rump of the silvery blancmange, which bubbled and gurgled. Pimple leaned over and noticed his recorder was running slowly. A quick flip of the replay button proved his replacement set of batteries had all but expired and Mrs Fish, although naturally ponderous in speech, spoke even slower and sounded a lot like the chap who does the Film trailers for American films. He would need to prevail on Georgie's vibrator and thought he would do this whilst his mother carried Mrs Fish, under her arm, back to flat 3, presumably to get her into her sea bed and to discard the track suit bottoms into Georgie's garden to be collected by the foxes.

None of this was missed by Georgie who applied a tight grin and directed it to Pimple, whispering it may be marigold time sooner than he imagined, she said in a chafing manner. 'Good-oh,' Pimple said, and Georgie clipped him around the ear and declared herself the winner.

You see – blow me down with a feather, it was a game after all – wasn't it?

FOURTEEN
THE PROFESSOR, THE JOURNALIST

THE PROFESSOR WAS UNAWARE HE HAD BEEN called upon. He was unaware he had become the focus of attention, or at least his private man parts had, being pre-occupied as he was with fondling those naughty bits; a hefty hand of bowyer's sausages thrust down the front of his trousers. This was disgusting enough, but was exacerbated further, as the facial hedge had miraculously opened up in order for him to sport a vacuous grin, accompanied by a distant stare through ping-pong ball eyes. Unfortunately the focal point of the gaze corresponded exactly to where Pimple was located, a little bit to the side of the Mediterranean; Greece to be exact. Aedd used the snooker cue to point to where all were looking, except Mrs Fish, who had recently departed under the arm of Dame Pimple with much accompanying squelching and gurgles of a disturbing and not particularly aromatic kind, which the moose dealt with on the run, so to speak, with some well-judged atomised Dettol directed as if the tail of a comet. She had the bottle clipped handily to her sumo wrestling belt, which nipped into the waist of her bell tent dress.

Aedd prodded the Professor again, mentioning the fly region, a geographical turn of phrase, though not technically accurate in this case except he did expand by pointing out that the Canadian Province of Manitoba was colloquially known as, *the state of a million black fly*, by all accounts. Thelonius stirred from his reverie and presumably inappropriate Frisian Tun thoughts of Pimple minor, who, in turn, was looking dejected, having lost convincingly, the clip-em around the ear game.

'The nether regions,' Aedd said in a jocular fashion, pointing at the Professor's privates with the cue, which seemed a little out of character for a hermit geographer and then, as the jocularity was enjoined by everyone except the Professor, he ventured further into the unfamiliar role of stand-up comedian. 'The Netherlands I presume,' swinging the cue to Holland and this did bring the house down and, one has to imagine that below the facial hedge, Thelonious was blushing and, if he wasn't, he jolly well should be, Georgie thought.

'Professor, if you would oblige us please, in the nicest possible way of course,' and Aedd paused, getting into the swing of winning approbation for his wit, which unusually did not come this time. The mirth had to be solicited by him saying, 'It's a joke...' and the laughter was duly received, if not wholeheartedly jolly and enthusiastically embraced by all.

'Oh, did I miss something funny,' Dame Pimple commented as she returned, seeking her previous seat nearby the recently devastated Canadian lake, not wishing to stray too far from her natural habitat, however much it had been destroyed by Georgie's revealing tumble. She allowed her hand to smooth over Georgie's Shirley Temple curls as she trotted by, lingering to caress an ear lobe and, as she was passing that way, she clipped Pimple around his ear by way of establishing the recommencement of the second set of the game, which wasn't a game; *or was it?* Smoothing his own ear, Pimple noted a warm smiley exchange between mother and his lover, which left rather an unpleasant taste in his mouth, acrid, as it still had a lingering after burn from his proximity of the exiting Mrs Fish.

Georgie swung and made contact with

Pimple's other ear. 'That's because you have been eating pencils Everard, and now you might understand why I may be reluctant to kiss you.' He had openly expressed his thoughts, but disguised his look of horror with a superb head swerve causing Georgie to swipe at clear air as she came back for a second volley. There may be no actual rules to this non-game, but Pimple thought he was pretty good at it as he had horizontally swerved his head, whereas Georgie, in her trajectory calculations, had allowed for a duck, so to speak. He couldn't resist a victory grin, which whilst applying to real effect, caused his head to be momentarily stationery and as a consequence, and ironically, he became a sitting duck, so to quack.

If he was honest with himself, Pimple was starting to get a bit fed-up with this non-game, which at first had its amusing characteristics, especially when one was talking taps and affectionate clips. However, Pimple thought, if he did not put a stop to this, and soon, we could be talking direct punches to the old noggin and we are not talking earole targets, we could be looking at socks to the hooter.

A new non-game? Perhaps?

. . .

The professor was rather grateful for the clip-em and the possible introduction of the sock-em game as a distraction from his recent sojourn to the Netherlands, his embarrassment ably disguised beneath his facial bush and all in all, had to admit, it had proved a pleasant interval if rather unfortunate for being caught. However, he did think Pimple had appreciated the overt gesture and innuendo, which he also considered was subtly conveyed, not realising Pimple would miss a cannon ball in the head, so, subtle probing looks stood no chance, though the odd clip and sock seemed to be hitting the target.

The professor considered he might like to have a little word in the shell like of Everard later. All he had to do was get Georgie off the scene and it appeared he might be able to achieve this by way of encouraging the Canadian wildlife to be more interactive on his behalf. Maybe with a visit to the Isle of Lesbos?

Aedd displayed great patience, considering they were waiting on the Professor, who seemed to be musing on something of a rather more engaging significance as he stared, no longer into the middle distance, but longingly at Pimple. This was not the case however, as Aedd was bathing in the reflected glory of his witticisms. Eventually the Professor stood and Pimple observed him head, not to the volcano but towards him and the anal lips appeared, cartoon like, to swell up as he blew a not particularly incongruous raspberry, which rasped and slowly morphed into a pouted air kiss onto the Professor's, previously mentioned Bowyers sausage fingers, where presumably a Dutch aroma lingered and he patted Pimple's cheeks with them. Pimple sniffed, whether aromatically curious or about to cry, it was difficult to tell.

'Oi you, Foxtrot fucking Oscar, mate,'

Oh dear, Georgie had betrayed her origins, which were from Peckham Rye, South London and interestingly not far from the Duchess's Hither Green, Town Seat, as the old crow would likely fly. Dame Pimple could not resist enjoining the rebuke and by so doing, threw herself into the spirit of the rejoinder and idiomatic manner. 'You 'eard 'er you ginger beer, tucking fart, keep yer Alice bands orf me boys 'ampton or you'll get a fick ear and me daisy roots up yer Kaiber pass.' Dame Moose reflected on her skills of imitation, as Aedd pointed the cue to the East End of London, mentioning in passing that she sounded a lot like Dick Austin and Moose was heard to mew a bellowing, "Ooooo-err", as though blissfully grazing in her natural Canadian habitat.

Georgie smiled and with her eyes, beckoned the moose whilst removing Pimple's hand from her intimate folds and, using a combination of arm leverage on a rather limp lad and a jousting type kick she had picked up watching the Tai Kwando in the Olympics, she removed Pimple from the settee and allowed mater moose to take up residence in the vacated seat and erogenous zones. Now, as you would likely imagine, a young lad only just being introduced into the ways of the adult world and, a rather seedy one at that, as well as the clip-em and sock-em game, would be mightily confused at this juncture. Well, you would be right, as Pimple felt compelled to say something, and forcefully.

'Now look here. I say. This is not on, just what are the rules? Is it clip-em, sock-em or boot-em up the bottom? I think a fellow needs to be cut a decent break if he is to stand a chance, don't you know.'

Georgie looked at Dame Pimple and together they giggled like two schoolgirls intimately attached. 'Oh shut up, Pimple, for Christ's sake,' Georgie said and this sentiment was echoed by his mother.

'Yeah Everard, shut yer trap or I'll shove the professor's privates down yer frote,' Dame Pimple said, continuing with her amusing London accent.

To be fair, the Professor looked as though he considered he had moved on a few bases, not that this was noticed by Pimple who simply said, 'That's not fair, shoving things in the mouth is not in the game at all!' And Georgie and Dame Pimple collapsed into another hysterical heap and the moose took advantage in an intimate way that seemed, all in all, to be much appreciated by Georgie, as both women rolled on the volcano, driving Pimple, just as he was beginning to stand, into the open embrace of the Professor.

The only one not seeming to get enjoyment from the scene, apart from Pimple, who steadfastly maintained his best fed-up face, even when he sensed and in a not too unpleasant way, his bottom being stroked by something, was Aedd, who being patently disappointed his stand up routine appeared to have been relegated to a mere supporting act, said, 'Can we please get on, I am meeting Bea Flat later. She is coming to see Birmingham and help me wash-up.'

'Oooh err missus,' Georgie and Dame Pimple said, from the floor, as if holding their handbags to their faces and not a hint of posh appearing to return at any time in the near future.

Putting his arm around Pimple, in a caring but surreptitiously suspicious and overly familiar way, the Professor made to start, when Pimple made the mistake of bending over to check his batteries, thus permitting Thelonius Monkspot to cheekily goose our reporter, in a Canadian Tundra way. Pimple whooped and flew horizontally, past the volcano and the collapsed Canadian lake. Aedd said, slipping back into his stand-up role, 'I say, was that a Canadian Goose?' And this elicited more hysterical giggles from Georgie and Dame Pimple, so much so they declared they had nearly wet themselves and had better pop off to the bathroom, whereupon Pimple said this sounded like a reasonable and sensible thing to do, especially as Georgie was without under garments. This observation caused even more major guffawing and cosseting, as the two women headed off to relieve themselves, so to speak, mentioning maybe the professor should carry on as they couldn't give a toss about the bit where the man from the Council turns up, not realising that this was, in fact, the nub.

'N'ube' Aedd responded and he swung in the general direction of France, to land the snooker cue on Paris, which was a strange coincidence as Georgie and Dame Pimple discussed they might share an Eiffel Tower (*shower*) together, and Aedd approved of this geographical innuendo.

FIFTEEN

THE PROFESSOR

THE SILENCE, SUBSEQUENT TO THE LADIES retiring to *powder their noses*, was palpable, just a gravelly groan from Pimple as he made to stand for the second time, having been knocked down, again, by his mother and his lover in their indecent haste to ablute in a monumental Parisian manner. Well, he knew all about that, but all the same he felt a sense of helpless abandonment; jilted, not valued, except by the Professor that is, who had leapt enthusiastically to assist Pimple to regain his left footing.

'Professor...' Pimple said in a friendly enquiring way, lest he offend this man who was helping him, '... I would not want you to think I do not appreciate your assistance and your caressing is certainly easing the odd bump and bruise, but can you tell me why you insist upon fondling my buttocks?'

The professor responded, light footed and clearly twitching in several departments. 'I am a Professor of economics, Pimple, my dear old chum,' as if this was all that needed saying, but the professor reacted to Pimple's further look of enquiry, not realising this was the naturally vacant Pimple appearance. 'If I am not mistaken, you may have some lose change within certain crevices, economically speaking,' the Professor added, a transformed look from amour-propre to letch-proper, and he did not let up with his confident economic task, which is what you would expect from a Professor of Economics, Pimple supposed, going along with it, but feeling he should maybe get involved if only in a manner to guide and assist?

'Oh' Everard said, pushing the Professor's hand away and feeling his bottom for himself, 'where?'

'Please allow me?' the Professor said, and Pimple thought he saw a tongue pop out from the hedge and lasciviously caress the rosebud haemorrhoidal lips.

'Thank you Professor, I am most exceedingly obliged. It may be some pocket money I lost a short while ago, now that I think on it?'

The Professor duly obliged, suggesting this

all might be a bit easier if Pimple removed his trousers whilst Aedd maybe refreshed himself with a second flush of Darjeeling?

Aedd, himself feeling a sense of geographical rejection, got up off his chair and went to the kitchen, via the foothills of the Himalayas pointing en-route to the Darjeeling region, but was conscious nobody was particularly interested. So he busied himself with thoughts of various flushes of tea and Marigolds, to resonant Whoops, Hooohs and Haaahs from the bathroom, which Aedd imagined was a result of splinters, or maybe scalding Eiffel Tower water. He made a mental note, passing Mont Blanc and on into the kitchen, to throw the sideboard out onto Georgie's lawn. Maybe the foxes could use a sideboard in their den, or was it a coven?

As previously mentioned, Aedd was a geography teacher and other subjects were not only of little interest, but often served to confuse – thus he stuck with what he knew, Geography.

The professor, enthusing over Pimple's loose change department, was unaware of the return of the ladies until he reacted to a firm boot in his own lose change area. 'Ow' he cried and bearing in mind the boot was a hoof and from a disgruntled, albeit recently sated moose, then "Ow" was likely an understatement and probably an indication of just how preoccupied the professor had economically been.

These academics eh, they can be so amusing in an absent minded sort of way, Pimple thought to himself.

'Just what is going on here?' The Dame enquired, having regained her posh demeanour and mode of conversing, the cockney, she presumed was likely brought on by conversation about Jack Austin and a pent up urge, latent from yesterday evening's bathing deprivations.

'Oh hello, mother, did you and Georgie get splinters?' Georgie and the Dame allowed their eyes to elevate to the Battle of Trafalgar. 'I heard the noises and the professor thought he felt some lose change and was lending me a hand to locate it. You remember I lost some pocket money recently? How's it going by the way professor?'

'Er, not so well Pimple old chap, perhaps we can reconvene another time?'

'Another time my loose change department,' it was Georgie, referring to Pimple's posterior very much as though it was her personal property we have to assume, as she collected the trousers of her erstwhile lover. She managed a passing look at his bottom and wondered if she could maybe assist in the loose change hunt, perhaps whilst wearing her marigolds, in a synchronised mode and mentioned this in passing to Pimple, pointing out she knew just how distressing it can be to be separated from one's pocket money.

This declaration from the adorable Miss Georgiana, was met by an approving whoop from Pimple and peculiarly, Pimple noticed an approving nod from his mother. Now that was odd, Pimple thought.

Aedd returned with a second flush and stood gazing around the room for a suitable depository for the tray, painfully aware he was now without a sideboard and no Canadian lake, or, for that matter, any other horizontal geographic furniture that would be situated at an appropriate height for high tea at a low table, so to speak.

'Let me take that from you Aedd, dear,' said the Dame obligingly, to the obvious relief of Aedd whose arms were developing an ache, the geography teacher not being of a comparable stout construction as a Moose.

'I say Aedd, old bean, I recall a delightful log of Battenberg from yesterday. I have to say I would appreciate a slice or two of that right now as my headache, following the conclusion of the clip-em and sock-em game has eased somewhat and I find myself a tad peckish. Georgie and I skipped lunch to attend to other matters, don't you know, didn't we love?' Pimple said, turning to Georgie in time to get a sock on the hooter. 'I say, I thought the game was over?'

'Have some Battenberg, dip bleedin' stick,' Georgie said, with a hint of Peckham Rye and a sardonic chuckle, confusing Pimple, as he did as he was told and took a slice of the now proffered harlequin cake. Aedd had collected the gateau, crossing a continent, presumably to Battenberg in Germany, thence onto Mont Blanc and into the kitchen, wherever that was, Switzerland logically, and all silently without anybody being aware.

Massaging the numbness from his nose with his cake free hand, Pimple delivered a piece of the delightfully looking sweet confection to his mouth with the other, savoured the marzipan covering and light texture of the angel cake and felt immediately comforted.

Georgie breathed sensuously into his recently clipped and thankfully, peanut butterless ear, 'Alright, my love, how is your headache? Would you like me to sooth anything else?'

And, like the cake, these hot feminine words had magical healing and remedying properties, so the gesture, words, and hot breath of Georgie eased the headache and mollified the ill feelings he had begun to harbour, which were close to generating a green bile in his stomach. Least, he assumed it would be green as that was the colour bile generated in Pimple's mind. His only worry now, having eliminated all of his other concerns, was where his pocket money was and, Georgie had said she would help him find that and, with her marigolds. So at that Battenberg moment in time, Pimple Minor felt tolerably well.

Whilst the Professor makes his way to the volcano to at last impart his story of the man from the council, which may take a little time as his step did not truly mince, as there was a hint of the butch about the bushy man, but he did have a delicate mode of placement of each foot that suggested either ballet training at an early age, or, he had, as Mrs Fish before him, erupted man magma in his pants, in an intercontinental way.

My money's on the ballet.

The professor, still prancing elegantly towards the volcano, does give me a chance to mention by way of an interesting diversion, my observations as I reside in this pseudonymical female form. This experience, I feel, may help the floundering male in his understanding of the womanly psyche. You will have noticed that Pimple was becoming like a festering boil (I do so like that little joke), and the puss of anger was likely to erupt (notice the volcano reference – that's geography fellas, or ladies, of course, though I am not sure ladies like pimple puss jokes and, are likely to erupt with their own verbal magma if the male persisted) at any time and could cause more than the odd ruction in a masculine sort of form and not necessarily from a side vent.

Now take note - Georgie, being all woman and me being merely a pseudonym, was able to see that this would do the story no good whatsoever and so, a little hot breath in the earole department of a man, mention of washing up delights that could be coming his way, even if it came with the risk of some chafing and also, by way of resolving a problem that might pray on a man's mind, like missing loose change, a hint at assistance in finding his pocket money, and, "et voila". There you have it, the eruption is defused with all and sundry well and truly comforted to Battenberg levels and indeed, excited at imminent pleasurable prospects – that, gentlemen, is the female way.

Whereas, in comparison, the male way of resolving such a situation, which I can of course advise on as I am a man, although I have to remark I am finding the fish net stockings and intercontinental pants rather exciting, all donned I hasten to add, as a need to get myself into

245

character don't you know; I am after all, a method writer. A man would of course smash the place up and do similar damage to any face that may be conveniently nearby and presented itself as a likely candidate for being smashed.

Calming, I point this difference out as simple musings. The Professor waits patiently for me now and with his toe he plays with the crumbs of a pain au chocolat that he, by way of a grinding circular movement, a bit like demi-pointe in ballet I have to presume, having already gone through the basic five steps of warm-up, Battement Tendu, he does so with his be-socked toe.

You recall this is a Scandinavian household and so, despite the danger of splinters when abluting, no shoes are worn.

And so the professor ground the French pastry crumbs further into the throat of the volcano, thus risking a blow-out at some later stage. This could be through the mouth of the volcano or a side vent that we had previously established existed when Georgie had sat on the Canadian Lake and fallen over in a bare faced effrontery to the Canadian Territories. I can still recall the mental picture when I wrote that and I don't mind telling you... Aedd interrupts.

.   .   .

'If you wouldn't mind not treading the crumbs into the volcano Professor, I would appreciate it, boyo,' Aedd said, not disguising his Welsh irritation at the damage already done to his unique rug, presented to him by the Portsmouth and Southsea Amateur Volcano Club.

The professor thoughtfully scratched at the hedge surrounding his unmentionable lips that Pimple thought sounded like Mrs Fish scratching her backside, encased as it was then by a Margaret Thatcher tweed skirt, which now was presumably in a den of Tory foxes or a coven of Thatcherites somewhere.

'The man from the council,' the professor said.

Thank the Lord he's started Pimple thought, as the professor carried on as if addressing a class of Greek boy students in a lecture on battement tendu and they were hanging on his every word.

'I was there when the man from the council arrived and, my initial thoughts were of the power the Duchess must wield, as the local authority officer arrived the very afternoon following the morning of the Pioneer corps meeting. All, as duly threatened by the Duchess and minuted by General Maxim, who had stamped the approved minutes in his Prussian way and posted a copy through every door of Frisian Tun; within the hour.

So it could not be said that Dick and Duck, names that I actually like and find appropriate for a private detective agency by the way, were not warned. However, following the delivery of the minutes to my own Duchess unapproved home, I visited Dick and Duck to seek what wise council should prevail. I was aware, by reputation only I might add, though appropriate when you consider how matters panned out, that Dick could be a tad volatile and could also, at times, be considered a loose cannon.' He stopped as Aedd pointed to the Battle of Trafalgar on the ceiling and the various cotton wool canon puffs. The professor thanked the twit geography teacher and moved on, 'Or, bazooka.' This brought a smile to Aedd and diverted his attention from the volcano.

'I have to say,' the professor continued, 'Dick's response when I asked if he had seen the minutes was completely in accord with his reputation, but shocked me nevertheless.' The professor paused again, stretched his leg and duly pointed his toes, swung his lower limb horizontally outwards, then back to the crater mouth, effected a gentle caressing movement of the pain au chocolat residue, beautifully achieved and all without the aid of a bar.

'Oi, get on with it yer fucking Pansy.' Georgie shouted, seemingly still rooted in her natural habitat of Peckham Rye and moose looked on as if she appreciated the roughness in the woman. A little bit like her son appreciated Georgiana's nocturnal earthiness. 'What the fuckin' 'ell did Dick say?'

The professor was undeterred as he considered his *demi-pointe* had lost none of its elegance over the years and he put this down to regular practice at the bar in C&A's. Experience enabled him to block out the jeers of "ginger beer" from the local patrons, especially Dick Austin, who had made very little progress subsequent to the Neanderthal era. The Professor continued, 'He said to me in a manner and mode I found quite accommodating, "Come in tosh, and park yer jacksey", which I also presumed to be my bottom on a chair, as he held one of the dining table chairs for me and, mentioned in passing, he'd seen the minutes and I quote further, "Wiped me bottle and glass with them".' The professor tittered, clearly reliving the moment as a mental image.

'What happened then?' Georgie, thinking she was asking all the questions Pimple, the pull-titser, knob-head reporter, should ask, but was ineptly slower at phrasing them. Pimple was aware of this perceived shortcoming, which he put down to a temporary misalignment of grey matter within his brainbox, due in part to excessive rounds of clip-em and sock-em, as well as a delightful pre-occupation with the prospect of Marigolds and, the sunny thought that after this evening, he could be up a few bob as well if Georgie could come up with his pocket money.

'Oh, for pity's sake professor, get on with it!' Pimple said rather aggressively.

Georgie noted that some of her feminine guile may have worn off and, we may be getting close to the masculine way of resolving matters and so, as you would expect of a woman with guile aplenty, she fondled Pimple's bit and pieces. There you go, back to square one.

'Well, after I had taken my seat at the table,' The professor said, 'and Duck, whom I consider a lovely woman by the way and it is incongruous to my way of thinking how, or why, she ever hooked up with Dick, had given me a cup of Girl Grey, as she called it...'

They all ducked, not because it was clip-em or sock-em time, but because the snooker cue swung at an unexpected and rapid horizontal velocity to point, not to India, as you would not unreasonably predict and everyone had anticipated, which is why the cue took everyone by surprise, as it headed to London, to wit, Downing Street in particular. Aedd naturally accompanied the directional geography with an agreeable, he thought, elucidation of the thought process that explained the odd direction his cue had taken, mentioning said tea blend was named after a British Prime Minister, Earl Grey. They ducked again as the cue swung, of all the places, to the huge country of China and Aedd told everyone, in his Bristolian accent, about "them rickrack fings they 'aves in Chinall" (*the rickshaws they have in China - but how they say it in Bristol*) and then back.

'Duck! It's the foothills of the Himalayas,' Georgie called, by way of an anticipated warning, mid-duck herself, indicating where the cue should have reasonably gone in the first place. Georgie awaited the reasoned explanation she knew would be coming from Aedd, which it did.

'Most of the Earl Greys you find use a poor quality tea base from China.' Everyone ducked, but the anticipated cue swing did not occur, they were safe as he had already pointed to China, the logical explanation of that. 'This is like palming yourself off as landed gentry when all you own is a Barbour coat and pink corduroy trousers... ha ha ha,' and Aedd laughed heartily, as if he was once again the front line act at the Apollo, Hammersmith. 'Earl Grey, in truth, should use the finest Darjeeling from the foothills of the Himalayas and, add to it the hand-picked bergamot citrus from sunny southern Italy.'

'Whoooah, wotsamatterwivyou!' Now that came as a surprise as the cue clipped Pimple on the top noggin, en-route to Italy, causing an outburst of fluent Italian and just a passing thought he would rather like a garibaldi biscuit, after enjoying so much the Battenberg. Pimple had spent his first term of A level English Literature, inadvertently in an Italian class, before the teacher pointed out the error, which Pimple had explained away as, and here you can understand the confectionery reference. "He liked the garibaldi biscuits" and the teacher did too, and so they spent the next term in temperate conversation over tea and garibaldi's, whilst the teacher allowed the error to sink into Pimple's limited brainbox; one of the reasons adopted as to why Pimple Minor had flunked knitting, having spent those academic moments in an Italian sojourn, and thus the lack of early tutoring was put down to the C grade he achieved. However, the mention of Garibaldi in his paper on needlework bumped him from a D to a C, Garibaldi being an embroidery stitch much used by Italian Mama Mia's by all accounts, and he made his dissatisfaction known, and the examiner let him know what he could do with his Italian dead fly, fucking biscuits.

Aedd was continuing, despite the lack of interest in the fucking tea, and the reason for the, bergamot citrus '... used to create something altogether more gentrified,' he said by way of completing the Earl Grey discourse, whilst tapping his foot in an irritated manner.

The Earl Grey talk had concluded, and Aedd allowed a broad grin to be applied by way of confirmation the Professor may continue, and the snooker cue came to rest beside Aedd's lengthy spider's legs, awaiting another geographical reference. This was now beginning to be known as the geography snooker game, equally as exciting as clip-em and sock-em, but infinitely more dangerous if you were slow of wit and reaction, as Pimple could testify.

SIXTEEN
THE MAN FROM THE COUNCIL

THE PROFESSOR ELEGANTLY HALF-SQUATTED, his knees flat out and in line with his not insubstantial child bearing hips and loose change area, which coincidentally were contained in Nijinsky styled pink corduroy trousers, though as upper middle-class cognoscenti would know, they could equally be of a mustard hue. He held his arms horizontally that Pimple presumed was more ballet tosh, likely Battement Fondue and, as he rose, he pointed the toes of his right foot, elegantly exposing in his yellow sock, a potato (*an amusing colloquial expression for a hole in one's sock*). His thrusting big toe looked like a banana sticking out of a bowl of custard, which amused the professor's audience inordinately. He then swung the pedal extremity back to the pain au chocolat, now well and truly wedged into the mouth of the volcano, coming to rest with his feet looking like they were only just supported off teetering broken ankles, facing in different and unnatural directions.

He was ready, and everybody was pleased about that. 'So, I parked my Jacksey, fully expecting Dick to join me at the table with a cup of Girl Grey and was surprised as he shuffled off to the very large Georgian paned sash window at the front of the room. He dropped to the floor and, bearing in mind his only hinted feelings that I suspect may be genuine homophobia, in the gay abandonment sense, as he had previously mentioned to me I could mince as much as I liked as he wasn't that bothered. He, it seems, was more interested in the Isle of Lesbos, saying that in another life he had been a thespian, for some such reason he did explain yet still eludes me...'

'Hah, the Isle of Lesbos! I knew you would know Professor. Now, whereabouts is that?' Pimple asked and contemporaneously ducked, fully expecting the snooker cue to head off to Greece and thus coincidentally he avoided a sock-em swing from Georgie, but was hit with a clip-em by his mother as he had inadvertently strayed near Canada. 'I say, this game was suspended, I thought?'

Georgie smothered a laugh but whispered and breathed into Pimple's ear and, equilibrium, and indeed a subliminal simmering animal energy retained for later nocturnal expending, was restored to the otherwise unusually agitated Pimple.

The professor struck his poncey Dame Margot pose and continued unabashed, unlike Pimple who had been bashed, but instantly mollified. 'Duck, seeing my confusion explained that Dick had positioned himself as lookout walrus, keeping an eye out for the man from the council, whom, he had assured her was coming as he had wiped his bottom on the Pie and Mash minutes before she'd had a chance to read them.

"Is he coming yet?" she called to Dick, in what I could only describe as a sexually suggestive and provocative voice. He replied, "I think so, come an 'ave a butchers." Which is butchers hook, look, in cockney parlance,' the professor explained, advising also people to duck as the cue swung to London. 'If I might make a suggestion Aedd, since I am discussing Dick the cockney ex-copper and likely to be so for a little longer, we can safely assume we all know where London is and, if we didn't before, we certainly do now, so can we desist from pointing all the time to our capital city please?'

Aedd thought about this for a while, then

countered, 'Alright there, boyo, to be sure, an all, an all, guvnor?'

There was a murmured, 'Yeah, we're sure' and that seemed to satisfy Aedd and the Professor.

'So, Duck went to have a butcher's hook, which enabled Dick to get a gander at his wife's Alan whickers.'

'Whoa' it was Pimple in a very Italianate accent, *still fancying a garibaldi is my guess,* 'what's a gander and, what are Alan Whickers?'

The professor duly obliged as he had started to consider himself a bit of a "conosser", as Dick would put it, of cockney rhyming slang, since he had become acquainted with Dick, who, despite his patent homophobic parlance and pretences, had made a fast friend of the Professor. But, then again, he had also told the Professor he was an enema. The Professor assumed he meant enigma, but since he agreed with Amanda that he talked a load of shite, maybe not? 'I still have to determine the rhyme in gander, although some say it is to take a long and lingering look, stretching the neck like a goose,' the professor said introducing an academic note. 'It means to look at, much in the way of butchers hook, look, and may have something to do with goosing?' He looked at Pimple, who blushed and ducked, fortuitously as it transpired. 'As this seemed to be the prevailing thought process of Dick, this would seem a logical conclusion and I am reliably assured by Duck that when he mentions Alan Whickers, he means Amanda's knickers.' That elicited a blush from Georgie, as Dame Pimple patted the pocket of her girl guide, tent dress, which contained Georgie's pink lacy unmentionables.

The professor continued, the haemorrhoids having formed a bloated grin, which Georgie threatened to smother with Anusol, then shove the tube up his Aristotle, bottle and glass, so to speak, unless he pushed on a bit faster. And so the professor did, although still smiling, as if recalling the picture of a walrus staring up the skirt of a very attractive Duck, or it may have been the prospect of the Anusol tube? Yes that would be it, as his speed of speech seemed if anything more languorous.

'Yes, well, coincidentally, as Dick was gazing heavenward and Duck was patently enjoying the experience, a weedy looking fellow tapped the window with the resultant effect the walrus headed skyward, like an Apollo rocket, causing Duck to flutter to the ground, pole-axed and, with many ruffled feathers. However, it all resulted in jolly good humour all round, as they giggled and chuckled and wriggled as if they were very much enjoying each others close and intimate company, to the consternation of "the wimp at the win-der", as Dick later called him.

"Er, Er, I'm the man from the council" the wimp said, calling from outside the window, tapping again as if they were not aware of the presence of this short and skinny, weed of an oik, a just pubescent boy and, this caused even greater mirth from the elderly couple, rampant on the carpet. The wimp tapped again and Dick told him to "feck off". Wimp looked shocked, not that Wimp appeared unused to such rebukes from people reacting to a visit from a wimp from the council, but it was not what one would expect in this very posh part of town, oh no. The answer had to be he had no awareness of the sitcom *Father Ted*.

Anyway, after a short interlude of jollity and frivolity on the carpet, Duck genteelly rose and padded in the direction of the front door, laughing at the oomph's and aaarghs that emanated, walrus like, from behind her. Dick was on the move and, despite the spry agility he had just ably demonstrated after being startled, these lumbering movements were more in keeping with the sea mammal characteristics that were a consequence of his actual size, apparent preoccupation with Yoga and, if various explanations are to be accepted as fact, serious injuries received whilst on a covert operation for the filf.

Dick was just about vertical when Duck reappeared with the man from the council, who, although Dick had previously said was a wimp and a Jessie, referring also to a girl's blouse the lad did not wear and, that the boy had been dressed by his Mum in a suit from Sainsbury's, I must say, I found the wimp all-consuming. He was attractive in a short arsed non-Greek sort of way, as the boy from the council was definitely challenged in the height department and, as he stood beside Dick to shake his hand, the difference in size, height and bulk, was bald-faced.'

Which remark, coming from the overweight bushy professor, was a bit rich!

Thelonius continued, 'The lad, with whom I was starting to feel a sexual simpatico, announced himself as Dominic Wimpole, and he was from the Portsmouth City Council, Planning Enforcement Department. Ironically, he looked like he could not enforce himself out of a paper bag, upon which, I feel compelled to mention, I found a cute characteristic and, I might add, I sensed the affection to be mutual as the lad could not stop staring at my lips.'

Pimple thought he could imagine that would be the case, but Georgie actually said it, whilst applying a mild sock to the Pimple hooter, which did take him completely by surprise, but she followed it up with a less than gentle tug at his bits and pieces department and he was instantly mollified.

See what I mean – and most blokes are not even aware it goes on, preferring to retire to a woman's boudoir, proverbially black and blue, than face up to the truth. Denial, that's what it is and, if I were not writing in a female guise, I would sound the clarion to all black and blue men and I am not referring to the stockings, we, as men, wear on occasions, as the mood may take us.

The professor continued, 'What happened next, I have to say, changed my whole view of Dick Austin, whom, as I was mentioning a little earlier...'

Georgie thought it was more than a little bit earlier and said, 'Get on with it, you ponderous old woolly woofter', simultaneously smiling warmly at the professor, and then to the renewed in confidence Pimple. Both men were instantly mollified and she thought to herself, Christ, it's so easy.

Stone me!

'What happened next that so enhanced your opinion of Jack Austin?' the moose asked, expressing a casual interest and applied her request in a polite and genteel manner that belied the size and form of the woman.

'Well, as I said...'

'Yes we know you said!' Georgie was getting irritated and Pimple took evasive action, prudently as it transpired.

'What did I just say...?' the professor challenged, matching Georgie's irritation.

'That you had an epiphany that completely changed the way you considered Jack Austin,' Georgie replied, taking into account the next anticipated dodge and swerve from Pimple, and thus connecting with a Brahma of a sock to the Pimple hooter, just as he asked how to spell epiphany.

'Hah! That's not it at all - so there,' the professor reacted, but it was Aedd who grabbed the attention,

'How do you know Epiphany Bootlegs? She teaches biology at St Winifrede's.'

Wishing she had not started this, Georgie agreed she did not know Ms. Epiphany, and apologised to Aedd and the professor in turn.

'Yes, well, I thank you Georgie, I think this makes me the winner...' the professor responded and Georgie sighed, which was again fortunate for Pimple, as it took all of the steam out of the subsequent unexpected clip.

'Yes, you win, please tell us what happened next?'

So you see, men do have one or two subtle weapons in their arsenal, other than a full frontal assault with as much brute force as can be mustered. There again, I consider the clip-em and sock-em game, which was clearly invented by women... oh I give up, consider me mollified – the professor's continuing anyway.

'So, we gathered around the table and Duck very kindly got the Wimp from the Council a cushion to sit on, so he would be more or less comparable in height with the rest of us, and the boy opened his pigskin valise, which he mentioned had been a gift from his mother when he got the job at the council. Dick asked why she would get him a vase, giggling uncontrollably, but noticed the joke was not considered amusing by Duck and as many know, he tells most of his jokes for the benefit of Duck, under the erroneous impression she liked them so much, to which Duck noticeably sighed, as Jack Austin was also want to speak his thoughts.

"It's a valise Mr Austin", the half-pint from the council said, referring and pointing to his briefcase. "Call me Dick, son," Dick said. "Son?" the milksop replied, looking confused in a pathetically hopeful way, "are you my father?"

And here we have it...' the professor said, '... the moment when any thoughts I harboured Jack Austin was a pig ignorant, chauvinist tart, of a homophobic disposition and a more than suspicious copper, changed, for Jack Austin looked deep into the eyes of the wet rag from the council and asked, "Do you not have a father, damp rag from the council?"

The wuss replied, "I do, I suppose, but I've never met him. I would quite like to find him and I would not be at all displeased if you turned out to be him." The boy went onto say he had done a bit of asking around before coming, as all of his other colleagues, when they heard it was Jack Austin they were to visit, strangely, all needed to return their library books.

I don't mind telling you there was a tear in Dick's eye, which I can also tell you, Duck says is not unusual, as Austin's gruff whale like exterior disguises an equally namby-pamby bloke inside and apart from the height and weight differences, it was just as likely Dick Austin could be the jelly fish from the council's dad. Duck also went on to say this would not be the first lovechild to appear on the horizon since she had paired up with Dick, and she also had had firsthand experience of her husband being a namby-pamby, jelly fish, milk-sop of a wuss, with well known scaredy-cat tendencies.'

'What happened?' it was Georgie, her hitherto well concealed maternal instincts rose enthusiastically to the surface and, Pimple was the beneficiary of this latent blossoming, as she affectionately rubbed his cheek as though she was about to take the skin off, before shoving his face onto her bosoms for a comforting suckle, albeit outside of her flowery blouse, then the pink lacy brassier, whereupon Pimple conjured the picture of her breasts he had committed to memory that morning, lest he be deprived of any future viewings.

You may recall?

• • •

The professor was not about to allow his discourse to be distracted by any mammary action and he continued, his voice elevated as though his ballerina tights were pinching, 'Dick stood and put his arm around his new son, who shared the glint of a tear, "I would be very proud to be your dad, sissy from the council," Dick said and, the sissy boy melted into the first flush of tears, followed in short order by Dick and then Duck, who both smothered the lad. I couldn't resist crying myself and joined them and under the pretence of a reassuring cuddle, I tried to feel Wimp's buttocks but got the loose change end of a walrus, which shockingly he responded to, though I did note he was looking at Duck and grinning. Duck looked back confused and was even more befuddled when Dick announced he would name his new son, Angie Son. Well, the raspberry tart from the council burst into a flood of tears of Noah proportions, for it turned out he had no real name, other than a list of denigrations and pointed out that his mother had Japanese origins and Dick and Duck felt this explained everything.'

The professor could see the sea of confused faces in front of him, 'I have to say, it did confuse me for a while...' and he left it at that and it looked very likely the sock-em game would soon be transferred in a Greek goatherd fashion to the professor, but he started up again, after dabbing a cheek of many stray tears that were now beginning to soak the facial bush.

'After the group hug, with fringe sea mammal benefits for me, we returned to the table and Angie from the council took the minutes of the Pie and Mash meeting from his pig's skin valise, and flopped them on the table. They were immediately recognisable, as you rarely see these days the typescript so familiarly used by the SS in the Second World War. They were also stamped in red and blue with words like Top Secret and Oomph Baum Bum Sterner, which is German for top secret, at least this is what Dick said it was, and he conversed in German to prove his point and that he was fluent, whilst goose stepping up and down the living room shouting, "Achtung Zimmer Blitzen babben", which apparently was get the Girl Grey on babes, in German, Blitzen being a Swiss chocolate biscuit I understand... though the Swiss were of course neutral and just collected the biscuit money from both the Germans and the Allies.'

Everybody ducked in unison, as the cue went from China, Downing Street and then, to the Darjeeling region, via Berlin and Zurich. 'So, Duck rose and went to put the kettle on. I do point out, lest you become too excited in admiration at the linguistic skills of the cockney, dubious filf, that Duck was definitely rolling her eyes during this episode, but I feel obliged to say, Dick's German impressed the hell out of Angie, the miniscule wimp from the council, and me, but Jack's new son was of the view his dad could do anything and it would be brilliant anyway. "And thus it is of such stuff voles are made." Or so Dick explained to me in his malacopperism way, as he waited for the tea.'

The professor was reluctant to mention Girl Grey or Darjeeling, aware now of the snooker cue consequences.

'Dick's new son, unless I was very much mistaken, had just been recruited as a mole in the Enforcement section of the Portsmouth City Council Planning department.' And the professor did an accomplished twirl that would not shame *Darcy Bussell*, they have a similar beard anyway, by way of emphasising the incisive nature of his relaying of the story so far of Angie Son from the council.

The moose stuck her hoof out and walloped the prancing professor and he started up again. 'Yes well, sorry – I digress in a dress,' he said and everyone agreed he had. 'Okay so, the stripling chip off the old block from the council, ventured a question to his new Papa, "I suppose I should see the poles dad", Angie said, looking up at Dick, whilst Duck and I drank our beverages.'

Never let it be said a professor does not learn from experience.

'And Dick took his son out to the garden and from the rear window we could see the pair of them, Dick bending down so he could put one arm around Angie's shoulder, the other arm waving energetically and, one has to add, it was waved in the manner of all good prima-donnas. Dick had a comportment to communicate the overall intention of the scheme, without conveying too much detail, which interestingly also changed every time he reiterated it for his son's benefit.

We heard Angie say, "Which scheme will it be, Dad?" and Dick tapped the side of his head with his index finger, which coincidentally was en-route to search out a particularly stubborn bogey that had, apparently, been bothering him all morning. At least this is what Duck said he was doing and she would know, having apparently assisted in the removal of the one that was blocking the current one with a knitting needle, earlier that morning.

"It's all in the noggin son, us Austin's" and he looked at Angie, as if to say, he was an Austin now and he should be proud of it, "we don't need to put things down on paper you see?" And miraculously Angie did see and commenced waving his arms in a similar prima-donna manner, eliciting an approving look from his dad, who, comforted his son was accomplished in the waving his arms about department, continued on with the removal of the stubborn bogey and this time he appeared successful. Least I guessed he was, as he flicked this fastidiously removed nose boulder over a particularly nasty neighbour's garden wall, mentioning to his son, the neighbour was a Pie and Mash member.

Angie looked perplexed, but as I said, he was besotted and his eyes betrayed a newly acquired, familial, though slightly oriental, reverie, and thus would believe anything Dad Dick said, being so joyous at eventually finding his father. Dick then explained to his more than curious wife, he had once had a fling, or was it a swing, with a Japanese midget, trapeze artiste and Angie looked completely overwhelmed as he explained that his Mum had been a trapeze artist, as well as being vertically challenged. He further explained his mum was a Japanese woman and she had always told him that his dad had been a swinger from the sixties. Dick nodded, and Angie nodded, as he would nod in appreciation of anything now and I must say that later, after Angie Son had returned to the den or was it the coven of iniquity, which is how Dick referred to the Local Authority, Dick said to me. "He nods like an Austin and has many trapezoidal qualities". He was unusually proud. His chest puffed out causing a coughing spasm, which coincided with more Duck eye rolling and I don't mind telling you, we shared a nonplussed moment at the reference to the geometric shape, but it did explain the Hai, Angie-son, Japanese name.'

And at that, the professor Jette'd back to his seat, spun, and allowed himself to sit back down in a manner that looked remarkably like the dying swan from Tchaikovsky's, Canoe Lake.

Aedd shuffled to stand by the volcano, thus replacing the bushy faced academic, who had so engaged the company with his moving, and graceful dancing, account of the visit of the man from the council.

SEVENTEEN
THE DAME, THE HOCKEY PLAYER

AEDD ANNOUNCED HE WOULD NOW TELL THE tale of the Priest and, as he said this, he pointed to Canterbury and sketched out the route of the pilgrims, from London to the resting place of Thomas Becket, who, Aedd elucidated, in what Pimple thought was likely an ancient English accent, 'Was Archbishop of Canterbury from 1162 until his murder in 1170. He is venerated as a Saint and Martyr by both the Catholic Church and the Anglican Community, don't you know? In days of yor that, is', and Aedd sort of sang this last bit in a strolling minstrel way, playing air lute, side-saddle on a donkey and looking a little taken aback this mode of chanting had slipped from his vocal chords, coincidentally noticing the professor seemed to be captivated

272

by his donkey riding posture. It is reasonable to surmise that by now, most people were becoming accustomed to the various accents and dialects, but this ancient one definitely sailed over heads, which were subsequently scratched, with no apparent ping to say, "Oh yes!"

'Days of Yor?' Georgie asked and something did ping, but it was her bra strap as Pimple had decided to test his finger dexterity for later on. She allowed him to continue to make a fool of himself for a while, thinking if she begins to detect any sign of internal warmth, she may undo it for him. She didn't, but this didn't stop Pimple, who carried on, unaware he looked like a mechanic lying under a car, puffing and blowing and cursing ripe expletives, as he struggled with a rusted on nut.

Aedd was only momentarily distracted before he answered Georgie's astute question. 'The Middle Ages I think, though history is not a strong suit of mine, but you know, Chaucer and all of that?' Aedd replied, not so confident now, a hint of nervous laughter muffled into the palm of his upturned, non-cue hand, having realised he had not gotten away with his amusing ditty and perhaps he was not, after all, a natural wit.

'I have heard of Chaucer, of course, but how is this relevant to the Priest visiting number 5 Frisian Tun and the Austins'?' Pimple asked, in a polite and enquiring manner, having given up on practical car mechanics, though he was aware Georgie would soon need servicing. He was conscious Aedd was a geographer and although they are often presumed to be insensitive to brick bats of the verbal kind, as you would expect of hermits of a general nature, Pimple had become aware in the last day or so of a certain vulnerability, a frailty even, in Aedd's internal constitution whenever his knowledge of any subject, other than geography, of course. Pimple wondered a little on that also, and as he did his wondering so he accidentally pinged Georgie's bra strap and, in a pained reaction, she clipped him around the ear.

Pimple was not to be distracted however, by a game that might not even be a game and Aedd did look hurt and, if Pimple was not very much mistaken there was a tear forming in the corner of his poppy out eyeballs that currently had the distinct appearance of a far eastern mystic in meditative table-tennis mode. Pimple was aware also, as a sensitive journalist, it should not be underestimated the torturous emotions that must be endured as a person relates and, as a consequence relives, a traumatic event. Though Pimple was at a loss to imagine that the visit of a Roman Catholic Priest would be viewed as traumatic, but then again, what with the recently exposed shenanigans in the Catholic Church? Maybe we would need to have our backs to the wall, as it were and Pimple, if he had a choice in the matter, would opt most definitely for the Horn of Africa and eyed his spot lest it be a race for the best places in the world when the time came.

Aedd recovered, his moment of reflection seemingly concluded, so he explained further, 'I just thought it sounded like the Pilgrim Tales,' a brief glance to Canterbury, 'you know, The Fish Wife's tale, The Professors tale and, the Japanese man from the Council, the Priests tale, the Knights tale as Dick Austin is soon to be knighted, and Duck always says he is an Actress and, there's a tale there I can tell you, and so on, and more especially the story of Blanche? John of Gaunt's wife. Lady Blanche-Teapot, see? And Chaucer, by coincidence, was also an Intelligencer, an old term for a spy. Can you not see the similarity, Pimple old chum? Though...' Aedd reflected, which involved almost dislocating his jaw as the ruminations became more animated. 'I have to say it is a lot like *The Canterbury Tales*, Pilgrims' Progress and all that, but where in this instance, nobody goes anywhere.' He chuckled at his aside and welcomed a restrained polite hee-haw in reciprocation and in recognition of his raconteur resourcefulness.

Aedd did wonder, reacting to the dumbfounded looks on everyone, which was accompanied by what could only be called a post chortle, stultified silence, if he had made his point, but felt, in that innate sense one has on such occasions when one has made a complete tart of oneself, he had not quite hit his mark. So he persevered, like the turnip he clearly was, except turnips have green tops and his was red, ginger in fact, and even carrots had green tops. 'There is, you see, a passing similarity to the *Canterbury Tales* I think, although, as I just intimated, nobody goes anywhere, unless you count the gangster who clearly departs this world for another and likely Hades, down under, having travelled pilgrim like from the East End of London, or it may have been Hither Green?' And, Aedd laughed at this supplementary witticism, swung the cue as a sort of nervous reflex action, to point to Australia and took a couple of noggins on the way as it was completely in a different direction to Canterbury, or London, for which people were prepared, as you would expect.

Aedd did seem to have a point Pimple thought, aware he had acquired a mate in Mr Austin, although he was still unclear if he was his mush and, he was unsure what a mush was and, now he was a chum of Aedd's. For a virginal chap who had no friends only two days ago, this has to be seen in a positive light, which Pimple did, feeling himself heartily cheered, knowing also that the Professor had expressed a desire in mating, so that could be three, or was it four? Pimple paused in thought, wondering if his dearest Georgiana was a mate or a lover. Pimple laboured with his thoughts, which is a natural state of affairs and, additionally he was still confused in a Chaucerish sort of way, which he assumed to be similar to liverish or just generally out of sorts, as to where a Sherman tank and a bazooka might appear relevant, even in a modern day setting of an account of the Pilgrims' lack of Progress to Canterbury, or anywhere else for that matter.

Pimple was most definitely befuddled and this contributed to a sense he should feel out of sorts himself, which bearing in mind his inept showing in the sock-em and clip-em game, his patent lack of success with Georgie's bra strap and motor mechanics, it would not be unreasonable to presume. However, despite all of this and all of the evidence that suggested he should be out of sorts, he was in fact, buoyed, as he now had some friends. He also presumed that once we passed the Gangster's tale, things may become a little clearer in the relatively modern day armaments conundrum for his article on the trauma suffered in Frisian Tun.

Aedd also appeared improved in mood and demeanour, which Pimple put down to a mutual chuffness in establishing himself as a chum of Pimple minor. He continued, and for the benefit and comfort of the professor, mentioned that Father Mike O'Brien was reputed to bat off an unorthodox footing by coincidence and, having got through what he considered an informative preamble, Aedd readied himself for the main course, but was interrupted before he could get going.

The sound that caused the interlude was that of a lyrical melody, not from the Middle-Ages, and this was played, if Aedd was not very much mistaken, not on a lute but on a Greek Bouzouki. It was not an unpleasant sound and quite tuneful as it transpired, in a Zorba the Greek fashion. Certainly it encouraged the professor to once again take to the floor and he began side stepping with his arms held outright, his hands twirling in an artistic way, pretty much as he had done at the start of his battement fondue. Sidling and dipping his knees this time, once again the professor proved he was unusually light on his feet for a big bushy man, obviously, as he batted in a quite unorthodox way, priest like even and certainly Georgie felt like crucifying him and, may have mentioned it as *Zorba* the professor minced by in Greek dance.

Thelonious pranced in tune and ducked in tune, as the snooker cue swung to point to Greece. The relatively un-nibbled Battenberg went flying as Dame Moose stood and smashed the plate in the fireplace, along with the Battenberg, which, being of a different consistency, constituent parts and weight as a china plate and, despite Galileo's theory, went in a different direction and attached itself, ironically, to the map of Germany and, if Pimple was not mistaken, directly over the town of Battenberg. How spooky was that Pimple thought to himself, although he could not confirm this as the map was covered in Battenberg cake, where it stayed momentarily before sliding past Croatia and Slovenia and eventually to the floor and the Mediterranean; a small section of blue lino with Corsica immediately evident.

Still, Pimple thought, as he watched the gradual descent of the cake, it was a marvel it had survived uneaten but he knew his mother was not partial to marzipan, which was annoying as he rather liked the almond confection that Chaucer likely called Marchpane. He curtailed his gateau perusals in order to open his mouth in amazement to watch as his mother hoofed and perambulated the floor, for her movement, whilst formidably rhythmic, could not pass for dancing and could only be assumed to resemble a Greek moose boogie. However, she gambolled with gusto, in a similar way to the Professor, adding every now and then a "Whoopah" which Pimple thought was likely Greek or could be his mother covering up a fart, which she was also known to do frequently, often blaming Stanley, the long suffering Pimple hound who was of a Bassett variety and thus was often out of liquorice all-sorts.

Eventually Dame Pimple eased her boogying in order to answer her mobile phone that nestled in the folds of Georgie's Alan Whickers, which in turn nestled in the capacious pocket of the bell tent. 'Hello?' she said, wiping her brow with Georgie's unmentionables that I just mentioned and. she casually gyrated in Greek as the tune that alerted her of a telephone call played on in her head.

The professor stopped and delicately picked his way back to his seat in a shared poncy ballet esprit de corps, bending his knees in an overtly revolting manner that made everybody think he had moose parped as he descended to a sitting position, whereupon he pointed his legs and toes horizontally outward, as though he had now, inexplicably, become a flailing Cossack.

Pimple ducked, but realised it was only a Cossack thought going on his head and the cue remained stationery, as did Georgie's clip-em hand. 'You have a mobile phone mother?' He remarked in a squeaky voice Pimple would have expected to have now grown out of, along with the eagerly anticipated occurrence of a beard bristle or two. All of which is what should be expected to accompany his loss of virginity; least Pimple thought so.

Georgie clipped Pimple around the ear, 'Pimple, your mother is on the phone!'

'But she says we shouldn't have mobile phones as they give you cancer of the grey matter,' he said, defending and resolutely bracing himself for a sock or a clip, but neither came, just a whispered word in his shell like.

'Shusssh, be quiet, there's a good boy,' and she soothed his brow and let him settle and then clipped him around his shell like and, as he reeled, so she followed through with a sock on his conk. 'Now shut up,' but then made a show of unclipping her brassier, taking pimple's hand and directing it forthwith to an advanced bosom position, so desirous of many boys of an impressionable age and, in a most efficaciously mollifying way.

Whilst giving the appearance of being mollified, Pimple's emotions still churned below his perfunctory equilibrium, only marginally distracted by the breasts, both of which he had already seen. As such the sumptuous tits held not so major an allure as to distract his principle thoughts, both of which currently resided in the Pimple grey matter, which conveniently remained uncontaminated by mobile phone micro-waves. His distraction was of such intensity he allowed his hand to fumble around within the now loosened cups of the Georgiana lacy pink brassiere and, almost as if he were an expert lover, he was inadvertently titillating the mature woman who now bore an uncanny resemblance to a sex starved Shirley Temple. This was way beyond ordinary synchronised levels, not that Pimple had noticed his involuntary skill nor, the ardour that was emanating as a consequence of his unpractised manipulations. Pimple was preoccupied with loftier matters. He liked a game as much as the next chap, but clip-em and sock-em was getting ridiculous and he would be insisting very soon the rules be written down, but instead, decided to listen in on his mother's telephone conversation sensing a need to be informed.

However, he was to be further distracted, because he noticed, being an aware sort of chap,

Georgie was now addressing him in guttural tones that resembled very much the earthiness from their previous night of passion.

The mater moose though, was absorbed in her telephone conversation, otherwise she may have partaken of a little of what her son was only just becoming aware. 'Yes, Mercy, I was most disappointed you did not show yesterday evening...' She continued listening to a very much one sided conversation that could only be Dame Pimple's hockey and bath time companion. 'I cannot see you at the moment Mercy darling as I am most agreeably engaged in the description of events that took place in Frisian Tun a short while ago.' She listened some more, appearing to have difficulty in getting a word in, but eventually blustered, 'Everard is doing a human interest story, don't you know and, has also had his brain's fully examined in an intimate way, if you get my drift, by a really beautiful woman who looks uncannily a lot like Shirley Temple.' Clearly this was all that was needed to quieten Mercy, though she must have pressed Dame Moose for detail. 'Yes, darling, I know you like Shirley Temple, which is why I mentioned it. It is why I dress to look like her. It's for you always my dear,' and everyone became aware the dewy eyed moose was completely cowed by her conversation with Mercy Mudstone.

Georgie was dumbstruck. She had of course worked out Dame Pimple was conversing with Mercy Mudstone, a woman who intrigued her in a jolly hockey stick way, but could not see how the dame could bear any resemblance to Shirley Temple, even if you ignored every characteristic of the former 1940's child film star and added back a stout moose. But, she could see why Mercy would like the look as she had been inexplicably attracted to Dame Pimple herself, in a *Specsavers* way.

Georgie stopped her thoughts, aware they had excited her, more so, as Pimple's manipulations had taken on an urgency that suggested he had now realised where his hand was, realising also that by female thought transference...

A skill that I am convinced exists but not quite if you are a pseudonym.

... the moose antennae, which ordinarily would be called antlers, had picked up the message loud and clear and so the dame dropped to the floor for a more intimate gaze, in a grazing manner, at Georgie, whilst pretending to, walrus like, look for a runaway coin. Thus the dame's substantial hindquarters retreated and raised themselves skyward, causing Aedd to back away towards the Sahara, a dry and barren area, which interestingly summed up Aedd completely. His mouth had dehydrated due to pre-performance nerves, so to speak, or not.

Georgie subtly shifted her body, discarding Pimple's hand, caring not where it went afterwards and allowed her mode of attire to appear ever so slightly provocative. 'Delores, my darling, was that Mercy Mudstone?' she asked, in a voice Pimple recognised as heading south to advanced earthiness.

'Yes, my sweet,' the Dame answered, unable to control her panting, as she grazed the carpet by way of disguising her lusting thoughts of the exotic Temple regions and not in a geographical sense, because the temple regions would likely have been sub-tropical India, if you excluded those that remained in former Inca countryside, completely the other side of the room.

'Do I gather she is interested in the Frisian Tun story?' Georgie queried, shifting down in her seat slightly.

'She is,' Dame Pimple replied with erratic moose pants.

· · ·

That is a reference to the lady's breathing, not her Alan Wickers, as it would be hard to imagine erratic knickers – nope, now I say this, I have conjured this in my mind and not an unpleasant distraction it is too, though not on a moose.

Georgie seemed less distracted than Pimple.

Or indeed Sue Narmee, the narrator...

'Then she must attend us and I insist she do it now,' Georgiana was assertive, and Pimple noticed his mother simper and obey in response.

Delores was up and pranced very un-Greek like, but with a more natural and accustomed moose gait, as she gabbled to Mercy, turkey like...

A country adjacent to Greece and, we understand, the Turkish people dance in a similar fashion; Whoopah.

... to get herself down here now. She passed on the address, closed the call and dropped back to the floor with a thud, saying, 'She's on her way.

Oh Georgie, you will simply love Mercy. She is such a handsome woman, in many ways more beautiful than myself,' sounding as though this would be an impossibility.

Pimple noted Aedd's eyebrows head north as did his own and they met, if he was not mistaken, on board HMS Victory, shortly after Admiral Nelson had been mortally wounded, but before Hardy had kissed the blind, one armed Admiral, who was partial to the odd sailory heavenly bliss, *kiss,* apparently.

Aedd allowed his ginger slug eyebrows to return to a normal angle of repose and looked to the Professor, who was humming Greek tunes to himself, tapping his pointed toes and gazing in a glazed and most inappropriate manner and, looking like he could not possibly explain either. Aedd followed the professor's direction of sight to Pimple and if the sinful grin on the disgusting lips was anything to go by, the professor's thoughts were completely un-moose like, musing as he likely was about a scantily clad Greek Pimple goatherd, playing his pan pipes in amongst the sand dunes of an hallucinatory transoceanic beach.

Goats, what would goats be doing on a Greek beach?

. . .

But, in fairness to the professor and his fantasy, he didn't particularly care about the goats; he had standards, such as they were.

Now, I appreciate you will all be looking to me as a female pseudonym, to explain, especially to the men, how a moose can consider herself attractive and if this was the case, what on earth could Mercy Mudstone, hockey player of some repute and not averse to bathing either, which I know most men find a bonus in a woman, look like, compared with, say, a Shirley Temple Moose?

Relaxacat readers. I use a jazz term, as I picture in my mind Thelonius Monkspot tapping his pointed toes and gliding in his thoughts to the lyrical tunes from a bouzouki, within sand dunes blessed with goats and a scantily clad, pan pipe playing Greek Pimple, goatherd. I can of course describe Mercy when she arrives, which judging by the excitement she conveyed to Delores on the phone just now, which only me as the author was aware, as I didn't mention it, but surely you guessed, she would be here any minute.

I can't be expected to explain everything, except, where women are concerned, I have often noted they are fast friends with moose like creatures and describe them in delightfully feminine tones, as if the visual evidence would not be immediately apparent, so a man could be clearly entranced in anticipation, initially, and so sorely let down in eventuality; such is the lot of men, I imagine, well, I know.

Even as a womanly pseudonym, because I now consider myself womanly in a pseudo-psychotic way, I can offer no explanation to my male readership other than to say, it is a 'thing' and as a man, for despite the recently acquired penchant for stockings of the fish net variety and incontinence pants, we all know I am a man and, aside from times when nobody is looking, I most definitely do not mince, we, as men, know all about 'things'.

Enough said, Aedd is about to talk on The Priest and my head hurts, as my partner in life and love and all of the machinations of a human relationship, is an enthusiast of the clip-em and sock-em game and, may have invented the rules.

I must ask her to write them down; blimey she wants her stockings back...!

EIGHTEEN
THE HOCKEY PLAYER, THE GOSSIP COLUMNIST

AEDD ADROITLY MANOEUVRED HIMSELF around the currently undulating and flexing, up until now considered inflexible, posterior of Dame Pimple, giving as much room as possible for he had noted throughout the afternoon the Dame occasionally lifted one of her huge hind-quarters from her Canadian habitat, to parp one out. Steadily he made his way eventually to the wall and the map of Ireland, avoiding France for obvious Mistral reasons.

'Father Mike O'Brien...' Aedd started, placing the flat of his hand on the County of Wicklow and speaking in an Irish accent, '... you would be surprised to learn, did not hail from Ireland,' and he moved to London that had attracted so much attention around the Bow bells area just recently and, Aedd surprised further by pointing to Orpington, which whilst being technically a part of the London Borough of Bromley, anybody who is anybody in the geographical world knows, Orpington is in Kent.

'Now, you may wonder why I make the point of informing you Father Mike O'Brien was a man of Kent.' They all nodded, acknowledging also the accomplished switch from Irish to an estuarine manner of speaking, except Dame Pimple, who bellowed up Georgie's dress in a manner characteristic of a rutting moose, chewing the cud.

I'm not sure if I should have mentioned this, I cud of said something else...

'Well, I will tell you, it is because his tool is incredibly bent,' and Aedd rolled up laughing, enjoying being the opening act at the Apollo once again and amazingly, this time, everybody did laugh, even Moose, but her laugh was muffled as she had made it to the heavenly Georgiana folds. I know this sounds like a geographic region or indeed a geological term, but I have to make clear, it most certainly wasn't and the fact that it wasn't, was a source of growing ire to Pimple.

'Yes, well, enough frivolity,' Pimple said, clearly irritated, although Aedd was patently still amused at his little joke but, Pimple had lost his sense of fun and told Georgie just what he thought. 'Georgie, I say, this is most seriously unpleasant and I jolly well thought you were my gal, so to speak?'

Georgie, in a condition of heightened senses, was thus insensible and let go a serious expletive accompanied by a sock that would fell a passing moose striking square on Pimple's nose. The aristocratic nasal protuberance stood not a chance.

The ensuing gushing of blood from said fireman's hose, Aedd pointed out, still speaking cockney, was not unlike a side vent would react if a volcano crater mouth had been bunged up with, say, un pain au chocolat.

This was all very entertaining of course, but Pimple reacted in a way he had never before and thus surprised even himself, as he took Georgie by her Shirley Temple wrist without so much as a please or excuse me, thinking that would be a lesson for his gal. He pulled her to him and she spun, as a Latin American dancer might, into his arms and her head flicked up and, as Pimple looked down at the stunned beauty, so his side vent (nose) spurted more red magma as if his mouth had been full of a French pastry smothered in raspberry jam and thus stoppered. Pimple's blood spurted to cover Georgie's face in a rather consistent way, the puffy cheeks particularly noticeably so, as a laminar flow edged slowly down towards the Mediterranean (floor).

With the occasional energetic burst sprayed over his mother, as he reacted to her standing up, presumably to stampede somewhere, it was at this moment the Pimple conscience kicked in, a fleeting thing, but later he could recall thinking, "Oh Blimey". This naturally shocked Pimple to the core, as it would any well brought up gentleman, as blimey was up there on the Richter scale of retorts, so high in fact, it is likely to be the cause of earthquakes and, as we have just seen, volcanoes.

Of course he could have used gosh, but honestly, it would not have been so powerful, Richter wise, though his nose was goshing.

Sensitively, Pimple examined Georgie's bloodied face and in that all to brief moment of goshness, her rocket fuelled expletive was forgotten but his blood continued to boil, which was unfortunate of course as the mouth of the volcano, for there is no doubting this was Mount Pimple, a Volcano that had been brewing for many years, was temporarily shut, and Georgie had only herself to blame on that score, as she had told him to shut it. Thus the rising blood that not so long ago had been virginal sap, and we all know how tame sap is in comparison to blood on the boil, increased dramatically in pressure when his volcanic thoughts turned to Georgie. He detonated onto her even more copious amounts of blood, some of which had lumps that could only be described as Magma snot.

Pimple felt charged and Pimple charged and he began dragging his floozy, for in his mind there was no doubt Georgie was a cunning floozy as she had gotten beyond the peanut butter barrier that would stop any ordinary floozy dead in her tracks, as had been ably proven to date throughout the whole of Pimple's passing manhood, so to speak. And, speak he did, with an assertion comparable to a red blooded male. 'With me, now!' He said in a charging way to Georgie and his comportment and tone suggested he would brook no gain saying, nor any continuance of the clip-em and sock-em kind.

In his heightened emotional state, that

ordinarily would be a subdued category of heighten if you recall, but just now was heightened to a pinnacle and definitely not subdued, he held Georgie by her shoulders, turned her and thrust her past Mont Blanc, thence to British Columbia and on toward the door, a casual passing side glance to the Swiss mount, causing him to spray a very white Mont Blanc with energised claret. The spatter pattern of red on white, curiously took on the look of the Arsenal football club shirt. "Ooo, that's nice", Georgie managed to say, as Pimple dragged his gal, grabbed the orb like door knob, wrenched open the door and pushed Georgie through and slammed it behind him.

He grabbed her again and not in a polite way, but in a belligerent manner, having considered the scruff of her neck but eventually settling on the wrist once again. He pulled her to the front door and opened it, roughly.

When I say he opened it roughly, I mean in manner and deed, belligerently, not that it was more or less open – clear? Good.

'Oh, hello Mercy, Mother's just through there,' Pimple said, pointing with his free hand, as the other was otherwise engaged in a wristy belligerence and then, having greeted Mercy Mudstone as would be expected of a gentleman, with just some minor blood spatters on the face of the stout centre half hockey player, and gathering himself and Georgie, he pushed past. Mercy was unfortunately oblivious of the threatening belligerency in Pimple, which was understandable as it was very likely Pimple had never heard of the word belligerent let alone been it before. As a consequence of the Pimple zeal at becoming at last in his life, belligerent, and by-passing Mercy in a belligerent manner, he caused Mercy to fold over, like a collector's hockey player cigarette card and tumble backwards into the bathroom, to collect a splinter in her centre-half backside.

Mercy simultaneously called out to announce the fact, evidently also in pain, 'Everard, I've a splinter and, rest assured, I shall be telling your mother of this, my lad.'

Ordinarily of course this would freeze the blood in Pimple's veins, but it was the Pimple arteries that were currently in the ascendancy and they were pumping red hot, so, almost casually when you think he could have responded in a belligerent manner, he called back to his mother's hockey colleague. 'Fuck-off, you old cow,' but in a relatively polite manner, as you would expect of Pimple minor when addressing a bathing companion.

Georgie, who since passing Mont Blanc had been consistently expounding, "Ooooh's and oooh-errs", intervened only with a casual remark that, coincidentally, she was an Arsenal fan and continued in a repetitive way her "Oooooooh errs". As Pimple reasserted his belligerency, Georgie offered an exaggerated "Oooooooh" which was to articulate her distinct dismay at the Pimple language and her amazement in that ordinarily she would have taken this up with Pimple, possibly preceded by or followed up with a sock to the hooter, but all that was forgotten as Georgie was definitely sensing an "Oooooooh err matron" moment or two. Her lady organs fluttered as a consequence of the treatment now being dealt out by her manly Pimple.

Down the stone steps he towed her and, she noted again in passing, he was not mincing, picking, or even behaving in a gingerly fashion. Georgie was just managing to stay upright as he pressed her into her flat, offering a mute apology she decided to ignore lest it spoil the event for her, and through to the pink fluffy boudoir whereupon he set about undressing her in a belligerent way, which Georgie was appreciating

very much thank you, and expressed it thus;
"Cooooooh..."

Now, I am aware as a man, my male readers would expect me to describe in detail all that followed in dear Georgiana's overly pink boudoir, fuchsia in parts, which may have been better served as a more subdued coral, but you would be mistaken and, as a pseudonym, I find myself frowning on such lewdness, so typical of a man.

As a male reader, if indeed you are a man and I know it can be confusing, especially if you are in fish net stockings and intercontinental pants, you may well have forgotten I am writing this account as a female and thus, I fancy, I will be obliged to leave a lot to the imagination.

When I discussed this aspect of the novel with my partner, she said that would be correct and a lot of men finish early leaving the remainder of the lovemaking to the imagination of the woman. So you see, I was correct. However, speaking to my female readership, and you males may find this of casual interest, it has often come to my attention women cannot always comprehend the singular importance to a man, of completing any task at a speedy rate, if one's country is playing in a football international or even, though I agree to a lesser extent, if you had promised to meet a mate down the pub.

So you see, I was tempted to write on a steamy boudoir scene as I almost became carried away with the moment and, as I typed, so I found myself "Ooohing and Erring", but I had to step aside from that temptation. Things were happening in the bathroom and I refer not only to the splinter in Mercy Mudstone's lady's bottom area, but other activities more relevant to this story than a steamy, phonographic sex scene; just for the record.

At the same time Everhard was belligerently Pimple-handling Georgie en-route to her pink pastel hued with cerise highlights and, curiously deep blue net curtains, boudoir, Mercy was introduced, although she would ordinarily have preferred such a first meeting to be splinter-less, to the gloriously beautiful Cecelia Crumpet.

Cecelia had missed the relative comings and goings of a volcanic kind in the hallway, as she was at the time wriggling entry via the bathroom sash window, her upper torso and a large proportion and, as we have already determined Ms Crumpet's body was noticeably well proportioned or indeed generously endowed, relative to her lower limbs, all of which had gained entry, but the remaining sections of calf and feet were struggling, as Ceeley's shiny patent, azure blue, wellington boots, were not complying.

Cecelia, a bright woman in every respect, noticed she was not alone and if Mercy had not been visually aware, coincidental to her own equally unorthodox entry to the bathroom, neither person intent on ablutions I hasten to add, one would be inclined to argue she was particularly aware of the cursing that emanated from a woman of fine bone structure This being obvious to a hockey player, even though it be more or less horizontal and crushing itself through a sash window that fitted Cecelia like a snug Marigold.

Cecelia immediately thrust out her arm, which had a hand on the end, ready and willing to shake another such appendage. 'How do you do? Cecelia Crumpet, Gossip Columnist of the Portsmouth Evening News,' Ceeley said, introducing herself to Mercy.

Mercy, sitting, as she was, partially on the bathroom floor and partially on what appeared to her to be a splintery section of a sideboard, a part of a drawer she amusingly observed, as she fingered the rim of her own drawers to seek the source of the sharp pain, was aware she needed to introduce herself in response. So, with just a casual glance back to her bottom, which had been bared in the splinter region by a prudent tugging of the finger along the bloomer edge, the reinforced gusset department, she thrust her spare hand out to Cecelia. 'How do you do, Mercy Mudstone, inside left and not centre half, as is often erroneously thought by many, for the Southsea Maidens hockey club, 1st team, vets.' And they shook hands.

'Inside left?' Cecelia asked politely, trying to ignore what were patent; "Ooooh's and errrr's", and the odd "matron", emanating from the semi-basement, garden flat, just below the bathroom.

'Yes my dear, inside left. I am particularly good off the left foot, as it were.'

'Do you not mean, so to speak?' Cecelia replied, still trying to free up her last wellington and aware that Mercy was ogling, whilst offering a kindly meant helping hand.

'That as well. I say, you are particularly scrumptious,' Mercy said, drooling slightly. 'Let me help you,' and Mercy offered her spare hand again, not being able to resist exposing and rubbing her sore bottom with her other, and to be fair to Mercy, this was not overt in any way other than affording her an opportunity for a soothing stroke by way of female multitasking, whilst on the way to help Cecelia's unorthodox entrance.

· · ·

Whilst Cecelia is being helped through the sash, which may take some time, as I suspect Mercy was using delaying tactics, I amuse myself by thinking it would be quite funny if Pimple were to remark to Georgiana at the coincidence of his first meeting with her in the same bathroom, splinters and all. But, as mentioned above, he was currently engaged in a belligerent and a thrusting, not very polite, carnal exchange, with said Georgie. Least that is what I like to think, although it might be as well to note also, that it is close to kick-off for the match, England -v-Sweden, and we know how men can be at sex, faced with an impending kick-off.

You would now be aware also the soundproofing in this flat conversion, that should never have received planning consent, was not all it should be as was ably demonstrated by the noted resounding, "ooooh's and err's", so it was safe to say, Pimple and Georgie would not be watching the match. Mercy looked askance at Cecelia as her last boot made it past the sash and they heard, quite clearly and distinctly and in particularly earthy tones, that emanated not from the earth as you might reasonably expect, but from a woman's voice, that "Ooo'd" a lot, and then inexplicably and quite clearly said, "Fuck me, you Pimply bastard" which, judging by the

302

subsequent sounds, Lord Pimple duly obliged, despite it being very near kick-off time.

There, and people said I couldn't write sex scenes, but it has had to be cut short as England just scored – Hoorah unless you are reading this in IKEA over your meatballs, in which case, 'Come on you ginger top Vikings!'.

NINETEEN
THE GOSSIP COLUMNIST

CECELIA, WITH HER CUSTOMARY AIR OF composure and confidence in anything she faced or tackled, duly obliged Mercy in the removal of the splinter, providing complementary soothing. Mercy, smiling her appreciation and amusement at the manifest carnal noises emanating from below the bathroom floorboards, suggested, as she secured Cecelia's hand, that perhaps they should join the others and, with Cecelia in tow, immediately headed off to where she assumed the living room was, confident she would find it, eventually.

Upon entering, Cecelia and Mercy became aware their good humour and patent jolliness was not shared by Aedd, the professor or Dame Pimple, although the Dame was pleased to see

Mercy and took in her colleague hockey player's look of fascination, as she in turn, took in the look of the map room and the Battle of Trafalgar on the ceiling. It transpired that Cecelia had been here before and took the décor and battle scene in her stride, as did Nelson of course, except he was short in comparison to the lofty Crumpet and, he did not survive a sailor's kiss, where as Cecelia, in contrast...

Aedd did not immediately react to the entry of the two new women, being focused as he was and in an evidently irritable manner, on his restorative cleaning to the *Hesse* region of Germany, in particular the removal of Battenberg from Battenberg. He'd not got to Arsenal's Mont Blanc yet. His stern face fractured only as he took pleasure in the odd crumb of marzipan and angel cake, otherwise he mumbled unremitting dissent and objection, through tight lips, at the desecration of Europe and, looking to the rug, he mentioned to himself, by way of a mental memo, accompanied by tutting and much eye flicking to Cape Trafalgar, he still had to free the mouth of the volcano of pain au chocolat.

The professor remained seated, his vacant eyes established he had his inscrutable face on behind the bush. He mused, God knows about what, but he was pointing his toes and appeared to be playing air pan pipes whilst the fingers of his hand danced delicately across the Dutch part of his trousers.

'Aedd, daaaah-ling,' Cecelia called silkily, siren like, subtly luring the Geographer onto the rocks of the volcano with expertly fluttered eyelashes and pouted coo's, a brief mention, 'Oh, is that Battenberg daaaa-ling, my favourite.'

Aedd left Germany, vertically rising a foot or so in the air and coming down firmly on the mouth of the volcano, thus ironically, compounding the congestion of pain au chocolat. He was unable to disguise his astonishment, which turned slowly and cautiously to frustration and subsequent embarrassment, as he looked up to Cecelia from the volcano mouth. She could see him contemplating his wearisome dilemma, decongest a volcano or an intimate greeting kiss for Cecelia...

I know what I would do, and I'm a woman; well, not really.

So he did what any red bloodied geography teacher would do and, on his hands and knees, he set about unclogging the volcano, knowing this could save the room from a severe side blow-out, whilst nodding to acknowledge the arrival of Mercy Mudstone with, astonishingly, Cecelia Crumpet! 'Oh, hello Ceeley, how nice... you will excuse me, pain au chocolat you know?' and he chuckled nervously, as he pointed in the general direction of France, but his face became rigid, as clearly Ceeley was volcano bound and he had only just managed to extricate a small portion of the flaky pastry residue. However, the racy journalist looked like she didn't much care for problematical confection, volcanoes, or even geography teachers for that matter.

'Aedd, daaaaah-ling...' and she stroked Aedd's Brillo pad hair whilst conjuring a face that suggested it was a most pleasurable experience; an accomplished actress it should be pointed out, notorious even. 'I hope you don't mind me joining you, but as I have just interviewed Lady Blanche-Teapot, I considered I might be able to contribute some thought-provoking detail to Pimple's article.'

'Er, well, er...' Aedd said, nervously rising from the volcano with most of the mouth and throat cleared, coincidentally attempting to clear his own vocal chords and, by way of explanation, he presented Cecelia a miniature mound of pain au chocolat residue in his upturned palm. 'Lava...' he gestured, more confident now, being

307

on territory he knew women found fascinating and he was right as Ceeley responded.

'Oh yes, dear boy, how lovely.' She smiled sweetly at him and Aedd purred as she knew he would. 'Now, be a love and put the lava in the bin and get back here, I imagine Pimple and Georgiana will be back up soon. I do not think he will be interested in England versus Sweden, do you?' And she said this ducking, in a knowing and practiced manner, as Aedd pointed generally to England and if I am not mistaken, the IKEA in Bristol, with a swathing left hand that came back to rest on his red hair, whilst the snooker cue swerved to Sweden. 'Yes Aedd, well done, now tell me how is the exquisite Bea Flat? I hear she is now front desk, first violins in *The Nun's Orchestra* (for those that do not know, St Winifrede's Roman Catholic School and Convent, in Portsmouth, has a famous Orchestra of Nuns, known as the *Nun's Orchestra* – see the next book, the nuns are in it a lot, and some on roller skates?) or is she conducting?' she asked, not particularly interested, chuckling as she answered her own question, 'Conducting, of course, unless she has taken Holy Orders in the past few weeks.'

'She's er, err...'

'Good dear, I'm so pleased to hear it,' not that she had heard anything, Ceeley was not known for her patience either. 'I will be taking Pimple for a walk later...' she added, like she would be taking the dog out, simultaneously pointing to her azure blue wellingtons scattered in the hallway, as if everything was explained. '... so I will talk about the Duchess and then maybe you can resume your little chit-chat after I return with him?'

Aedd felt he should assert himself, but knew from the sensation in his stomach and the continuing parching of his mouth, he couldn't, so he didn't, but he did manage an accomplished, and in view of matters, quite impressive, 'Er, err...'

'Yes dear, I know, was it your turn to talk?' She said sloping her head provocatively. Aedd nodded and she stroked the gingery fluff on his cheek that passed as a geographer's beard. He considered whether to err-sert himself again, in the time honoured masculine way, but she stopped him with a look that bordered on a knowing smile, a smile that would whither the resolve of any man on his vine and so, a geography teacher was toast. 'Be a good boy and make me some tea please, and none of that girl grey, pansy, shite. I would like monkey tea, and Aedd...' Aedd nodded in nervous response, as he prepared to leap into action, but awaited further instructions, hoping she would see he was being a good boy, '...

I know where the fucking jungle is or wherever they grow tea, so toodle off to the kitchen without passing GO, there's a good boy,' and she showed him upside down walking fingers, which all in all he considered a little unnecessary and, when her back was turned to greet the returning Georgiana and Pimple, he pointed to the Indian Jungle and together he and the professor folded in half and shared a conspiratorial naughty boy's giggle.

'Aedd, I told you, I know where the jungle is.'

Aedd looked horrified and instantly recalled Jack Austin had confided to him that women had eyes in the back of their heads. He shivered and reflected on the unnatural balance in life, but then thought, in an innate sense of self preservation, he'd better get the tea or it would be the naughty step, which had only minor ameliorating consequences as it was not very far from Tibet.

The naughty Steppes of Asia Minor (not Pimple Minor).

'Cecelia?' Pimple at least managed more than Aedd's initial response and managed also to accompany this with a beaming smile, as he retracted his arm from Georgie's narrow waist, reacting in confusion as he got a reproving glance from Ms. Crumpet at the action.

'Yes, Everard, it is me. Now pop over and give me a little kiss,' and she leaned forward, expectantly, 'spit spot,' and proffered her beautifully powdered and perfumed cheek, tapping it with a perfectly manicured finger with blood red polished nail, indicating Pimple should kiss the one on the left, just up a bit and over to the right from the lightning slash, dynamite, red lipstick painted, sumptuous lips.

Pimple stood stock still, mouth agape, but Georgie was able to synchronise this for him with a tap on his bottom. 'Go and kiss the lady Everhard, you sexy creature,' and she allowed that final remark to tail off into a subterranean grumbling tone, to hang in the air and, as he turned to look at his gorgeous Georgie, she reinforced the earthy note with a lascivious grin, smoothed his bottom in a practiced manner and sent him on his way to Ceeley with another tap. All in all, Aedd thought, looking through a crevice in Mont Blanc, the crack in the kitchen door, a most attractive look on a most attractive woman, but far too racy for him, he preferred, or at least felt more secure with a Nun's orchestra conductor, inter-alia, mature and mumsey tectonic plates.

Pimple nosed his way through a barrage of perfume and kissed a glorious Cecelia cheek that was cool to his lips, which in turn were still red hot from recent energetic kissing and, he dallied in his smooch, noisily sucking in the smell of a gorgeous Crumpet through a nose still congested with claret and bloody magma. He luxuriated in the flavour and sensation, which meant he was left unprepared for the European second kiss, as Ceeley turned and presented to him the opposite cheek. He caught up and felt very French, may even have inadvertently oui'd himself. Ceeley seemed to take pleasure in Pimple's out-and-out awkwardness and, looking to Georgie, as Pimple floundered the second embrace, she ignored Pimple's attempt at a return visit to the original cheek. 'Dearest Georgiana,' Ceeley said, 'how is our boy coming along?'

Pimple allowed his shy and easily startled and, newly created Gallic shrugging look, to develop to one of watching tennis, presumably *Rolland Garros*, and thought he felt inexplicably discomforted, which of course Ceeley had long ago noticed before he became aware.

Georgie replied, still with a lot of rasping earthiness. 'I was initially of the view this was going to take longer than we imagined Ceeley, but now, just now... I'm not so sure...' and Georgie seemed to be pondering on this, aware Pimple was even more discomfited and would likely realise this in a minute or two. 'He has shown remarkable promise in the last half hour or so; perhaps a week should do it?'

Cecelia looked pleased. 'Thankyou, Georgie that would do nicely. Now, if you don't mind, I was going to step out with Everard after I tell everybody about my interview just now with the Duchess.'

Aedd could be heard to mumble from the kitchen, 'It's my fucking turn.'

'Tea, Aedd, there's a good boy.'

'Yes, Ceeley, just waiting for the kettle to boil,' Aedd replied, a lot clearer, but with the humbleness and humility you would expect from a tea making, football buttoned cardigan wearing, geography teacher, focused on his allotted task in Switzerland, a neutral country, so he at least felt secure from injury.

This seemed to settle Georgie and Ceeley. 'I noticed your wellingtons, so presumed you would be off for a brief sojourn with the lad.' Georgie simpered, looking deep into the Pimple, blue eyeballs that had glazed with a shine suggestive of Ceeley's wellingtons.

'How perceptive of you daaaaah-ling,' Ceeley replied, as she gestured with her head for

Pimple to take a seat. Pimple duly responded, wondering who would sit next to him, but as the monkey tea arrived, so Georgie slid on the shiny leather to land beside him and snuggled into his armpit, caressed his thigh, noticeably taking in his musk for he had not showered at the request of Georgie as she said they would do it later, together. Pimple imagined they were likely going synchronised swimming, maybe with Marigolds, as Ceeley slid in to take up the other armpit.

Aedd tumbled in through the Mont Blanc door with the tea. 'Er, it's *PG Tips*,' he said, resisting the urge to point to Sri Lanka with his elbow, but inadvertently pointed to Pimple's armpits, mentioning, by way of additional information for Mercy and the Dame who were posh, the term monkey tea derives from the telly advertisements featuring monkeys, 'A strong tea sometimes coined as *builders tea* – "coo-eeh, Mr Builder, light refreshments"', and Aedd laughed, timidly mimicking one of the monkey adverts, also realising biology was not a strong subject for him, aware he still pointed to Pimple's armpits where Georgie and Ceeley were well and truly ensconced.

Dame Pimple rose from her seat calling out as she did so, "Coo-eeh light refreshments", an indication to everyone she may be excessively posh but she was familiar with the monkey adverts and she went across to Aedd, took the London Zoo chimpanzee tea party tray and tea pot and, having previously consigned the Khyber Pass telephone, temporarily, into the Pacific Ocean, she settled the tea on the table beside British Columbia and retook her large armchair. Mercy responded to the Dame's patted signal and settled herself on the arm of the chair and allowed her bottom to slide on the polished leather, in the manner so recently accomplished by Georgie and Ceeley, but with less of an elegant flourish. She slid to eventually reside on the moose lap.

Aedd could not resist a thought, accompanied by a naughty giggle, that maybe Dame Pimple was a reindeer and this was Lapland, but was brought up sharp with an admonishing stare from Ceeley and he followed her eyes to British Columbia, where there are no reindeers only moose, aware he may be on tricky ground. 'Tea, Aedd, there's a sweetie and then I can the make a start, you don't mind do you, love?'

'Er no...' Aedd asserted, fighting to keep his voice from squeaking, 'ladies first, eh?' And he wobbled and chuckled, pleased he had said something that re-established his male dominance.

Looking to Birmingham, Ceeley

acknowledged Aedd in order to keep the children happy and observed, 'Didn't you have a sideboard daaaahling, where is it?'

'Up my arse.' Mercy said, responding to the shocked looks on everyone's face, except Ceeley's of course. 'Well, it was, or at least had been,' and Mercy explained about the kindness offered her by Cecelia and it emerged Dame Pimple was not best enamoured of Cecelia Crumpet.

'Floozy,' Dame Pimple remarked firmly so all understood her drift, and Pimple thought she was sifting through her handbag looking for the peanut butter jar. 'Ceeley Strumpet if you were to ask my opinion,' the Dame added sniffily. Whether that was posh or simply following a peanut butter scent, Pimple could not be sure.

Fortunately nobody did ask for the moose opinion and Ceeley seemed quite inured as she made her way, with cup and saucer, to the volcano. With her feet, she toyed with the residual crumbs at the mouth of the volcano, her red painted toe nails, recently exposed by the removal of the azure wellingtons, exotically complimenting the geological strata diagram. 'I have just interviewed Lady Francesca Blanche-Teapot,' she announced. Ceeley stopped, so that Dame Pimple could say, "Big deal, strumpet". Then continued, 'I thought this would help your story along Everard daaaaah-link...' smiling warmly at Pimple, who felt the feminine potency inveigle its way into his collywobbles, a sensation Georgie and Dame Pimple picked up on with mixed reactions. 'Did you know Lady Blanche has just made a statement to Bernie LeBolt that will appear in tomorrow's editions, saying she was at first harassed by Mossad, then the CIA and, followed by a deformed Frenchman with the appearance of a hunchback George Clooney who, by all accounts, was French intelligence? If that is not an oxymoron?'

Pimple tittered, suggesting he had intelligence and grammatical comprehension hitherto unknown of, but in fact, he had just laughed at the Ox reference as he looked at his miffed moose mother. Apart from Aedd and the professor, who also sniggered at the Ox reference also, there was stunned silence, so much so Dame Pimple's passing of moose bottom breath hitting the atmosphere, having progressed unimpeded along the line of least resistance, skidding as it did along the leather armchair, resounded more than she anticipated.

'That's a good one Delores darling,' Mercy said, and the Dame nodded acknowledgement as the two women sniffed in posh appreciation.

Ceeley moved a little further away from the volcano, towards the fresher environment of the

Sahara and Aedd visibly relaxed, even choking as he was.

'Yes, well, I thought I would follow this up from the gossip angle, you know, "Barmy old aristocrat bat, imagines the CIA and Mossad came a knocking", and so on, but thought also we could blend this with your story Everard. What do you say?'

'Rather,' Pimple said excitedly, happy to blend anything with Ceeley.

This seemed good enough for Ceeley, although she had hoped for a little more articulation, but Pimple was clearly still stuck between various sexual reveries and not a little confused that Georgie was not showing any signs of jealous irritation and, his consequent ducking and diving had all been for nothing, other than good practice. He was no fool and, although we are expecting the rules for clip-em and sock-em anytime now, it is always prudent to get in the practice.

'Tell us about the Duchess, please.' It was the professor soliciting inquisitively, scratching his facial privet that Pimple thought likely had birds nesting and he was encouraging them to fledge.

Ceeley seemed pleased the professor was showing an interest, but she was also aware the Duchess and the Professor have history, and we are not talking *Chaucer* and a non-trip to

Canterbury, or John of Gaunt's wife. 'I will Professor, but a little of the background, a lot of which I hasten to add does come from Jack Austin,' and she fluttered her hands to suggest this could be in the realms of fantasy. 'So must be, just a tad pinch and saltish, if you get my drift, but I will be checking it all out and if verified, I can say it will make fascinating copy.'

They all nodded to say they would take this with a pinch of enthused salivation rather than salination, even the Dame, who had allowed her curiosity to be piqued, to temporarily by-pass her floozy antlers.

'When I spoke to Jack, I refuse to call him Dick...' the dame warmed to Ceeley just a little as she nodded her approval at that, '... he told me the Duchess is not all that meets the eye.' She left that hanging, being the mistress of suspenders, as Pimple and now Mercy, both could testify, as she wobbled her hand to indicate *a bit iffy*. 'Well, it turns out that...' She stopped as the room looked up in reaction to a buzz, 'what's that Aedd?' The buzz went again, several times.

'It's the bozzer.' The Irish accent that had been noticeably absent of late and Pimple felt unusually comforted by the Dublin'ish, up a bit and to the left, tones.

'The bozzer?' Cecelia asked, unable to disguise her irritation, a peculiarly feminine

319

irritation Pimple found intoxicating, which also says a lot about Pimple's sense of self-preservation - der.

'The door,' Aedd answered, but clearly not enough information passed to defuse Cecelia and remarkably, he picked up on the signal and so expounded. 'Yes, it's a lovely door, of western red cedar, which weathers particularly well in this seaside environment. It's from British Columbia you know,' and he swung the cue to where the Khyber Pass had been, but now, incongruously he found himself pointing at the London Zoo chimpanzees' tea party tray, which Cecelia did not find so incongruous and mentioned it in passing as she swerved backwards, ducked and dived, in a casual and practiced manner.

'Aedd, you fucking turnip, answer the bleedin' western cedar will you...' Ceeley said, as her head swung back to upright, '... daaahling.'

Georgie reacted. 'Are you from Peckham Rye, Cecelia love, only I never realised before. It's where I'm from.' Cecelia was even getting a tad fed up with Georgie, but whereas she would have released some pent up invective to a man, she replied politely to Georgie, whom she liked. 'Catford, darling, still, South London,' and for the benefit of the passing geographer, 'not too far from Lewisham.'

The bozzer still continued, suggesting the prospective visitor was insistent on entering or that the person was as thick as two short western red cedar planks, either way, Cecelia thought this all suggested it was a man rather than a woman calling upon them. With an extended sigh that Pimple and Aedd noted came from pouted red painted lips, which in turn, and once again, had a peculiar effect on the Pimple collywobbles, Cecelia requested Aedd should see who it is. Only she said it more how they would say it in Catford, or even Peckham Rye for that matter.

Anyway the message was conveyed and Aedd tripped the light fantastic to the hallway to answer the bozzer that was now bozzing rhythmically and Cecelia thought to herself, was that *Ave Maria*? But left that thought as she lowered her eyes from the Battle of Trafalgar to anticipate who entered through the door.

TWENTY

THE PRIEST

THE GRAVELLY BOZZING MORPHED INTO A less than tuneful wheezing squeal of hinges that could do with an oily drink, which was immediately supplanted with a discordant whistling, not hinges straining for lack of oil but a thinly disguised *Ave Maria*, straining as if the *Virgin Mary* required a powerful laxative. The sound increased in piercing volume as it echoed in the hallway and thence all eyes, previously fixated on the map room door, swivelled to Cecelia who expounded, not so affectionately, 'Feck me gently, it's the bloody priest,' said in a *Father Ted*, Catford accent. A suggestion of South London and Tipperary, which was much appreciated by Aedd, who followed up from behind the father and appeared to overtake the vicar of Christ to get to snooker cue?

And so it was that father Mike O'Brien entered the living room with Aedd bringing up the rear and sacrilegiously butting into Maria's constipated aria. 'I'm just about to talk about you,' Aedd said, trying to squeeze past. 'So, you will have to wait your turn, as Cecelia has already jumped in front,' and Aedd wanted to stand still and stamp his foot, to emphasise how serious he should be taken by Cecelia and indeed by the priest, but Mike was not stopping and, although he was known to bat in an unorthodox manner, he had not, as yet, developed eyes in the back of his head.

The Priest, who had visited Aedd before, was unmoved by the striking room decoration and went directly to the Professor and pecked him on his forehead, demonstrably avoiding the bushy beard and pursed, expectant, rose bud lips. 'Thelonius, how are you old chum?' No Irish accent, but Aedd had previously mentioned that although the priest had an Irish name, he was from Orpington in Kent, and thus had a contorted willy.

'I am well, Mike and, rather taken with Pimple.' Two pairs of left footed eyes swung their gaze to where Pimple sat. 'What do you think? The look of a Greek goatherd on a sun kissed beech, playing the pan pipes whilst tending his flock in the sand dunes, no?'

Mike considered the Greek tableau and Pimple visibly withered beneath the priests all seeing gaze, tucking himself behind Georgie's flowery print blouse and floaty out skirt, appearing as though peeking out from behind a powerfully scented rose bush.

'Geek goatherd, maybe?' Mike answered, chuckling, and his purple sprouting broccoli cheeks, wobbled independently of his beetroot pug nose, which was fixed steady by steel wire rim glasses. The priest was known, at times, to display an off-the-catholic-wall sense of humour.

Mike O'Brien was a big man, dressed in a black suit that made him look slimmer than he likely was and, younger, as he had to be about sixty. Aedd knew this as Father Mike had been a friend of Jack Austin "Forever and ever, amen", least this is what Austin had told him and Aedd would have told everybody else if Cecelia, and now the priest himself, had not shown up and pushed in. Aedd did not even feel like disguising his fed-up face, which had a peculiarly county of Munster appearance; Corkish.

Mike took two long strides towards the Sahara, skirting the Volcano and swung around to face everybody. He settled, a hand resting on the Sudan and, swinging his priestly hips, he nudged Aedd across to another continent, Europe, Belgium to be precise, mentioning he did not appreciate the Munster scowl. 'Stop scowling Aedd, boyo.' A Welsh accent that suggested he knew Aedd well, but did not ponder as Aedd would have. He went straight in, taking the limelight as was his style. 'For those who do not know, I am Father Mike O'Brien and I have been a friend of Jack Austin forever and ever, amen.' The father chuckled, glancing briefly to the Benelux countries as Aedd had moved slightly away from Belgium, heading to Birmingham where he felt more comfortable, though he could not disguise the fact that the Priest had stolen his joke, which he was about to steal from Jack Austin.

The Father, who stood like a giant devilish predating raven in front of a barren and parched part of the world, had a commanding presence and all eyes were riveted on him. Even the never to be underestimated Cecelia ire, was diffused. 'Cecelia, my love. As beautiful as ever and, Georgie, how does it go, is he doing well?' and his piercing raven gaze fixed on the Greek goatherd.

Startled this gay priest was so perceptive, Georgie replied she needed a week or so, but was most encouraged. 'Good... good,' and Mike swung his ink black, faux pious eyes that pierced through a veined purple complexion that to an intimidated Pimple, looked like the devil stealing a look from behind a draped altar cloth, to gaze upon himself, who in contrast was a shrinking violet, except he had shrunk behind some dearest bellisama Georgiana roses. Thence to Cecelia and the priest remarked casually, 'Mmmm...' tutted, '... I see.'

'Well, I am pleased about that you old raspberry tart, now, what are you doing here?'

'Ceeley, calm down, dear.' A remark guaranteed to have the opposite effect on Cecelia and, judging by the impish grin on the father, he was aware of the likely effect on all of womankind, but continued, trusting in the protection of the cloth. 'From his window, Jack saw you go into the Meddlesome household and presumed you would be interviewing The Duchess and so I, in that I mean, we, had a natural curiosity to find out what was said?'

'Well, if you hadn't interrupted me I was about to say... *dear*,' Cecelia retorted.

She stopped because Aedd had found a miniscule amount of masculine bravado, probably sourced from the nearby Midlands, Mercian Mudstone as likely as not. 'Excuse me, Ceeley, *you* were going to say? Neeee-ah, yoooh-yah' He emphasised the "you" in his Japanese accent so his vocal signals could not be misinterpreted, even if you found the Ninja like stance he had adopted, in comprehensible, which unfortunately prevented him traversing the world to get to Japan to reinforce the effect, which was to demonstrate he was not a man to be trifled with, in a spongy, cowardy custard way.

'Oh shut up, Aedd,' Ceeley reacted.

'Righto... er, boyo.' The bravado evaporated and the Japanese accent whimpered away to a Welsh valley, bleating lamb and Aedd began to wonder if he should have pointed out Japan or China, to reinforce his ninja point. A matter to reflect upon he thought as he relieved himself of his ninja stance. I think more practice isn't it, he thought to himself in Welsh.

By way of an interesting informative, I can say, and most men can testify, the masculine assertion of boldness and even outrageous audacity, in front of a beautiful woman can be fleeting and so, boldness was really rather audaciously ambitious of Aedd, when you think about it, or so I am informed by my pseudonym. However, although it may appear to a man that such levels of courage may seem to be easily cast aside by a woman, it is in fact, and in truth, greatly appreciated by ladies, who will generally expect such shows of bravado and knowingly be aware also, of just how taxing it can be for a man.

For the benefit of my women readers, you should know that men take great solace in the sure and certain knowledge they are fully appreciated and that by not carrying through such masculine irritation, which could be accompanied by immeasurable smashing up, all as previously mentioned, it demonstrates that men have a sensitive side and, Ceeley demonstrated just that, by stroking the Aedd ginger downy face fuzz. He mewed – see what I mean, the ginger ninja was thus mollified – now you don't see that in the Ninja films, but if you did, it would more or less appear to be a normal day in a Tokyo suburban library, in other words a boring film – ahh so.

In real life, it happens all the time in Japan, except they're not ginger, I think, maybe ninja though? I must ask Jack Austin's new son, Hai Angie Son

It became clear father Mike was a tour-de-force and Aedd and Cecelia would have to be content to sit this one out. Mike O'Brien was assertive, bold, and audacious even and, in such a way that confirmed he had no lasting interest in womankind, other than their spiritual salvation.

Thus immune, he announced he would tell people about himself, and then set about this task to demonstrate the veracity of his intentions, by stepping forward to take his stand on the volcano and brushed aside some flaky pastry with the toe of his polished Vicar of Christ clodhoppers...

Note that even in Denmark or Sweden, churchmen do not remove their shoes - or so I am told, probably because they have smelly feet and holey socks.

... and he spake unto them, as if giving the Sermon on the Mount...

Not on a horse, but a mountain, well, a volcano.

... and not just a suspect diatribe about himself from a volcano.

Later to be confirmed in tablets, paracetamol likely as not as Georgie was already complaining of a headache, which worried Pimple for their prospective evening diversions, or perversions, of Marigold delights.

'When Aedd called to talk with Jack and Mandy.' He stopped, Aedd had his hand raised. 'Yes Aedd?'

'If you are going to tell this story please get things right, it's Dick and Duck.' Aedd felt certain he had established this as his terrain and so contented himself in allowing the priest to continue, but made sure his wobbly head conveyed to everyone else this was a victory, however Asia minor and, would have been established irrefutably if he had not genuflected afterwards, but this is what happens if you are a cowardy custard, ginger Ninja, faced with a powerful left footed priest.

'Head. Shut it, Aedd,' the father replied.

'Righto, Father, so,' Aedd said mimicking *Mrs Doyle,* 'would you like a coppa tea father? Oh, go on, go on, go on...' and Aedd giggled, made the sign of the cross thus excusing himself from damnation, genuflected again and mentioned Mary and Joseph, just to be sure, to be sure, in an Irish accent. The plea for personal salvation was clear, beyond any true religious zeal on his part.

Mike O'Brien, who could be quite

intimidating if he wasn't talking about curtains and colour palettes for his cathedral, nodded. Satisfied he had the volcano, with no further risk of interruption, Father Mike resumed. 'Is this pain au chocolat in the mouth of the volcano, you do know it could cause a side vent to blow?'

Aedd sat there with his head shut and just Mmm'd, a satisfying grin that said to anyone who gave a flying crucifix, he had told them so, and ever was it so, forever and ever, amen, but cautiously stepped away from the danger zone and crossed to his home base of Tara in order to gain spiritual strength from his Irish Regal heritage and, began sipping Darjeeling second flush from a saucer, in the manner of his Irish King ancestors.

The father continued, 'Aedd.'

Aedd jumped, 'What? I've kept my head shut,' and he looked pleadingly at the father for forgiveness, for something he was not aware he had done, so catholic, and for holy confirmation from the others his head had remained perfectly shut.

'Six our fathers, Aedd,' Mike commanded.

'What, six? What have I done?' So much for the sanctity of the confessional Aedd thought, aware he had only confessed to himself, but knew the priest knew exactly what he had been thinking. Aedd gave up his futile self-justification and said, 'Okay father, so,' in Irish. Well, he was in Tara wasn't he and he slurped some more tea from the saucer. It was magical, mystical even and, he sensed the presence of his four feathers.

I think he meant forefathers – so you see how intimidating Father Mike can be.

Mike continued, still looking at Aedd and Aedd thinking here it comes, Hail bleedin' Mary's, but it didn't. 'Aedd, I know you have been telling people Jack Austin is more than just a retired copper.'

'How do you know that?' Aedd asked, panicked, before the father could continue to explain or make his point, or point out Aedd's head was no longer shut. 'I haven't have I?' And Aedd looked around to everyone, eliciting support, which did not come. Aedd swung his gaze back to the priest, 'Oh alright, but just a little bit, you know, were...' and he fluttered his hand underneath his armpit to the disgust of the women in the room and the total understanding of the men, who fully comprehended a gentle breeze of man-musk can be irresistible for women and, the odd bushy faced professor.

This included Mike, as he nodded and surveyed the whole room with his penetrating expert interrogation, holier than thou, angelic, gobshite eyes. 'Well, Aedd, you would be right of course and, of course, I would expect everyone here to keep that an absolute secret.' He specifically looked to Cecelia and for balance, to Pimple behind the roses, almost as a matter of horticultural and journalistic courtesy, 'that includes the gutter press as well. Do I have an understanding?'

'Gutter is about right with that Strumpet,' the Dame managed to say, before she received the priestly stare, almost as if it came from the Almighty himself and she shrank back into her moose habitat, which currently was the heavenly folding embrace of one, Mercy Mudstone, whose face, coincidentally, currently had the look of the folding rocky geological strata beneath Birmingham.

'Do I have an understanding?'

They all nodded and said, "Yes Father," said like *Mrs Doyle*.

'I will know if it leaks and, I will know where to come if I find this out. Am I understood on that?' He waited again and got a similar affirmative. 'Good, then I will rely on you Ceeley and you Pimple, to write things in a discreet manner, but you can rest assured what I am about to tell you is Gospel,' and he crossed himself, mentioned Mary and Joseph and the priest's face brimmed with absolution before it needed it, as he knew he was not about to relate the absolute truth, being a man from MI5 himself, although he was truthfully a left footed priest.

So Mike began his half-truth. 'Jack Austin and his wife are now completely retired, but in their former existence, they were MI5.' He allowed for the intake of breath that he noticed was not so marked in Cecelia whom he suspected already had an inkling if the twinkling in her eye was anything to go by. 'I would not want you all to run away with the idea they were action men spooks, so to speak. They were quite the contrary, although some of you may recall that in some recent, shall we say, scrapes, involving Jack Austin, you would be forgiven if you did not comprehend that.' More nods, Aedd looking pleased he had been forgiven and wanted to ask if he still had to say his Hail Fathers, or was it Our Marys, but kept his counsel as Mike continued. 'It's hard to credit, Jack Austin was always the cerebral spook and in truth, is the clumsiest and practically the most inept man on earth and is, was, kept as far away from the sharp end of business as could humanly be possible. But, and some of you may already know the man, around Jack Austin,' he flung his hands out as if preparing to be crucified, a thought that flashed by Cecelia's mind coincidentally, 'well, around Jack, things happen.'

Father Mike O'Brien allowed this to sink in while he swivelled his eyes along the length of Frisian Tun and back, to indicate that despite all of the denials, earnestly meant and delivered, it is very likely Jane Austin truly was responsible for the partial destruction of this delightful and idyllic, some might say decorous, middle class street, where they lived. Probably. Well, most likely.

'Are you saying...?'

'Stop there Georgia,' Mike reacted, putting his hand up.

'Eeeeh!'

'Eeeeh?' Mike asked.

'Yes, Georgeeeey, not Georgia,' Georgie said.

'Ah so,' the priest replied in Japanese, thinking of Jack's new son Angie, and Aedd adopted his ginger ninja pose, the one Father Mike uses most Sundays when he threatens you with the blood of Christ if you don't eat your bread up.

'Oh shut up you flaky ponce, are you really even a priest?' Georgie was not impressed and Pimple wondered if he should mention the clip-em and sock-em game to the father, who he had taken a shine to and felt it only fair he be warned, wondering also if he could be his mate or indeed a chum, possibly even a mush.

'Dearest Georgiana,' and Mike applied a smug Pride and Prejudice victory grin, 'I am indeed a priest and what is more, I married the Austins in the Roman Catholic Cathedral and arranged for their Papal blessing, so ner!'

'Ner?'

'Ner.'

'What's ner?'

'What's in where?'

'Oh for Christ's sake,' Aedd said.

'Make that twelve Our Fathers and throw in a Hail Mary or two, Aedd. Do not blaspheme or bring the Lord's name into disrepute.'

'Twelve?'

'Yes, twelve - Ner.'

Aedd was dispirited and glanced to Rome, but no help came. Father Mike O'Brien had that all stitched up, as anyone who knew Mike would know for certain.

'Now, walk me to the door, Cecelia. You are taking Pimple walkies, am I right?' Mike gestured his pious head to the door, 'Patent azure blue wellies, Ceeley?'

'I thought it would rain, Mike, and yes, I need to talk with Everard.'

Mike looked out the window, 'Do you want rain?'

'I quite like the rain and wind along the seafront, don't you?'

'No, Ceeley, but if you do,' and Mike made a really devout face and looked up to the Battle of Trafalgar, but was likely looking beyond the Spanish Cape. He waved his hands like a magician. 'Okay, Ceeley.'

Aedd looked out of the window to the relatively cloudless and sunny sky, back to Mike, to Ceeley, and to Pimple, thought about discussing cumulonimbus cloud formations at fifty thousand feet are not likely to drop rain, but they should watch out if it dropped to, say, six thousand feet, but in the end settled for a Gallic shrug and pointed to France and thought no more of it.

TWENTY-ONE
THE JOURNALIST, THE GOSSIP COLUMNIST

CECELIA AND PIMPLE, WITH FATHER O'Brien in tow, crossed the narrow lane that was Frisian Tun, and stopped outside number five, where Amanda Austin's head and shoulders were visible over the garden wall. She was tall and rested her chin on her folded arms on top of the wall; a comfortable *look-out*.

'Mike's out and has Ceeley and Pimple with him,' she shouted, turning her head back to the partially open, expansive, Georgian sash window that reflected the setting sun to cast a tawny tinge across the forecourt, which was poetic if you were a poet, but otherwise blinded the shite out of you, so much so you frustratingly could not see into the window.

· · ·

And we all know how much we like to peek into other peoples' windows.

Therefore, you couldn't see the walrus, but its presence was suggested to the nosy passersby, by a distinct bellowing, walrus like, a wriggly grandchild, one very wriggly Meesh, an 8-10 year old girl and a ginger border terrier, all on top giggling, woofing. Little walruses at play with granddad walrus, an altogether agreeable summer evening sound of familial bliss.

Amanda received a flipper like tap on the glass, acknowledgement from Grandfevvers Walrus. More squeals of delight, the kids tickling the exposed flipper pit.

'How did it go Mike? Girl grey, or are you going back for a pray?' Mandy asked, smiling; they knew each other well.

'Coffee would be lovely. I'm not doing mass this evening, but when I get back we are all watching *Pride and Prejudice* again, and again, and again, amen, for the umpteenth time. Heavenly Father, help me', and he glanced at the cumuli-nimbus that may have dropped a few thousand feet. 'Since Jack became Jane, my life has been blighted by genteel manners and how do-you-do's.'

'Shusssh, Mike.' Amanda put her finger to

her mouth, 'He will hear you and then I'll have to watch it with him tonight, all five hours. Crikey, I'm sure you did that deliberately.'

Mike grinned devilishly, went to let himself through the gate that stuck, booted the bottom as he lifted it in its hinges and it squeaked open, it sounded like a hymn.

'Ave Maria, Mike?'

'No thanks, just had one...' and the priest folded over and giggled. "Ave... a good walk you two. Pimple should you not have a Mac?' The priest called out to the couple as they departed, seafront bound.

Pimple looked around him as the glorious reddening evening sky bathed the stuccoed villas a blood red, dulling the evident pock marking of bullet holes. He embraced the warmth of the residual heat of the day and the proximity of Ceeley and thought the priest must be barking mad as well as a left footed spy. 'I'll take my chances Father,' and he smiled back at Amanda and the priest as Ceeley had already begun to tow him away, her arm in the crook of his elbow.

As they strolled, Pimple resisted looking at Ceeley. She was gorgeous, he knew, and although he had gained a little in confidence in the past twenty four hours, he was petrified to his marrow, even so, he could not deny his excitement. Amanda was aware of Pimple's conflicting feelings and she gave him the most beautifully warm and womanly smile. He was a mouse being toyed with by a big cat who could devour him anytime. He was enjoying it and, not only was he not picking, he was walking a lot less gingerly.

Ceeley's azure wellies galloshed and scuffed the pavement and then were then silent as they hit the grass of Southsea common, the vast expanse that was the approach to the seafront and ancient fortifications. 'Everard,' he turned to face her and reacted in the collywobbles department. It was her coquettish grin, the shape of her long oval face enhanced as it tilted; oh God, he loved it. 'You can look at me you know.'

So he did, pleased he had got away with his previous surreptitious glances and now he took in her every feature as though it were magnified. 'I, er, er...' thank God Pimple thought, he'd managed to say something, and in a baritone that would surely have disguised his nervousness.

'Come here, Everard.'

She had stopped and he was walking on, oblivious, absorbed in his own thoughts of being the cat's first course, before she got onto the cream, 'I, er, er...'

'What, Everard?'

'I er...'

'Hmmm?' she sloped her beautiful head,

enquiring.

Pimple would have squeaked were he not already a dead mouse.

You know when a woman goes "Hmmm", it resonates in a man? Well it does and, I can reliably inform my readers of that fact being a man. Furthermore, as a female pseudonym, I also have a canny insight into the thinking of both women and men, which may account, for those who wondered, for my success in life generally. Yes, I can tell you a "Hmmmm" resonates. Interestingly though, it can be either a sexual resonance or it can be fear? And here nature plays a diabolical game on the man, as generally and, unfairly, it befalls upon the man to determine if he should be frightened or aroused sexually.

I appreciate a woman may tell a man there are signals, but if you have a pint with any fellow at any bar he will always say, "What bloody signals, I didn't see any bloody signals". As a man, if you recall I am, I can tell you that it is nigh on impossible to tell or see any signals and furthermore, the natural default position of a man is to be sexually aroused. A thingy bob scientist, who studies these things, could probably explain it as an inherent desire in man to sustain and procreate the species, dating back to when caves were viewed as places for wimps and Jessies, and this may well account for why men often are frequently losers in the sock-em and clip-em game.

Pimple was relatively inexperienced. Almost a day and a half experience if you include the glorious Cecelia dalliance on his orange box, and who wouldn't, which for most men is all you need to sally forth and confidently conquer your woman with a winning smile and wondrous banter of a sort women find fascinating, like, say, "We don't need to find a cave, we can have sex behind that bush. Caves are for wimps and Jessies and think of the money we will save on a hotel cave".

Pimple though was mindful of his relative inexperience and was not aware of the natural default of a man, and so he went defensive and shaped to duck or parry a sock or a clip. He was therefore shocked when Ceeley took his hands away from his face and planted a kiss, summarily on his lips that had already prepared themselves to scream in pain, as their natural default position.

'I er, er...'
'Yes, I know, Everard darling.'

· · ·

You see, women are all knowing, although I think they just have the confidence to carry off the act that they are all-knowing. The problem is men do not take the time to practice being all knowing and sometimes they just assume everyone knows they know, all, if you know what I mean?

Ceeley slipped her arm back into the crook of Pimple's elbow and he was captured, drawn in as she applied her tractor beam, which was not as agricultural a sensation as the term may imply, although there was no doubt Everard Pimple was like a recently dug up turnip. She gazed into his face. She was five foot ten of fulsome woman, a black haired bombshell fit to burst, to Pimple's six foot four of beanpole, fit to embarrass himself in the trouser department and, satisfied with the look of bewilderment on Pimple's slender face that had the bloom of a naive blush she so adored, Cecelia walked on and he naturally followed.

Well you would if you didn't have warp drive to break free of the tractor beam, wouldn't you? And then of course she had him by the crook of his arm, so photon torpedoes would be out as well.

· · ·

'You know, Everard, I've been thinking.'

He stopped as he thought he needed to concentrate in order to formulate a reply he was sure would be needed. But, he was still in the tractor beam and so was obliged to mention a few errs, but did loll his tongue to demonstrate he was not intimidated by aliens, was quite au fait with the dalliances of women and, knew how to titillate them.

'Put your tongue away, please,' he pulled it in immediately and wrapped it around his inner cheek, the appearance being he was hiding a gob stopper from his teacher. 'Very good, Everard. There is no need for you to loll your tongue unless I specifically request you to do so, okay?' He nodded and shifted his tongue to the opposite cheek and pretended to casually examine his inner mouth as a natural way of being a man in considered thought. Coincidentally, he considered rubbing his cheek but was too late and also he didn't want to lose that one stiff bristle.

Ceeley was not fooled, 'Everard?'

'Mmmm?' Pimple said in response, it being hard to say anything coherent to a teacher, or a woman for that matter and especially a female teacher, without giving the game away; any boy will tell you that.

Ceeley, being a pragmatist, looked like she

might put aside the gob stopper and move on. 'I've been thinking we should write this article together.' She looked at him, received the anticipated "err" and proceeded with her expressed train of thought. 'I have a by-line and we can share it, *Crumpet and Pimple*, sound good to you?'

'Coo' he said, marginally better than "err" she considered, and carried on.

'There is more to this story than just what you have learned so far and that which I will impart to you later.'

He looked at her quizzically, the first time as a reporter with the sniff of a story and not a love sick dewy eyed Pimple. 'Coo, er...' this time said in a manly journalistic manner.

Well you can't have everything at once Ceeley thought to herself, comforted Georgie would sort him for her and she settled down to enjoy her walk, in what was a darkening summer ambience, with, if she was not mistaken, cumuli-nimbus rapidly descending to, circa six thousand feet. 'What do you think of Georgie, Pimple?'

Pimple was thrown by this. He had put Georgie to the back of his mind, having resolved already on an excuse that Cecelia and he were talking journalism, should Georgie seek one, to explain what he was doing walking with another woman and striding out in what could only be called a man and woman intimate fashion, reminiscent of how a boy and girlfriend might walk.

'I, er...'

'You seem to get on well, the two of you?' She carried on walking, tugging him along with her eyes to the front. They had just passed the fountains outside the castle and Pimple was aware of the threatening clouds behind the fortifications, the lustrous residual red sunlight ruddily bathing the castle's lighthouse.

Ordinarily Pimple knew all the names of the parts of the fort, but as most men know and women should be aware and, I may have mentioned earlier, rational thought tends to go out of the window or arrow loop in this case, when a man is aroused and in close proximity of a sex kitten. This can only be perceived as compounded when being questioned about intimate details of a peculiar kind, between said man and another woman, and is complicated further if all had happened in the past day or so.

Pimple answered, "Er, coo".

This seemed to satisfy Ceeley, who casually turned up the collar and hood of her anorak, to protect her neck from the fat drops of rain that began to spatter, bringing before it an earthy tang, which was Pimple's excuse for a big sniff.

'It's an earthy tang,' he said, thinking coincidentally of Georgie's earthy manner of night-time talking.

'What?'

'The rain?'

'What about the rain?' she was irritated; it doesn't take much.

But this is one of the reasons why women prefer caves; in fact likely found the bushes got stuck up their bums (Just sayin').

Pimple pressed on, committed to his interesting fact, confident in the certain knowledge Ceeley would find his discourse fascinating, eventually. 'When it hasn't rained for a long time in the summer, and when it eventually rains, it brings with it an earthy tang. Sort of irony. Not ironic,' and he giggled nervously, which inadequately disguised a long and hard sniff, as if to demonstrate the veracity of his claim. She smiled at him, a broad and warm smile that went directly to Pimple's collywobbles department. He noted in his mental book, that he may write one day, *How to be with a woman and not appear a tart*, that he had elicited this response without even lolling his tongue. He must be getting better and he stuffed the sniff technique into his brain ledger, thus displacing the tongue loll move, not aware this loss would please Ceeley inordinately.

'Everard?'

'Hmmm?' he was enjoying this walk now, the rain refreshing as it dribbled down the back of his neck and he became fascinated as the blobs appeared ink-black on the powder blue material of his shirt. She looked at him and thought he looked sublimely happy and wondered if she should disrupt this reverie.

Well, you know what happens when a woman sees a man is in a blissful reverie don't you and, Ceeley was all woman and, wasn't this after all the task of all women, to keep men earthbound.

'Georgie...?' she mewed, still enquiring, watching him wriggle on the end of her line and noticed that immediately he looked shattered as he crashed and burned.

'I er, er...' he wondered if that would be sufficient and sniffed to see if this would help matters along a bit, so he could carry on dreaming and looking at his shirt that had the look of those ink blot cards psychiatrists show you. They say they are butterflies when anyone could see they were a crowd of demented zombies. He sniffed a default sniff; he was a natural.

'Do you have a cold coming on?'

He looked at her as if she was a dimwit and even declared in thought to himself, maybe she was not aware of the ways of men? A simple innocent? 'No!'

She did not press as she looked at him and amazingly took pleasure in the sight of the beanpole in front of her, the lanky streak of aristocratic piss who, as he stumbled along, presented the raindrops an almost impossible task to hit him, just a few spots on his powder blue shirt that to her looked like a butterfly.

'Why do you ask about Georgie?' He turned to look at her and at last, she noticed his eyes did not dive for cover. They were blue and glinted, moist, and his daft blond haystack hair was flattened onto his pointy scalp; he looked like a Norman soldier. 'I like her, but...'

'But what, my dear?'

He was thrown by the affectionate way in which she addressed him, 'I er...'

'Yes?'

'I am concerned we, er, had thingy. You

know?'

Now she tormented him. 'No, what thingy?'

'Thingy,' he said, as if all should now be clear, he'd even fluttered his hand, not realising this was the cat playing with the mouse before the cream course.

'Did you have sex with Georgie?' She was onto the cream.

Pimple went scarlet, a rouge that matched the redness of the sky in the west, where the black cumulonimbus had not yet reached. 'Yes, and I am worried.'

'Worried, why? Was it not nice?'

'Oh Ceeley it was wonderful...' he pulled himself up, inherently knowing he should not be speaking like this to another Goddess, especially in a squeaky mouse like voice.

She was a little disconcerted herself and wondered at that. 'Well, what is the problem?'

He screwed his courage up, which if you recall is connected to the Pimple face muscles and he coughed out his worries to this most beautiful of agony Aunts. 'We used no thingies and what if she got thingy? I mean, I would marry her, of course, but what would mother say? And father for that matter? I don't earn enough to support a family and, where would we live and how do you look after babies, and then I think...' he'd run out of steam, but was mainly disarmed by the fact Ceeley had removed her arm from the crook of his elbow and amidst a torrential downpour, was folded over in hysterics and, as she raised herself back up and guffawed to the open heavens, her hood fell back and her raven black hair became instantly plastered to her beautifully rosy cheeks. Ceeley steadied herself and faced him again, this time with only mild tittering and Pimple noticed the rivulets pouring down her face, black lines running from her eye surrounds, flowing alongside her hair lanks, a drip hanging off her Romanesque, strong nose. He took all of this in as he felt both her hands cover his face and draw him in and... Oh my God. She kissed him. Fuck me gently, she kissed him hard and on his half open mouth.

Georgie had taught him this. It's so a woman can get her tongue in, you see.

Pimple was in a blissful rapture and, Cecelia lingered. So, he kissed her back, feeling as though he had permission. He did, and she replied in thrusting tongue movements.

Told you.

. . .

He thought it would look lovely if they lolled tongues, together, so he sniffed as she grabbed his rabbits bum and pulled him to her. So the sniff worked he thought.

She broke away and giggled some more. 'Oh, Everard, you are such an innocent.'

He was not so sure how to take that? 'I say, is that a good thing?' He was breathy for some reason and hoped it did not make him seem like an idiot, or was becoming asthmatic, as well as having a cold.

She seemed to consider her reply, her eyes though remained fixed on his and she was pleased he held her gaze. 'In your case, Everard, I think it may be, but I may also be able to put your mind at rest on one score.'

'What score, nobody said we were scoring this?'

She giggled again and said, 'Oh Pimple, darling, I'm not sure I ever want you to change, but needs must. You are aware how old Georgie is, are you not? Are you aware she is past the menopause? But it says a lot for you that you see beyond all of these things, not least she bats off both feet, probably favouring the unorthodox if it came right down to it.'

Now this did throw Pimple. It wasn't so

much the age thing, although now Ceeley had mentioned it, he thought he could see this now and it wasn't the style of batting that pricked his consciousness, he could see that and was not overly concerned, no, what concerned him and raised itself high in the library of life questions he had forgotten about, what was the menopause? Pimple did not consider himself a nerd by any sense, but he did know how to work a DVD machine and such like and, was aware of the pause button, but was not aware he should maybe have pressed this button when he was with Georgie and, even if he knew where it was, and even if he did feel he should press it, would he be able to locate it at the delicate moment so to speak, thus preventing the risk of fertilising Georgie. He was not even aware women had a pause button.

Sometimes I forget I'm a pseudonym. Okay I'm back now.

Ceeley took pity on Pimple. 'Don't worry sweetie, everything will be okay.'

'It will?' She reassured him with a smile, 'But where is the pause button?'

She reassured herself, which coincidentally

reassured Pimple, with the thought Georgie knew what she was doing and it would only be a week or so. Ceeley fluttered her hand to herself with the resultant waft of intoxicating, raindrop drenched, earthy perfume hitting Pimple's energised and flared nostrils and he forgot absolutely everything.

Aedd let the pair drip in the communal vestibule, conscious of the presence of the almighty and, intimidated by the power of the priesthood to summon cumuli-nimbus and set them at around six thousand feet so they might precipitate. Aedd felt truly Roman Catholic, wallowing in guilt, as he looked at the drowned skinny, lanky rat, that was Pimple, and apologetic that he had not warned Pimple or given him an umbrella or a *drizabone*, a coat from Australia, glancing back to the map room and wondering if he should pop back and maybe point to the outback or something.

Georgie let out a piercing scream, accompanied by much ripe cursing that hailed likely as not from Peckham Rye. She hopped out from the bathroom, favouring her big toe on her right foot and into the vestibule with a towel in hand and, passed it to a partially soaked Ceeley. Everard just dripped; ironic isn't it? He was known as a drip. However, Georgie was aware that her Pimple had an earthy smell to him and, it caught her collywobbles on the hop, so to speak.

There was no need for explanation and Ceeley intervened. 'Georgie, perhaps you need to take Everard downstairs, he can minister to your big toe and maybe you could warm him up with a bath or a shower?'

Georgie's face illuminated with ill-concealed desire and energy and, remarkably, this surpassed all pain that may have emanated from a particle of sideboard in her toe and, et voila, Pimple was nervous again, but mainly because he looked back to Ceeley for a reaction. But the delectable Ms Crumpet just smiled warmly back at him, flicked her hand in a waving goodbye gesture and called out, 'Georgie, can we move on to the slow down techniques and explain the pause button, please.'

Georgie grabbed the drenched Pimple, encouraged him to the door, the steps, and into to her semi-subterranean perfumed pink (with fuchsia bits and dark blue net curtains) fluffy boudoir, where Georgie stripped Pimple and herself. She had no time for synchronised bra uncoupling and, dashing to the shower room, dragging a naked Pimple and sitting herself on the loo, she stuck her big toe into Pimple's agape mouth that was actually prepared only to receive her tongue. Remarkably, Pimple was getting to be extraordinarily experienced as he showed only a little surprise, which, when you think about it, is difficult to do anyway with a sideboard and big toe in your mouth.

As he softened the skin of the toe that visually looked enormous in perspective, he gazed into the eyes of Georgie on the loo seat and for the life of him he could not read her age. But, he had more important things on his mind, like, where would a woman keep her pause button and, as Georgie's toe popped out with a mild sucking exclamation, he had another thought that maybe he was supposed to have a pause button and he was dashed if he knew where that would be either.

Having ministered to the sideboard, Georgie and Pimple showered and she explained the slow down bit about making love to a woman and remarkably, Pimple seemed to grasp the concept in theory, but depending on how he managed in practice, Georgie thought he might be ready in less than a week, but maybe she would keep him on for the full stint anyway?

TWENTY-TWO
THE GEOGRAPHY TEACHER, THE POLICE INSPECTOR

Everyone reassembled in the map room at nine the next morning. Ceeley greeted Pimple with a kiss on the lips and he was sure he sensed a fondling of his bony bottom, but that may just have been his over active imagination.

Aedd stood prepared on the volcano, no French pastries today, he was not going to take any chances with a side vent blow-out. 'If we can get right to it, this has already dragged on longer than I had imagined and as it is a Friday...' he stopped and looked out of the window, '... I shall be seeing Beatrice after she finishes orchestra.' He leaned and looked out of the window again. Everyone else craned their necks to look in the direction of the window.

'What?' Georgie asked, as she leaned across Pimple, fondling his bits and pieces in a multi tasking fashion, a womanly skill greatly appreciated by Pimple minor.

'What do you mean, what?' Aedd replied.

'Just, what?' Georgie answered, but followed it up with a look that would tear the skin of yer. Pimple ducked instinctively, but there was no need, Georgie was feeling well disposed to Pimple at the moment. He had, likely inadvertently, found his own pause button, but there were many female buttons that needed her synchronised guidance on.

'It's just that Father Mike is back and, he's in the forecourt with Mandy, I mean Duck.'

Pimple ducked, before he realised he was talking about Amanda Austin. Georgie got up and Pimple fell on the floor. She sidled over to the window to join Ceeley and Aedd. 'Oh Yeah,' Georgie said, looking back to Ceeley and then Aedd. 'Did you tell him about your interview with Lady Blanche-Teapot, Ceeley?'

'Not in detail, just that I had interviewed the Duchess,' Ceeley replied.

'I imagine he still wants to know?' Georgie said, stating the blindingly obvious.

Pimple sneezed and the two women turned and looked at the poor soul nursing a distinctly unsexy sniff, unaware that Pimple was controlling his sniffing as much as possible, so as not to arouse Ceeley in front of Georgie.

It can be so difficult being a sex idol and I should know, in my male guise that is, and also being bone idle. Sadly in the sex department these days.

Despite his growing know-how, Pimple was not sure how he would handle that one, but luck was on his side, Georgie had not enquired as to the drenching walk he had had with Ceeley yesterday evening. Amazing Pimple had thought to himself, women just don't see things.

I did say Pimple was only relatively experienced, as women do see a lot more than men and sometimes, they see things that are not even there, honest. And then they bring it into a discussion when a man has completely forgotten and moved on to pastures new, in a conversational way of course, even if he had never seen the new pasture or even the old one before in his life, honest!

. . .

'He's coming down with something,' Ceeley observed in a Nightingale way, and shared a conspiratorial chuckle with Georgie as they made their way back to their seats, announcing that Father Mike and Duck were map room bound. Aedd spryly leapt toward the western cedar street door to avoid *Ave Maria* on the bozzer and thus avoid the suggestion it should also be whistled for all attending, in a congregational sense, for their spiritual benefit.

Father Mike entered. 'Good morning, I trust you and your families are well?' And he bowed quickly and stiffly. There was silence, then he said, in a very posh voice that Dame Pimple took as normal, 'I am tolerably well. I trust you did not get overly wet yesterday afternoon, young sir,' and he directed his gaze to Pimple. There was more silence, which did not bother Mike in the slightest and he went to speak again only halted, responding to the less than subtle visual request of Ceeley, conveyed by her eyes.

'You watched *Pride and Prejudice* last night?'

'I did ma'am, and a right rollicking affair it was too. I hardly slept a wink, what with the excitement and all, that Darcy, you know, when he comes out of the lake with his shirt all clingy and I know George Wickham is a bad lot, but I am sure I could sort him out, don't you know?'

Nobody did know, except maybe Georgie did and possibly the professor.

'Shut yer trap you holy ponce and I shall be most exceedingly obliged,' Georgie said, switching from Peckham Rye to Pemberley with an almost indiscernible segue to the uninitiated.

Aedd stepped in to stop World War Three. 'Sit down please, Father. I was going to tell everybody about you, but instead I will put Pimple in the picture regarding the day I was with Dick and Duck and the Police Inspector called.' Aedd looked to Ceeley to see if he was to be challenged, but she seemed distracted, wiping Pimple's nose with a tissue and then, she spat on the end and rubbed his cheek to remove a mark that turned out, after a period of excessive maternal abrasion and the removal of several layers of skin, to be a mole. She gave up and smiling, sat on the arm of the armchair, making Pimple, the filling in a Georgie and Ceeley sandwich.

Pimple said nothing, except "Coo", but he did rub his cheek to sooth it, aware that in this position he would be well and truly smoked in the sock-em and clip-em game, therefore it would be best to keep his mouth shut, though he did think cooing would be okay.

'What I couldn't understand was, why the police called? Why would Lady Blanche-Teapot call them? Did she call them?' Aedd asked, looking to the Father, who hummed *Onward Christian Soldiers* whilst perusing the Battle of Trafalgar, a picture of gobshite piety; a wafer would not melt in his mouth.

'Does it matter?' Dame Pimple asked, comfortable in the intimate folds of the settee with Mercy, which afforded a jolly good shared view of Georgie's cherished lady parts, and they looked like they were locked in a celebratory embrace, having just scored a goal in a hockey match.

'Well, it does in the turn of events you see, but why call?' Aedd asked, seeming to be preoccupied by the thought as though it was the first time this had occurred to him; it had only just occurred to him, but he carried it off well he thought. But, the women knew, and of course wouldn't mention it until it had completely slipped from the Aedd memory banks, probably just before bedtime.

'He was a policeman and so was Amanda, I mean Duck, so maybe it was social?' Mercy suggested, getting in on the act and cosying in with the moose, unaware the act of cosying had caused bellowing noises from the moose hindmost quarters.

'No, it was more than that and, this was a Detective Inspector from the Metropolitan

Police Serious Crime Unit. Er, something like that?' Aedd looked to Mike, 'You were there, Mike, what was her name? A cockney sparrow she announced herself as?'

Mike obliged, maintaining an almost smug grin toward the Cape of Trafalgar and various ships of the line, trying to work out which boat was the Victory. 'Her name is Della Lovington, Detective Inspector and a little bit were, if you get my drift,' he said fluttering his hand, but maintaining station at Trafalgar. 'England expects and all of that, nods as good as a wink to a blind bat though, eh?' He added in a celestial twat manner, and looked down to see if the nod had indeed been as good for the blind bats, whichever foot they were using.

'Is it?'

'Yes Ceeley. If a bat is in fact blind, you see...'

She interrupted, 'I know what your drift is, but...' and she fluttered her hand, and Pimple thought that seen in a prudential light, it could be misconstrued as a bat like flutter.

'Well, if you knew what my drift was, then why interrupt?' Mike interrupted as if fear was something he commonly met and trod its precarious path with relative immunity. Had he not heard of sock-em and clip-em, Pimple thought, but noticed the Father had placed himself out of range.

Clever buggers these priests.

'The point I'm making is that a bat, being blind, obviously would not see a nod, much less a wink, but with its sensitive sonar would pick up the movement.'

Ceeley sat back on the arm of the chair and gently, lovingly, fingered Pimple's ear lobe, which was large and floppy, but in proportion generally to the long and fulsome ears that could not in a million years be described as Indian, and had to hail from African descent, elephant wise; maybe they were taxi doors? Mike looked like he had been holy smoked and went to answer, hoping an intelligent response would appear as he moved his lips, in a confident masculine way, but Ceeley had not finished, although she did maintain the fondling of Pimple's lobe. 'What you are saying is she was another spook, MI5, is that right and, once again, I take it we are sworn to secrecy?'

'Yes, that bat would most likely avoid that nod,' he said nodding, avoiding the direct answer but applying a knowing visage, which was picked up by everyone except Pimple, who had drifted off, enjoying the sensations of an electric current of some meter in his ear lobe, en-route now and rather rapidly, to his collywobble department.

Aedd resumed, nodding himself and he could not resist a flutter of his hand under his armpit as he smiled at Cecelia. 'Yes, well, what was she doing down from London eh? Answer me that, clever clogs?' And he swung the snooker cue from London to Holland. No injuries ensued, the move was anticipated, but not the one to Hebden Bridge in the north of England, where, Aedd informed everybody, they still made clogs. The confusion and ducking was a sight to behold, Father Mike later told his mate in MI5, Jane Austin.

A suggestion that maybe Dick and Duck had not, after all, retired?

Cecelia was enjoying her Pimple lobe moment and whereas she could very easily have interrupted Aedd with the knowledge she had gained from her interview with Lady Blanche-Teapot, which information had allowed her to consider that all was starting to fall into place for her, she considered she would allow Aedd to continue talking about when the Inspector called. It may provide interesting background information to the article Pimple and she would write.

Aedd, of course, thought he was allowed to continue because he had asserted himself. Such is the lot of men and please do not enlighten (us) dear ladies, as bliss is not ignorance, it is actually bliss and, how rare is that these days – okay, I'm back as my pseudonym, so let's get on.

Ceeley stretched out from the arm of the armchair and nudged Aedd with her cherry red painted and pointed big toe, which were simply gorgeous, as was the rest of Ceeley, Pimple thought. The toe, the foot and then the long elegant and shapely leg, the whole ensemble looked so beautiful.

Aaaah...
Aedd thought, bloody cheek, but he did get on with it, starting as if still in deep thought. 'I am not sure if the breezy persona of this cockney sparrow Inspector was like a breath of the

proverbial fresh air she assured me she was, or whether she was disguising the fact she was a brazen hussy, brazening it, so to speak?'

'What do you mean' the mention of hussy had Mercy and Dame Pimple interested, so much so they swung their joint gaze from Georgie, a picture of Shirley Temple squashed in the armchair with Pimple, her legs akimbo, to Aedd.

'What I mean is...' and he looked like he was still trying to think what he actually did mean, '... is that she did not so much breeze in, as take the living room by storm; gale force. Interestingly, the walrus appeared unmoved and I had to look once or twice to see if he slumbered. Amanda also took the intrusion completely in her stride, getting the woman a cup of monkey tea before it was even requested. Not that any of this seemed to stop the motor mouth sparrow, and I quote, "Oi mush" she said to Dick, who reacted with a "wot?" and that was it. Silence reined as did the Queen, according to Della and then, Dick told us all about the Queen.' Aedd thought for some time and everyone allowed the Queen to rule, in silence. 'It was extraordinary how we got to be talking about the Queen, who Dick knows well, apparently.' Aedd still looked confused and adequately demonstrated this by rubbing his fluffy IKEA chin.

'He does know her well.' It was Father Mike, still intently looking at the Battle of Trafalgar, probably trying to see Hardy kissing Nelson. 'Della knows her as well, it seems the Queen likes cockneys, although I understand the Duke of Edinburgh is ambivalent, but does like a tin barf.'

'Tin Barf?' Mercy inquired and Dame Pimple seemed equally curious. Pimple was oblivious of any bath as Ceeley had allowed her hand to slip from his lobe department, down the front of his powder blue shirt and was stoking his chest. She was conscious not to rub too hard as Georgie had reported Pimple only had seven hairs and six of them were loose.

'Laugh – tin barf, larf,' Mike explained. 'They're bleedin' cockneys,' he expanded, in the parlance, a passable accent, which you would expect coming from Orpington where they spoke cockney with an estuarine lilt.

'Oh' a joint expression from everyone, except for Pimple who went "Coo". And it looked like he couldn't care if he lost one or two of those tentatively attached hairs, he could always grow some more before he drew his pension.

Aedd continued as if with renewed vim. 'Yes, so, the next thing we know is Della had poured her tea into the saucer, she apparently liked couth cups because they came with a saucer and quite uncouthly she slurped, noisily, her tea from the saucer, mentioning also the Kings of Ireland did this, and so it was okay for her. Dick confirmed this. I have of course checked and it is the case, which is why, considering my lineage, I have adopted this mode of tea drinking myself, being directly descended from Diarmait the 1st...' He turned to point to Tara, just up a bit and to the left of Dublin, but "ooohed" as Ceeley judiciously allowed her cherry reds to poke his "Khyber pass" she also said, in the cockney parlance she had familiarised herself with since she had gotten to know Jack Austin, sorry Jane, sorry Dick.

Aedd got on with it. 'Well, after we got past the Queen, this Inspector went on to talk about "Lady cha-cha" as she seemed to call the "bleedin' *Teapot* Duchess" and declared, "she was checking it out with Del-Boy" but all in all, I got the impression she considered Teapot was a bit "ginger beer", which I gather meant the situation was a little queer and she had asked someone called Derek to investigate. She then went on to talk about quiz night at the Gravediggers, the pub opposite Eastney cemetery, where, if I gathered correctly, she was off to straight after, in order to get a "good rogering" from her new husband, who I also gather, is the landlord of said "rubbadub", the pub.'

Mercy was fascinated. 'I've heard about that pub, it's like stepping back into Victorian times, spit and sawdust and only serves their home made ale and homemade stew; fish or beef, it is quite a place.' She giggled nudging Dame Pimple with her elbow, almost forcing the enormous woman from the settee, 'Get it Delores? Plaice, place, fish stew,' and the two hockey players rocked on their hind quarters enjoying the jest wholeheartedly and hugged each other as if they had just participated in another fortunate goal.

Aedd tapped his fingers on the side of the snooker cue, puffed out his cheeks and blew a stream of air up to the ceiling, like he was playing the flute. Father Mike noticed the cotton wool canon puffs flutter. 'If, I may move on... as I say, I am meeting Bea Flat after orchestra this evening and I may just go to the Gravediggers for some stew and ale.' The idea had just occurred to him and was aware, as he saw everybody duck, he could have pointed to the detail map of Portsmouth to indicate Eastney cemetery, but he couldn't be Kaiber Passed.

'So, what happened?' It was Georgie, irritated as she wanted to stroke Pimple's chest and wasn't all that bothered if she caused the loose hairs to fall out, if Ceeley had left any that was.

'I will cut a long story short...'

'Hoo, bleedin' ray' it was Georgie, her Peckham Rye strains almost as cockney as Della and Dick's, as her frustration grew. 'Ceeley, you do know for the time being the chest department is mine, don't you?'

'I am so sorry, Georgie darling. I got a little carried away,' she answered as she counted six blond hairs in the palm of her hand. 'Oh well,' and she sighed and it looked like Georgie was considering sticking them back on, but decided she might listen to Aedd instead – Pimple was in bliss.

See, it is a wonderful thing to be a man – least I imagine so, writing blissfully unaware, as a female pseudonym, but my subconscious persona informs me thus.

Aedd coughed. 'It is my turn, you know.'

'We know, now cut this long story short will you,' Georgie said, squashing her hand down the front of Pimples powder blue shirt a tad more energetically than she originally intended.

'I say, mind my hairs dearest lovely,

Georgiana...' and Pimple looked down at his powder blue shirt now unbuttoned to his waist. How did that happen he thought, as he scanned his chest; the hair department. 'Oh,' he was bald, save one stubborn hair, inexplicably ginger in hue.

To be fair, it looked like Mercy and Dame Pimple would prefer the long version, but they were also aware that they had Cecelia to come as well and that might prove more illuminating or at the very least more attractive to watch.

Aedd continued, blissfully unaware he was less attractive to watch than Cecelia.

See what I mean about being a man and bliss?

'I was conscious Della was a bit "were", so to speak and, she was, for all of her motor mouth front, circumspect in what she was saying in front of me, and when she told me to "fuck-off carrot top", I got the distinct impression she wanted me to leave. When I pointed out carrots had green tops, she did not seem at all impressed, but I have often noticed women are not overly interested in detail. I recall talking to Bea the other evening about the sub-strata of Birmingham,' he turned to point to Birmingham and got a cherry red up the Khyber again and realised maybe he should get on.

'Anyway, I digress...'

'Yes you bleedin' do,' Georgie's Peckham Rye cadence more distinct and Pimple thought no wonder a synchronised swimmer was not wanted in Frisian Tun, and yowled as Georgie clipped him. 'Don't speak your thoughts Everard, there's a good boy.' Blow me down, he thought, checking he had not said that out loud as well, but then was instantly mollified as Ceeley soothed the recently smitten lobe.

Aedd was fed-up and felt like a cup of second flush and so, rounded it up. 'Anyway, Della, went on to say she had mentioned something to Abe, Custard, and Bubba, and Burial had some MK something or others and someone called Jimbo could get a bazooka if Dick wanted one and there you have it, except Duck cautioned against the bazooka, but Dick seemed keen. Now I'm off to get a Darjeeling second flush...' and as he set off, so he swung the cue to the base of the Himalayas, clipping Pimple as it went by. He had been distracted looking down the front of his powder blue shirt at his one remaining, ginger chest hair, the previously robust one also in danger of losing its footing. He wet his finger and gently soothed his singular resilient hair that looked darker wet, and howled as the cue struck his haystack. 'Do I presume you all want Darjeeling or would anyone prefer Earl Grey?' This time they were ready as the cue ping ponged to China and thence traversed the known tea world, to pick up Downing Street the home of the former Prime Minister, Earl Grey.

TWENTY-THREE
THE GOSSIP COLUMNIST

ALL EYES WERE RIVETED ON THE DOOR between British Columbia and Mont Blanc, still red in hue with Pimple's sprayed blood and where beyond, presumably the Tundra or was it Switzerland, cups clattered in anticipation of Darjeeling, through a door, mysteriously painted like the Pacific Ocean, various Atolls evident though not the names; nobody was prepared to ask this of Aedd.

'I think Aedd is not best pleased,' Cecelia said getting up from the arm of the chair, smiling as she draped and dragged her hand across Pimples cheek, causing more fluff to fall out; she sighed and so did Pimple.

Pimple was sensitive about his hair growth and called after Ceeley, 'Hey, I was growing that,' and Ceeley returned his retort with a gorgeous brimming smile, gleaming pearly whites behind dynamite lipstick and Pimple settled back, mollified

Remember what I said about the mollification of men by women – I am actually thinking about writing a book, called, 'The mollification of men by Venusians' - that should do the trick and put the cat amongst the aliens.

Aedd settled the Chimpanzee's tea party tray onto the Khyber Pass table and distributed the second flush with the assistance of Dame Pimple, who joined the priest in a girl grey (Dame Pimple was getting into the swing of this cockney lark). This accomplished, Aedd sat himself down beside the Professor, who had more or less been oblivious to everything this morning, preoccupied as he was, imagining sticking the hairs back on Pimple's chest in a Greek goatherd manner.

'I interviewed Lady Blanche-Teapot yesterday.' Cecelia said, spinning on her toes to face an enraptured audience, except for the professor that is. 'This was at her request, I add and, it proved illuminating. She was obviously angry, still. I supposed this was to be expected because her Victorian villa had been destroyed. However, this seemed an almost casual aside, compared with the real reasons for her ire.' Ceeley allowed that to hang in the air and she watched Pimple eyeing her cherry red toes that were subconsciously stroking the top of the volcano – no prizes for guessing his thoughts, she thought, mildly encouraged. She further observed the Professor looking at Pimple and thought, no prizes there either. 'I think what shocked me was the vehemence in which she insisted she had been visited by the CIA, Mossad and, a bent looking chap, whom she said had the appearance of a deformed George Clooney, who was apparently, French Intelligence, if you will excuse again that possible oxymoron.'

Dame Pimple and Mercy giggled like two schoolgirls at the repeated joke, but received an admonishing look from Ceeley. They harrumphed like they had been caught by the Headmistress.

Ceeley continued, 'I have to say, it was all I could do to hold back the laughter myself, but Lady Blanche was serious.' Ceeley stopped as the noise Aedd was making, drinking his second flush from the saucer, was revolting her. 'Aedd, drink from the cup.'

'What? The Kings of Ireland do it,' Aedd retorted, his ginger Brillo pad vibrating with regal indignation.

Cecelia had to admit that Aedd had her there and there was no disputing it historically, but still she did dispute, as you would also expect of a consummate woman. 'Drink from the cup Aedd. That's what the feckin' Queens of Ireland would say,' and she smarmed a shark infested smile. Aedd had to admit she made her point well and poured his tea back into the cup, but just to show that he was not one to be cowed by a woman, he slurped from the cup.

'Quietly, Aedd.'

'Yes, your Majesty,' he responded, cowed, and mooed, but it was so quiet you could not hear it. It was a good moo as well, one of his better moos and he felt disappointed his personal safety dictated he could only do it quietly.

'I questioned Lady Blanche...' Cecelia continued, making a note to milk Aedd next time he moo'd at her, '... or Lady Francesca, as she said she preferred to be called, not liking her husband's name of Teapot particularly either and who could blame her, though Lady Francesca felt it her right to retain the associated title of course. My interrogation was faultless, even if I say so myself and yet, I could not trip her up. I came away believing her, not that this is

important in the large scheme of things. Pimple
and I will still write it, it's a good story and I
propose a headline: "Mad aristocrat bat visited
by foreign Spooks". You can imagine it.' They all
could, and Ceeley noticed Father Mike was on
the edge of his chair looking directly at her. This
confirmed for her that the Duchess was not
telling tales. 'I happen to believe Lady Blanche...'
and she left that hanging, '... and, I find it no
coincidence she is visited subsequently by DI
Della Lovington, so soon after calling upon Dick
and Duck, but what I want to know is, what
happened next? Why did the police dig up Lady
Blanche's garden, her pride and joy and, this
morning I went to follow up my story and she
had completely disappeared, but where to?'

At that the Priest guffawed and would have
fallen off his seat if the Professor had not
stretched out a hand to steady him. Father Mike
calmed, stood and walked over to Cecelia and
put his arm around her slim waist, his face still
emanating much contagious mirth. Ceeley found
herself infected and chuckled and the rest joined
in, not knowing why they were laughing. 'Sit
down, Ceeley. I will fill you in on the rest,
anonymously attributed I hope.'

Ceeley agreed the *anonymous but reliable
source*, and returned to the arm of the armchair
and draped her arm across Pimples shoulder

and, feeling herself possessed of a little devilment, she leaned over further, thrust her hand down the front of Pimple's powder blue shirt and tugged out the remaining hair. Pimple yowled and Ceeley smothered the yowl with a smouldering kiss and, he was instantly mollified, pain forgotten, male bliss resumed, albeit a bald chested bliss. 'Darling, if you are staying with Georgie tonight, perhaps you can ask your mother to arrange for the delivery of another shirt, there is only so much masculine musk a woman can take,' and she smiled to defuse any reactive feeling that may require mollifying.

'Yes,' Georgie added to Dame Moose, 'and if you could bring down some more pants, save me rinsing the ones he has through tonight, I would appreciate it as well, Delores.'

Delores replied with an obliging moose smile to assure them both that a suitable change of clothing would be delivered and Georgie and Cecelia seemed mollified, even if Pimple was embarrassed, but as we now know that was easily dealt with, and so it was. Father Mike watched on with a worldly wisdom that defied his calling, waited for the mirth to subside, quite enjoying the feeling.

'Why are we laughing?' It was the Professor who was enjoying the jollity as much as anyone, but, as an academic, felt it necessary to seek the source of such amusement.

The father duly obliged. 'It is that the garden was such a pride and joy to Lady Blanche-Teapot that Jack Austin came up with his idea, which was to inform the local constabulary, via the Serious Crime Unit of the Metropolitan Police, one Della Lovington, that he suspected bodies to be buried in the garden. A suitable revenge for the aristocracy not liking his *Capability Austin* garden designs I believe he said.'

This explanation served only to step up the volume and energy of the laughter at the ridiculous notion and that they recalled the police did swoop on the Blanche-Teapot arcadia, front and back and, the immaculate middle class villa gardens were completely devastated by clod hopping filf, none of whom could muster a grain of *Gavin* or *Titchmarsh* genes. However, as tears were dabbed and stomachs caressed to relieve the symptoms of such gaiety, they noticed the Father had adjusted his face to a semblance of incongruous piety, and they responded with a quiet that suggested anticipation of yet more revelations.

'The fact is, and this news was suppressed to enable the continuance of the investigation, bodies were found, along with some serious arms and cash.'

Ceeley jumped and now she scrabbled around in her bag for her little tape recorder that Pimple noticed worked immediately. He had to presume the beautiful Cecelia Crumpet did not possess a vibrator, or at the very least if she did own one, it was now missing its batteries and, he may have mentioned it, if Ceeley's reaction was anything to go by.

'Pimple!' Pimple blushed and Father Mike calmed the situation.

'Don't worry Ceeley, you will have the scoop and, I have cleared it you can release the story, not Bernie, but if you would not mind holding off for a day or two whilst Dick and Duck get their mallards in a row, so to speak, please, it would be much appreciated.' He tittered at his little jest, miniscule compared with the previous laughter, however, the impact was equally potent. 'You will get the full story Ceeley and Pimple, unabridged, with all of the background and, it is more widespread than Friesian Tun, I can assure you, but no recording, please.'

Ceeley was greatly intrigued, but focused on the here and now. 'What happened?' Ceeley enquired, enjoying the news in a relaxed manner, no longer tasked with taking notes or having to record the interview she knew would be immediately confiscated if Mike's connections were, as she imagined them to be, MI5.

'The serious Crime Unit took over from local plod, which were relegated to plodding duty, securing the site.'

'Serious Crime Unit? Was this Del-Boy?' Ceeley pressed.

'How quickly you catch on Cecelia. I think Pimple and you will make a good team.'

Pimple was broken from his blissful reverie when he heard his name, 'What?'

'Indeed, Pimple,' the Father said and Ceeley immediately applied her Venusian skills and mollified her naive Martian. 'Forensics were such that the remains were identified as local and London gangsters, one postman who was reported to have intercepted a laptop computer from the wrong person and, we believe the relatively new remains of one Cuthbert Wicker-Knees of number eleven, a poet who was known to wear a beret and flounce about Frisian Tun in an entirely inappropriate manner, who also supported the planning application for the conversion of these flats.' Mike waved his arms for no reason it would seem, 'He was also reputed to have been in favour of the Jack Austin poles, being of an avante-garde predisposition apparently.'

· · ·

Ah, that would be it. Father Mike was being a Prima-donna in a landscape architect sense. The silence reined, as did the Queen coincidentally, although only technically and by the overall consent of her people in the form of a Parliament.

This was big news and although the humour of the excavated pride and joy of the Duchess was still titillating the glee buttons, there was a sense of trepidation, a presentiment of a thought that this was definitely not over and, this was why the Father was here and why Duck and Dick the Walrus appeared regularly watchful and animated of late. Well, Duck was.

'Is this why I was steered here... and what happened?'

'Ceeley, I am about to tell you,' and he picked out his phone and speed dialled. 'Jack, you tosspot, if you wouldn't mind? I'm not calling you Dick, Jack... Jack, oh fuck off Dick.'

TWENTY-FOUR

A COCKNEY BARROW BOY (SOMETHING OR OTHER), HIS LADY SUPERINTENDENT WIFE, A COCKNEY SPARROW SPY, THE PRIEST.

THE BOZZER BOZZED AND THE SUSPENSEFUL silence was broken metallically and earthily. Aedd went to the apartment door and rushed back, in a dizzying hurry to stand beside East Asia, whether to elucidate on a conversation or to distance himself from an altercation, or even to be ready to expound further on tea, was unclear and almost immediately forgotten. The occupants of the room swivelled their direction of gaze to observe a bundle of arms and legs, a pretty face and a really ugly one, stuck within the portal to the map room, seemingly trying to gain access at the same time in an amusing manner, at least it was for the ugly one.

From behind could be seen a flailing set of

sparrow's arms, unrealistically attached to a Dodo body, but without feathers. Jack Austin, the ugly one, popped his head over the petit and beautiful, though scary Valkyrie, 'Allo my old Chinas,' he said.

The Valkyrie appeared to have decided who would die next, when Aedd pointed to China and elucidated, 'China plate – mate,' for the benefit of those still learning cockney rhyming slang and he swung the snooker cue to the Scandinavian countries, everyone ducked, anticipating a swing to London and Jack Austin ducked to dodge a right hook from Della Lovington. 'A Valkyrie,' Aedd espoused, 'in Norse mythology, is considered the Chooser of the Slain.

One of a host of female figures who select those who will die in battle.

'Spot on Aedd, my old Ginger mucker,' Della, a cockney sparrow chirped, having passed through the map room portal, smoothing her door jamb ruffled feathers. 'And, feckin' Dick here,' she pointed to the ugly one, 'is number one on that list and then you Mike, you ginger beer holy Joe tart. Della rarely entered a room quietly, or leave it, or be quiet whilst there. Whereas, Jack Austin, the ugly one, rarely entered a room quietly, which was a complete opposite to the way he frequently left, apparently, or so he told everyone, quietly, normally just before he left.

Aedd put in plain words this particular Norse mythology, as Jack Jane Austin, aka Dick, paraded around the room, nudging Della with his swinging hip as he passed by, sending the cockney sparrow flying to find seed elsewhere. Stomping like a man with tin legs or a carrot up his Khyber Pass and waving his hands in an impresario way, he was aware he was now the centre of attention, and would, for the time being be running the show; how he liked it.

'You will not be running the show, darling,' a soft, feminine tone.

Not Anthony, or Tone as he likes to be called.

'Now sit down, there's a love.' It was the long suffering Amanda, recently arrived, a delay that avoided any portal altercation, aware of her husband's doorway proclivities and she set about sorting out her husband, whilst the sparrow located a suitable perch. Amanda's husband was famed, among many other disabilities, to speak his thoughts. Many also considered this the onset of senility?

· · ·

Which nobody denied may be occurring, and is even mentioned in 'Merde and Mandarins'. Amanda did telephone the doctor, but then forgot his appointment – offered a feeble excuse, that she had been brutally kidnapped and both her legs broken – girls eh, say they'll do something one day...

However, Jack (Aka Jane or Dick) Austin had always spoken his thoughts. Another reason why he had been a back room brains Wallah at MI5 as he would never survive interrogation if he was ever captured, not because he had a notoriously low pain threshold, bordering on cry-baby status, but because he would reveal all before the interrogators had even sat him down and, be totally oblivious of the fact.

'Feck me gently, I was going to stand on the volcano,' Dick replied to Duck (Aka Mandy, Amanda), his wife, or, in the parlance, Jack's trouble and strife.

'I know you were darling (trouble) and that is why I stopped you pushing Mike out of the way (strife), he is not as young as he used to be, dear,' Duck said in a genteel fashion that defied the menace behind the message. 'Are you okay Della?' Mandy asked, and the sparrow chirruped that Dick was dead meat, but did convey she was satisfied with her current perch, having pushed the professor off his chair.

Dick looked shocked, did I just speak...?' Everybody nodded, getting into the swing of it as most people did after a while, a bit like the geography snooker cue and the clip-em and sock-em game.

'You did, Jack,' Mandy said

'Dick darlin',' Jack responded, offended.

'Dick, precisely,' Duck replied, an exasperated quack.

'Okay, I'll carry on shall I?' It was not a question and Mike took up from where he left off, but not before introducing the fuming, beautiful cockney sparrow as DI Delores Lovington (*now, Mrs Sexton of course – read Merde and Mandarins for heaven's sake, as Father Mike would say*). Della is from the Met Serious crime Unit, but not really, and he wafted his hand under his armpit in the manner of all good spies. 'Nothing that was supposed to happen, happened, but what actually happened, happened because of an inspired guess by, Dick.' Mike looked confused as he said that, and even welcomed Jack's indignant, unscheduled interruption, whilst Della giggled.

'It was not an inspired guess. I worked it out.'

Dick clearly needed mollifying, but before Mandy could soothe his inner turmoil, he managed to say further, 'I never get any feckin' credit.'

Della humphed, pushed the professor away as he tried to regain his Greek goatherd viewing platform. 'It's me what never gets the credit, bozo,' she said to Jack, and then to the professor, who was mounting a counter attack, 'Oi, feck off, bush face, or I'll shove the fucking Parthenon up yer arse.' That seemed to do the trick, as the professor retreated and settled on a secondary chair in the vicinity of the Sudan and reluctantly sat in his barren and quite uncomfortable chair, a peculiar smile appearing as he contemplated the Parthenon up his backside, whilst picturing a Greek archaeologist with the look of a goatherd. The professor, unwittingly, passed a discordant whistle from his rosy anal lips; pan pipes? Or he may be expecting an Admiral of the Greek navy on board anytime for a kiss?

Jack stopped his ranting as Mandy stroked his hand, having pulled up a chair to sit next to her husband. 'It was a guess, my lovely,' she said to her mollified ugly spouse, 'and done because you wanted to see the Duchess's garden destroyed.' She soothed his wavy wrinkled brow that looked like a gale force nine storm in the

English Channel. Jack Austin certainly was ugly Pimple thought, regaining a semblance of rational thought following the raucous invasion from the cockneys and one handsome mature woman, from, if he had to guess, Guildford, Surrey.

'I might have, maybe, Coo,' Dick said in a mollified voice that gently modulated as most mollified men do.

You see what I mean, even an experienced spook, albeit challenged in the vocal department and an established cry-baby, can be mollified, so what hope for lesser masculine mortals? Best to stick with bliss, which is of course what most men do, or they settle for oblivion, which usually follows shortly after bliss and, in the spare bedroom.

It was like a hypnotist had clicked her fingers. Jack Austin settled back in his chair and relaxed, just a casual throwaway remark, 'But you said, you thought you saw the Banana boys burying bodies?' A pathetically mollified Dick said back to his beautiful Duck.

The beautiful Duck leapt from her nest. 'J'accuse, Mon grand Morse.' She had struck and the lightning impaled mallard felt for his heart, which had leapt from his chest and was currently heading for France like a rogue Exocet missile. But he was, upon reflection, and after determining he was not having a heart attack, placidly pleased he was referred to as a big Morse, he liked that detective. 'Morse is French for walrus you feckin' eejit. And that's Irish for, feckin' eejit.' Mandy rounded up, having made her case, which was affirmed by a snort from Della; so no contest then.

Mike stepped in. 'Yes, well, you may have recalled Mandy's suggestion, Jack?'

'Dick, you plank,' Jack replied, his beautifully colourful mallard feathers beginning to ruffle again. He did not like appearing a fool. Everyone laughed and Jack looked around, 'Did I...?'

'Dick!' Mike exclaimed, riled himself.

The professor, currently stranded in the bleak desert of the Sudan, wondered if he should mollify the priest; were priests allowed to be mollified in the Catholic Church? Thelonious took a chance. Mike was attractive he thought, though clearly had no Greek or Goatherd characteristics. The professor pranced like Nureyev with arthritis, to Mike, and smoothed the Vicar of Christ brow.

'Fuck off yer feckin' pansy arsed, wanker,' Mike said, quite shocking Nureyev, who slinked back to the Sudan, more like Angelina Baller-fucking-rina after a major night out with the corps de ballet, a curry and subsequent diarrheal morning blues.

Mandy stepped to Mike. 'There, there, Mikey. You tell them what you know, okay, you're so good at it. Jack and I always say...' she stopped as Jack muttered, "Dick" and Mandy gave him the stare in return, the one from Psycho she sometimes gives him when he's in the shower. Mandy patted Mike's hand, switched her Psycho gaze briefly to the professor, smarmed a honeydew Mummy smile and a peck on the purple sprouting broccoli, holy cheeks, all for her little priest boy, who needed just a little bit of encouragement.

Mike was mollified. Makes yer bleedin' sick don't it? Whatever happened to smashing the place up? Oops! My persona slipped...

Mike carried on, having adopted a sickly sweet smile himself, only with a crooked mincing posture, coincidentally teapot shaped. 'We did not have to do anything, we knew it would happen without any prompting from us, and here it is important to note that not all of this was inspired deduction by Jack Austin.'

Jack jumped up and swung his hand with a pointy finger, 'Told you,' and sat back down with a blinding grin applied to his face that had to be painstakingly smoothed out by Mandy, who seemed remarkably practiced in the art. She then explained to her turnip that Father Mike had actually said, "NOT inspired deduction", and a deflated retired copper spook, now a private Dick, looked up at the errant priest and said, 'Did you?' Mike nodded, and Jack sighed his done up like a kipper sigh.

Father Mike beamed impishly, he had done that deliberately. He knew Jack Austin well. They went back many years, with him being the conduit for Jack Austin back to his contacts in MI5, who for the last fifteen years or so had been Del-Boy. 'What happened next was that we were approached by a chap who went by the epithet, Weasel. Although we had not disclosed our findings to the world, he knew what we would find in the garden as he had been Lady Blanche-Teapot's gardener. He did the heavy stuff, literally, all of which he revealed to us, in exchange for immunity.'

Father Mike was interrupted by the cockney sparrow, 'Immunity, which was clearly not worth the paper it was not written on since Weasel was now brown bread, and pushing up daisies in his own garden,' and she applied her sparrow's victory beak smirk.

Mike congratulated Della on her intervention and for stating the feckin' obvious, and he continued. 'Mr Weasel further suggested to us that Lady Blanche was related in some way with one, Keith Bananas, as if the filth and MI5 did not already know this... and, this is the trouble with eejit super grasses, although Weasel did look after the Duchess's lawn particularly well,' and Mike chuckled.

There was an audible intake of breath from the non-filf, non-spook, cognoscenti, as Keith Bananas, who had died not more than a hundred yards away from where they sat, was a notoriously vicious London gangster.

Mike allowed the jangled nerves to settle before he continued. 'What Mr Weasel said to us, apart from identifying the remains, was that Keith Bananas was not his real name.'

'You mean it was not, Keith?'

The tension was broken as everyone laughed at the casual and unthinking remark made by Dame Pimple, who clearly saw nothing wrong in the name Bananas, being aristocratic and thus accustomed to daft names, like her own maiden name, Devonshire-Wallop, thinking this marginally more aristocratic than Pimple, which was spot on, so to speak. And so Bananas seemed not an unreasonable name to her; it was one of her five a-day names.

Father Mike took up the cudgel, wishing to carry on without anymore gaiety, so to speak. He had that steely priestly look that can scare the bajeezers out of even a non-believer. 'What this did do is open up a number of different enquiries for us.'

'It did?' Dame Pimple was not even embarrassed, just a tad befuddled.

'What was his name, Mike?'

'Cecelia, you have that cutting edge, and I know you and Pimple will be well suited.'

Ceeley ignored the even more befuddled look on the Moose as she swung her gaze to Everard and, in that rare moment, she could see the likeness now, in a bovine befuddled characteristic way. She chose to ignore that. She considered that on Everard, befuddlement was okay, a natural look, okay, so long as he did not get befuddled too much. He had other characteristics that more than made up for his befuddlements, but she struggled to think of them just at that moment. 'I know we will be okay Mike, what was Keith Bananas name?'

'White.' Jack Austin spoke, his serious head on, rising and stepping up to the volcano.

'White?' Ceeley responded, astonished, not seeing anything remarkable about the name.

'Yes, White.' Mike said, but clearly Jack Austin wanted to say it.

'It was my turn, Mike.'

'Sorry Jack, you plank.'

'Dick,' Jack said.

'Yes, White, Ceeley,' Mandy said, at the same time stroking her riled husband and setting him back down in a very accomplished mollifying movement, lest he smash the place up.

'I'm sorry, Mandy, I don't see the significance,' Ceeley asked.

'Duck' Dick said.

'What?' Ceeley said.

'Her name is Duck, der,' Jack answered.

'Duck Der?' Ceeley answered, enjoying winding up a dick of a Dick, but her fun was terminated as Pimple intervened with an insightful observation.

'Do you mean, Blanche?'

Everybody turned to Pimple to witness Ceeley kiss him full on the lips. Pimple was befuddled at that as he had not lolled his tongue or even sniffed. 'Clever you, Everard. Lady Blanche, White, and she was related to Keith White, also known as Bananas. Ha, I see, so what did you conclude after that?'

'Are not bananas yellow?' Pimple enquired only to be studiously ignored by everyone.

Mike looked to Jack Austin, who now had his miffed face on and would likely need more mollifying quite soon, but Mike had seen this face before, ignored it and carried on, which actually miffed Jack more, and super-hero, *Mandy Mollifier*, was called into action while Mike spoke. 'It became obvious that Lady Blanche was a White and Weasel confirmed to us that Keith White often visited Southsea when he a juvenile delinquent, which is where Weasel met him and, they played together, became pals when Keith stayed with the Teapots. She changed her name to Lady Blanche-Teapot. We still are trying to track Lady Blanche down in the White family tree, but we are working on that and so, there you have it.'

'We have it?' Ceeley questioned, having left Pimple in a state of euphoric confusion, feeling like his body snapped and crackled with static rice crispy electricity. 'How did we get from Keith White to a half destroyed upper middle class street with several deaths?'

Mike looked to Jack, 'You going to tell them?'

Jack Austin looked like he was struggling to make a decision, whether to let them stew while he stewed, or grab his rightful place beside the lime-illuminated volcano? He chose the limelight, as everybody knew he would, even Pimple knew he would, as he came down from his sexual high. This had been an extraordinary few days for Pimple and he felt a clarity of mind he had not felt since he first picked up a needle to embroider.

TWENTY-FIVE
THE SPY

Jack stood and headed to the volcano. His mistake? He went via Greece, whereupon, he was tripped by a still stewing moussaka Della. As he fell, his legs opened and an audible parp ensued. 'Side blow-out, Aedd' Della shouted and giggled as did everyone, including Mandy, who respectfully appeared embarrassed for her husband.

Jack sniffed, 'Sulphur, Aedd.' He sounded a klaxon and made like he was a submarine diving, as the cue headed to the sulphurous lakes of the Canadian Territories, skimming Dick's diving head. After he had submerged, he sent his periscope up and looked to Mandy and she gave him her nod of approval.

'That was a good one, Jack,' she said,

respecting her husband's multifarious capabilities and knowing he will be happy now, everything else forgotten. He lost his miffed face and had on his mollified, superior person's face, the eejit, not realising she will want to talk about this later and she considered, just before bedtime would be appropriate.

Jack Austin wandered around a bit, lonely as a cumuli-nimbus, he told people, bathing in his presumed reflected glory, while others reflected and choked in his recent bottom cloud. He did not wander more than two steps from the volcano, just in case somebody decided to take his talking spot. You had to be very aware these days. Gone is the society of gentlemanly conduct and pleasant manners; Jack Jane Austin was a stalwart *Pride and Prejudice* fan of course. He was also famed for drifting off and this tried the patience of most people, except for the tried and tested Austin aficionados, who saw this as a form of respite, time to charge the batteries, so to speak. There was an intake of breath, which you have to do if you have been holding it in for so long, but also because he was now back on the volcano and was either going to talk, or parp another time, either way you needed to be on your guard and have sufficient oxygen to go the distance. In the event he did neither, he picked at the wrinkled skin, sunken into his vacant eye socket, pulled it and the suction caused a pop and he seemed rather pleased with this. Once again, Mandy seemed inured, but Mike knew she would step in soon, but didn't need to, as Ceeley poked him up his Khyber Pass with her cherry reds.

Now, here is an example of how a man can be ruminating and thinking about what he is going to say and is prompted to get on with it by a woman, who only a few minutes beforehand, could have been chastising that same man for not thinking before he spoke. To be fair, Amanda had more patience and it has to be said, loved her man, but even she had been known to kick Jack Austin from time to time and in various parts of his anatomy, whatever was convenient really. She was also known as a top champ in the clip-em and sock-em game; ironic isn't it? I mention this in passing only because it is just that, ironic.

'Okay, okay, blimey old Riley, can't a man fink?'

'No,' Mandy, Ceeley, Della and Georgie said in unison.

'Rightee-ho,' and he drifted off again and, as previously mentioned, this is normal. The Queen and peace reined for a while and then, he seemed to get some inspirational energy from somewhere. 'Well, of course Weasel fed back to Keef Bananas about what had happened, least we think it was Weasel, but on reflection it could have been Lady Blanche herself...' he drifted and swayed and, it looked like he was going to faint, but it was only another side blow-out and then he was fine, though nobody else was. 'So, what happened?' He asked the question of himself (*told you he'd drifted off*). Then he answered himself, 'Well, of course Keef Bananas popped down with a few of his henchmen and we, that is us meat pies.'

Mandy interpreted, 'Spies' she explained.

"Oh", resounded.

Jack carried on oblivious, so no change there then. 'We fancied a bit of a chinwag, but not formerly, under caution, if you know what I mean?'

'No?' It was Mercy and Dame Pimple.

'He means meet up with the police...' and Mandy crooked her fingers as exclamation marks, '... and under caution, definitely formerly under caution, Jack,' she asserted, 'to be interviewed about the bodies that had been found.'

'Thank you, Amanda,' Mercy the centre half, or was it left half and occasional hockey goalie replied, pleased there was a sensible one amongst them.

Jack went, 'Ner, Ner, fank you, Amanda,' in a not very good posh imitation of Dame Pimple or Mercy Mudstone and wobbled his head excessively. 'I'll do the talking if it's okay with you,' he followed up to his wife.

'Do the farting more like', she said behind her hand to Georgie, Pimple and Ceeley, and this went down excessively well.

'Please, be serious,' Jack remarked, and this made them all laugh more, even the professor, but Jack did carry on. 'A little dickey bird told us...' he was stopped by Della.

'That was me,' and Della, the cockney sparrow, clearly the little dickey bird, stood and nudged a miffed Jack from the volcano. The professor lunged for the Greek chair, while the sparrow was distracted. But Della was rarely distracted and she expertly tripped Thelonious and his haemorrhoidal lips kissed the Mediterranean, nearby Corsica and nowhere near Greece. Della continued, 'I had Intel the Banana boys were coming out of hiding, intent on mischief and mayhem, in the direction of, Jack,' and she pointed to a disgruntled Dick, at that time being mollified by a Duck.

Ceeley interrupted, 'And would this Intel be

Mossad or CIA or a deformed French Ox intelligence officer?'

Della smiled, confirming to Ceeley she was spot on again, but frankly it befuddled Pimple. Della continued, 'Ordinarily, this is an action for which I would approve and likely encourage, any damage to Jack the feckin' tosspot Dickhead Austin, but since Mandy could become, as the Yanks say, "collateral damage", I decided I needed to inform them and of course, provide Jack back-up, because he couldn't punch his way out of a bleedin' paper bag.'

'Oi, Della,' Jack said, irritated, and as a result, he decided to tell on Della to Mandy. That would teach her.

'I know sweetgums. I will tell her off later, get back into your paper bag, there's a love,' Mandy said, thus mollifying her eejit husband and at the same time packaging him up into a brown paper bag, like the proverbial kipper, knowing full well he could not escape, even if the bag was wet.

'Did I...?'

'You did, darling, but you did it so well.' Mandy applied the killer mollifying punch and, suitably mollified, Mandy soothed Jack's bottom parts and guided him back to the arm of her newly acquired armchair. She nodded to Della to carry on. Mandy knew that if you waited for Jack, you could be there forever and ever, amen.

So Jack sat on the arm of the armchair and allowed his attractive wife to stroke his thigh at advanced liberties position. He watched Della take on the mantle of narrator in this story of muck and bullets, which marked the seventieth anniversary of D-Day on the Frisian Tun beaches and, he remained oblivious – was this the Alzheimer's or a resultant effect of consummate mollifying? My money is on the mollifying. Mandy was brilliant at it as you would expect, she had had so much practice – ironic isn't it?

TWENTY-SIX
MI5 COCKNEY SPARROW, LADY BLANCHE

DELLA LOOKED AT AEDD, WHO LOOKED BACK at Della and, despite the enormous height difference, Aedd went where he was sent, Table Top Mountain, out of harm's way, though whose harm was debatable. Aedd remained prepared at a moment's notice with his cue and acuity in geography, but alas in little else.

'There's a good ginger-knob, stay there unless I need you, but now I mention it, a cup of monkey Rosy-lea wouldn't 'arf go down a treat,' and Della beckoned ginger-knob from the Horn of Africa to her with a crooked finger. Aedd obliged, and duly presented his fluffy ginger cheek as suggested by Della. She pecked him and blew a raspberry and sent him on his way. 'Two sugars in my mine please.'

Blushing, Aedd shuffled away, glancing back, 'Tea everyone,' a throwaway comment. He was going anyway and then he did, via Mont Blanc. He was no fool, he knew Della and, even heavily pregnant as she was, he knew it better to be out of the firing line and, was grateful to find sanctuary within neutral territory, the kitchen, or likely as not Switzerland, as Aedd, prancing like Heidi the Swiss goatherd, yodelled as he left.

Della spun her bird like frame and kicked off. 'So, Lady bleedin' Blanche, who is she?'

Jack put his hand up.

(Stop it; I am talking like he was at the back of the class, and not a hand up Mandy's skirt, though it was obviously an afterthought).

'Yes, Jack?'

'I know.'

'You do...?' Della replied; deceptively calm.

'Yes.'

'You do...?' It was Mandy and she had taken his hand off her thigh so she got the message through, she was not as deceptively calm as Della. 'Why haven't you told me?'

'Why haven't you told me?' Della was ramping up and she only had a 5 amp fuse.

Jack drifted off, (*You recall I mentioned he was prone to do this*) he was thinking of what they might have for tea.

'I've got sausages, Jack and, if you don't tell us who you think Lady Blanche is, I will shove them up your arse, one by one.'

'Where are the sausages from?' Aedd yodelled from Switzerland.

The professor was alerted, sausages up the proverbial being a lightening conductor, in a Greek sense. 'You will?' he said, his lips appearing to take on an anal life of their own as they quivered and pouted.

The kitchen door opened and Aedd yodelled again. 'Where are the sausages from?'

The Dame Pimple was alert and stopped looking up Georgie's dress for a moment. 'Are they Hampshire Free range?' returned her gaze to the intimate regions of the lady downstairs.

(*I hope you will pardon the play on words; Georgie lived downstairs you see and the moose was looking at her downstairs department; loses a bit in translation, doesn't it?*).

'Local Hampshire free range are the best,' Heidi the geography teacher added from Switzerland,

'and, if you get them from cattle regularly grazed on a southerly or western slope, they can be particularly splendiferous. Now, I know a farmer...' Aedd's yodelling was cut short and his bottom felt the need to pop back to Switzerland, in response to Della, who looked like she might shoot an apple off his head any minute and may deliberately miss and then, she would *William Tell* on him to the police; she could do that; would do that.

Ceeley stepped into the growing affray. 'Fuck the sausages, if you know who Lady Blanche, the fucking Duchess is, spill the fucking beans and, how about telling us how the last shoot out at the Okay Frisian Tun happened, while you're at it.' Pimple looked at Cecelia and thought, did these words really tip out from such a beautiful mouth and it was as if he was mesmerised by Cecelia's lips. She blew a light kiss to her Pimple and told him to start taking fucking notes.

Pimple reacted in a way that suggested manhood could be just over the brow of the hill. 'I can't take fucking notes, you dozy mare, Georgie has my hand between her thighs and you are holding the other one.'

Georgie and Cecelia looked at one another and, with sloping, wobbling heads and dewy eyes, they looked at their Pimple, smiled and aaahed, 'Isn't he lovely Cecelia?' Georgie said.

'Definitely coming on. You are doing a wonderful job dearest, Georgiana,' Cecelia replied and both women caressed Pimple's short back and sides, haircut.

Can you guess what ensued? Yes, of course you can and, if you can't then you have not been paying attention. Pimple was mollified. Perhaps his manhood is a little further away than the brow of the hill, maybe over the mountains and firmly lodged in Kathmandu, wherever the feck that is? Maybe Aedd will know when he comes back from Switzerland?

As a female pseudonym, I pity men, they are putty in the hands of women and, of course, pseudo women. As a pseudo man, I quite like putty and, when faced with a mollifying woman, my windows are apt to fall out.

Georgie released her charge and Pimple waved his hand free of pins and needles and, after Cecelia had returned his other hand, he went to collect his notebook and pencil from his school satchel in the hall.

Della showed all the signs of an explosion from a side vent and Aedd, risking life and limb, may have yodelled this from Switzerland, as the snooker cue appeared from behind the kitchen door and pointed to the volcano rug and in particular, the side vent.

Dame Pimple's phone sounded, the now familiar bouzouki dance theme and the professor launched himself across the room, to be met by a hockey centre half and occasional goalie. Together they Zorba'd, arms raised with the Dame offering the occasional "Whoopah" from the South Downs armchair.

Pimple shifted himself from the dancing danger zone, stood behind the sofa and watched with an open mouth. Father Mike blessed the dancers and joined in, as light on his feet as the professor. Jack leaned, as if to enjoin the Greek festivities, when events rather overtook his relish for Hellenic prancing.

Through the open bottom sash window, a canister entered as a projectile and commenced rolling across the Mediterranean. Jack shouted "Down" and dived toward the canister. Pimple, with hitherto unknown strength, pulled the back of the sofa and both Cecelia and Georgie, rolled backwards. Pimple held onto the sofa, turned his back and lay across his women, as an additional shield. Jack Austin reached the canister and as he rolled, he picked it up and hurled it back out to Frisian Tun, but missed the huge gaping sash.

He was never known as 'Dead Eyed Dick' – well, perhaps he was, but not in an aiming sense.

The flash bang detonated, a brilliant light and a resounding bang, shattering the glass and frames in the window. Jack's inept toss of the stun grenade caused it to hit the reveal of the window frame, though he did point out later it was on its way to Frisian Tun, albeit on a circuitous route and he was of course aware that ideally it would have been better if it had passed through the colossal gap in the window, but he was trying for an "in-off" billiards shot. "What a load of crap" Mandy is reported to have said in response and anyone who knew Jack Austin would likely as not sided with Mandy, realising this might be a topic of conversation just before bedtime.

The effect of the billiard style toss, was that the grenade blast sprayed shattered glass back into the room and peppered Della, which could have been worse had not the professor Jette'd to her defence and took the majority of the brunt of flying shards in his not insubstantial backside that similarly shielded Dame Pimple and Mercy. Father Mike had been knocked back through the swing door into Switzerland.

Jack oomphed himself up to see Mandy bloodied, still in the armchair, a dazed look, and he dashed to her.

Pimple raised the sofa to reveal Georgie and Cecelia, unharmed. 'Fuck me,' Pimple said, 'what the hell happened?'

Just then automatic gun fire could be heard in the hallway and shortly after, the map room door splintered and crashed open. There stood Lady Francesca Blanche-Teapot, in a plain but flowing dress, delicate, size twelve, flat white shoes, an ideal summery outfit, accompanied as it was with a liberty print silk scarf wrapped around her shoulders, to take the evening chill off; the evenings were still cool and this was readily felt by old cows. Oh, and she had a colour coordinated Kalashnikov machine gun, which had the tell tale stream of smoke trailing from the dangerous end that more than suggested she knew how to use it and, just had.

It was as if time stood still, just for a moment and then, there was the sound of crunching glass as the professor stood, both hands grasping his bloody behind. He leaned down and effortlessly lifted Della and took her to Europe. He leaned her against the wall, nearby Battenberg. There was noise from Switzerland and Lady Blanche fired a short salvo that disintegrated the swing door and a goodly proportion of Mont Blanc. A scream echoed from the kitchen and Jack shaped to help.

'Don't move, you fat bastard,' Lady Blanche shouted, betraying her Hither Green, shunting yard, roots.

Jack froze, looked down to Mandy, he wanted to ask her if he was fat, aware his bum sometimes looked big in chinos, but Mandy was clearly shell shocked. He felt like crying, but had to focus. He could not rely on Della; she looked completely out of it.

'Come out from the kitchen,' the Duchess called out, a little middle class respectability appearing to creep back into her voice.

'It's Switzerland, you-olda-lady-too,' Aedd yodelled back, no middle class decorum at all which, all things considered, was a not a particularly sensible thing to do and, if Aedd was relying on Swiss neutrality, he had a shock coming. The Duchess released another salvo and splintering wood, shattering glass and china could be heard, but no more screams. 'Okay,' Aedd said in response, unfortunately a bit like John Wayne...

. . .

Was there a map of the Wild West in the kitchen? It is entirely possible and nobody had been in to check,

... as he added, 'to hell I will,' would this guy never learn?

The Duchess fired again and as the plaster dust settled, a hunched Aedd appeared supporting a wounded Father Mike. The priest looked wan and pallid, just his beetroot nose, like a Rudolph guiding beacon through the fog of floating debris. With the priest draped over his shoulder, Aedd dragged Mike to the now upright sofa, where he laid him down.

The Duchess issued more orders. 'All of you who can stand, over to the wall,' and she gestured with the muzzle of the gun.

It looked like Aedd was prepared to challenge this order, when Jack poked him. Aedd grabbed the snooker cue from him, 'If you don't mind,' Aedd said. Jack was impressed, either Aedd was showing distinct bravery, or the Welsh Irish twat was more dim-witted than he had previously allowed. Jack and Aedd shuffled to the wall.

'What continent?' Aedd asked.

'What?' the Duchess replied.

'What feckin' continent, so?' Irish, maybe Aedd's warring ancestors were coming through and then, Aedd swung the cue to Africa. 'Africa?' And put his hands and the cue out in a *Julie Andrews* placatory manner, pointed to the wrecked kitchen and began to sing, "The Hills are Alive..."and was swinging back to Northern Europe, via Birmingham, when the cue engaged with the Kalashnikov and the gun spewed more bullets as the Duchess was unexpectedly caught off balance.

Pimple launched himself and seized the gun, but he had grabbed the hot barrel and, as a consequence, screamed in pain and inadvertently, barged into the Duchess whilst waving his hands like he was a bird trying to take off. Georgie and Cecelia leapt from behind the sofa to rescue Pimple and completely knocked the Duchess backwards and onto the floor and the ensuing salvo destroyed the French Navy.

No wonder Nelson won, although at a price as he still had to kiss Hardy.

Jack ran to the Duchess, tripped and landed on top of the woman, completely knocking the stuffing out of her. Her head banged back against the Malaysian Archipelago and she was unconscious.

Incontrovertible proof, if one was visibly challenged, Jack was a fat bastard.

Just then a loud hailer could be heard, calling for the occupants to make themselves known. "Friend or Foe?"

Jack lifted himself off the Duchess and shouted out, "Foe" and dropped back down and giggled in the earoles of the just recovering Duchess, which was just as well as a salvo of machine gun fire chewed the red brick surround to the window.

'Fucking Ada, Cisco. It's me, Jack Austin!'

Cisco, head of armed tactical, replied through the loud hailer. 'That you, Jane? You said you were a foe.'

Jack shouted back, showing that he too could be a tad temperamental and, in his poncy artistic manner, 'It was fucking dramatic irony you, tosspot. Oh, and it's Dick. Oh, and get some ambulances and a Medivacuum helicopter.'

Jack, or really Amanda, had arranged for tactical support, guessing in Jack's view, or reasoned one by Mandy, that something would happen. It usually did and around Dick, Jack, Jane.

You could hear chuckling from outside and this disturbed the eerie peace that often follows on from deafening gunfire and ear-splitting bomb blasts. 'The Medevac helicopter is on its way. We're clearing the Waitrose car park now. Can paramedics come in and I have Jimbo and Del-boy here, Jack. Can they come in as well?' Cisco asked.

Jack, entering into the spirit of the game playing out, got his handkerchief out from his pocket and began waving through the hole, where the beautiful Georgian sash window had once been, mentioning that seen in a prudential light the opening was not that large and could be easily missed if tossing, say, a grenade.

'Put that disgusting rag away, Jack.' It was Mandy. She seems okay Jack thought to himself, aware his wife had this thing about handkerchiefs that he did not wholly understand and insisted on a clean one when going out? 'I am okay,' she said, 'a few cuts and a ringing in my ears,' Mandy replied.

'Well answer it then. I can't hear anything,' Jack said, slipping back into his normal dozy twat, self.

Mandy sighed, it was okay, at least he had

put his disgusting handkerchief away and, she reflected on how peaceful retirement had not been and, realised this had been the first case for the DaDa Detective Agency. So she should not be surprised.

TWENTY-SEVEN
THE DUCHESS REVEALED

A LIMP VOICE EMANATED FROM CENTRAL Europe. 'Jack, who the fuck is the Duchess?'

Jack picked up the Kalashnikov, left the sash window and crunched his way across the Mediterranean to Della; everyone ducked. If you did not know that Jack was like a monkey when he held a gun, then your second sense of self preservation would have informed you to take cover. 'Whoa,' Jack exclaimed, surprised as the gun began automatically spitting bullets. Jack fell back with recoiling force and that did it for Nelson and his fleet. It was Pimple, who had become a man in the past few days, in more ways than one, who took the gun from Jack and lobbed it out the enormous gaping hole that was the window and as the gun hit the garden terrace below, so it began spitting more bullets. Cisco, head of armed support, ordered that the whole area be sprayed with return fire.

Pimple pushed Jack back to the deck, having just managed to stand, but conveniently he fell beside northern France and was able to converse with Della, who, worryingly, was regaining a lot of her former inner Valkyrie strength and vim.

He raised himself to a crouch, 'How're you, sweet'art?'

'Cut to bleedin' ribbons you tosspot but otherwise, okay... the Duchess Jack?'

'The baby? Is everything okay,' and Della could see he was genuinely concerned about her more than obvious pregnancy and recalled his daughter Alice had, not so long ago, lost a baby following a dog fight; Della was touched.

'Yes, Jack, thank you. All is fine sprog wise, how's my boatrace?

Jack looked at Della's face, 'Superficial stuff, babes, you'll be back to normal soon, though what Jonas sees in you God only knows,' things were slipping back to normal already.

'You know who the Duchess is don't you?'

Jack nodded and turned as Jimbo and Del Boy entered. Jimbo, an MI5 minder, immediately put plastic cable ties on the wrists of the Duchess, lifting her scrawny frame and depositing her back against the wall. Jack recommended the North Pole and further suggested the pole be shoved up her backside. Jimbo adjusted her position to be alongside the frozen wastes of Greenland and looked down into the cracked face of the old woman. He playfully slapped her cheek, 'Sit tight sweet'art,' Jimbo said and swung an enquiring gaze back to Jack, who was making his way to Father Mike.

Jack nodded to the now knowing, but confused Jimbo.

Jimbo called out, "Clear", for the paramedics.

'What was that?' Della asked.

'What?'

'That look you bozo. You and Jimbo.'

'What look, was it my film star look?' Jack grinned and applied his *Frankenstein's monster* face he erroneously imagined was *Ponce Brosnan*.

Della guffawed, '*Pierce... Brosnan*, you tart.' She winced, but carried on, 'How do you put up with him Mandy? You need a bleedin' medal, girl.'

'I have a Papal blessing and Father Mike promised me a sainthood if I married him,' Mandy answered, recovering her pith and poise, looking heavenward, but only seeing the destroyed two fleets; Nelson looking a tad dead and thus unable to prevent the Hardy, Heavenly bliss. She looked across to Father Mike, who looked like he might be able to put a personal word in with God anytime soon.

'Well you can put that saint-hood over the face of yer man there,' Della said, but noticed the fading priest as paramedics took over and began applying field dressings.

You can tell because they had grass stains on them, field dressings, get it? An amusing aside that. I thought it would ease the nerves you may be feeling after such a frightening episode, in what up until then, had been a jolly cosy book, slightly risqué in places with just a little goshness and, of course, we are worried about father Mike.

After a short while Father Mike was hoisted onto a stretcher and taken away and, through the gaping hole that Jack insisted wasn't that big, they could hear a helicopter landing in the nearby supermarket car park.

'Medivacuum,' Jack said unnecessarily, but amusingly.

Del Boy, head of field ops for MI5, called for order and stood beside the now righted sofa to speak his thoughts, but was bonked on the head with a snooker cue, 'What the fuck?'

Aedd obliged. 'If you want to talk, you have to stand on the volcano.' He gestured with his head and followed up, pointing with the cue to the rug, now cleared of French pastries and thus, relatively dormant, except there was concern that plaster debris and a few French ships of the Line may be congesting the side vents.

Del obliged the weirdo geography teacher and, sidestepping Pimple, who was in the process of being hugged to death by the divine Cecelia and the dearest lovely Georgiana, he made his way to the volcano. Thus positioned and looking incongruous, a shortish fella with blond soppy floppy hair, but with contrasting steely grey eyes, Del stood amongst war torn Europe, his backdrop a shattered Switzerland and pockmarked and battenburged Germany. Even the geological strata of Birmingham had not escaped damage.

'Okay,' Del started off, pleasantly, 'what the Jeffing hell has been happening here?' The pleasantness did not last.

Jack clambered over the centre half and moose, who were still stuck together in a comforting embrace, and he nudged Del off the volcano. He was about to opine and not everyone was looking forward to it, certainly the Duchess looked like she was done up like a kipper, visually, and fragrantly; something was fishy.

'Frankie.' Jack said, his remark directed to a shocked Duchess.

'Frankie?' Della reacted, hoisting herself up and looking like she would take over the volcano any minute and, would have done so, if the professor, in a Brahma of a reprisal, tripped up the delicate sparrow who went on another flying trip, directly into the laps of Mercy and Moose, who seemed not unduly disturbed by the pretty woman's presence.

'Fucking woolly woofter. And you lot from the Isle of feckin' Lesbos,' Della exclaimed.

Pimple broke from Cecelia and Georgie's combined embrace and pointed at the professor, 'You know where the Isle of Lesbos is?' He was looking to grab the cue from Aedd and pass it to the professor, so he could point out the said Isle, but was halted. Everyone had folded into hysterics.

Georgie went to assist Della to stand and afterwards sat on the vacated laps of Mercy and Dame Moose. She duly kissed their already pouting lips and called back to the dumbfounded Pimple. 'Look, The Isle of Lesbos, Pimple my darling.'

Cecelia took Pimple's befuddled head, turned it and whispered into his ear, pleased Georgie had removed all trace of peanut butter, 'I will tell you later, Pimple my love. I think you should come home with me. Georgie may be otherwise engaged tonight and, you will not need to get an absentee slip from your mother, I think,' she whispered, and as she did so, she smoothed the Pimple bottom with a gentle and caressing hand. Pimple was well and truly mollified.

See – simples, makes yer sick doesn't it, and I know many male readers were hoping for some more smashing up of the place, but this is a decorous, if saucy novel, so shut yer trap – there, that should mollify my male readers.

Della tai-kwando'd the professor off her chair, the argument proffered by the bushy academic that it was originally his chair, making no headway, as you would expect and, even if Della was minded to mollify the professor, it likely would have no effect, but if Pimple offered, that would have been a different kettle of fish, who had retired to her sea bed days ago.

TWENTY-EIGHT
THE ISLE OF LESBOS, 5
FRISIAN TUN

THE MÉNAGE A TROIS, OF A MOOSE, HOCKEY centre half (*left half*) and a synchronised swimming instructor, was becoming fever pitch, so much so that Aedd, concerned for the stability and construction of his armchair, interrupted Del Boy's flow to suggest the three women may wish to retire to the Isle of Lesbos downstairs, and he pointed with the cue to the floor, but everyone, even Pimple, knew he was indicating to beneath the waves of the Mediterranean; Atlantis?

Pimple relaxed into the gorgeous arms of the dazzling Cecelia, safe now in the knowledge that the Isle of Lesbos was of course unknown to the Terrafirma cartographical world as it resided below the waves. Everything was explained, Atlantis. He gazed into the eyes of his beloved Cecelia and she nodded, knowingly and, in a mollifying way that Pimple was correct. Cecelia knew you could not rush things, like, educating a man and, in Pimple's case, it would likely be a lifetime's work, but it was a task she was man enough for, she thought to herself and, *et voila*, she felt mollified.

See - self inflicted mollification — I wonder if I should write a dissertation on mollification of the male and subconscious female? Perhaps after I have written Women are astronauts who have been to Venus and men are on another planet, somewhere else and with no spaceship to get off.

Georgie lifted herself up and as the moose and centre half struggled to right themselves from the fractured and now decimated armchair, she went across the map room to Pimple. Smoothing the Pimple fluffy cheek, she whispered in the peanut butterless and as a consequence, floozy vulnerable ear, 'Pimple, darling, I think you are more or less ready.' She looked to Cecelia, who nodded her understanding and agreement.

'Cecelia will take you home with her now if you don't mind, my dearest. I will spend the evening with your mother and Mercy.' She left it at that. Pimple seemed comfortable in the knowledge and even more so in the arms of the blousy gossip columnist, but he grabbed the shoulder of Georgie before she could get out of range.

'Will you ask Mama if I can have a mobile telephone please, dearest, lovely Georgiana?'

Georgie and Cecelia stifled their hysterics tolerably well, enough for Georgie to say, she will try.

'You can borrow my phone from time to time,' Cecelia said and, Pimple was mollified.

Heaven help us. But, what you have to remember is that it is only a day or two since Pimple has had no peanut butter behind his ears and dealt with his virginal sap - one step at a time sweet Jesus; see, heaven may help him, or Cecelia...?

And the triumvirate of women, two hockey players and one swimmer, in a rather excited state, bordering on frenzy, exited the ruins of the cartographical room; Atlantis bound.

Jack suggested everyone retire to Mandy and

his Victorian Villa at number 5 Frisian Tun and, when he had told them the rest of the story, he proposed he would show them all how the poles will eventually look, as they were, "work in progress". He further suggested, if Del Boy and Jimbo could help him get the pole in next door's greenhouse back over to his own garden, he would be most exceedingly obliged.

It seemed not an unreasonable suggestion. Mandy was okay, the paramedics had put some tapes on minor cuts to her face and she was recovering from the shock of it all. Della seemed to have perked up as well. The paramedics suggested a visit to the walk-in centre if she felt the need, which she didn't. After getting Father Mike off to hospital and insisting the bottom department of the professor could maybe do with some attention at casualty as well, eliciting a little excitement in a Greek way from the bushy academic, they all followed Jack, who followed the Trois Ladies.

Pimple was heard to say as they passed the ménage triplets, disappearing into Georgie's Pied-a-Terre and presumably on into the pink and fluffy boudoir, "Ah so, the Isle of Lesbos". At last that was sorted and then he noticed the name of the entrance door, *Sappho-Villa Atlantis*. Now, how come he had not noticed that before? But of course, he had been overly excited and whilst walking gingerly, he had been concentrating on not picking or indeed mincing and now, all he had to do was work out who Sappho was, although he did think he was likely a jazz trumpeter called Louis, or was it Louise?

They crossed the curvilinear and tacitly cosy, though strafed and war torn lane that was Friesian Tun. Passed the secure positions that had been taken up by the Tactical Unit, Jack offering a passing derogatory comment to Cisco, which Cisco ignored as he didn't understand what he'd said as it was Jack's frontier gibberish; definitely slipping back into Twatdom. Then they waited while Jack looked for his front door key and, Mandy and he argued about who was supposed to bring the key, when Jimbo opened the door from inside.

'How'd you get in?' Jack asked. Not an unreasonable question he thought and saw everyone, except Mandy, standing behind Jimbo. Mandy and Jack looked at each other, followed Jimbo's line of sight to number five's own immense Georgian sash window, which stood fully open to anyone who wished to step through. 'I thought you closed that,' Jack said to Mandy.

'You said you were closing it and bringing the key,' Mandy replied.

'Dick,' Jack said, and then he offered, with a

flourishing hand and arm gesture, indicating Mandy may like to step in and, if the head gestures were anything to go by, Jack assumed he had won that one, he even mouthed a score, 'six hundred and one, I think?'

Mandy playfully punched his arm, stepped over the threshold, then stepped over Jack's foot as he tried a retaliatory trip; she knew her dozy husband so well.

By the time Mandy and Jack arrived into the dining room, everyone had found themselves a seat and were sitting, patiently awaiting an explanation of what had just transpired, what had happened in the *Battle of Frisian Tun* and, more importantly, who The Duchess was?

Jack sent Aedd to the kitchen to make monkey tea and some girl grey, thankful the snooker cue had been left behind in the battle zone of the map room. 'And none of this Laplander Sue-Shong or Nancy boy Darlin'-jelly, either,' Jack added and was vocally supported by Della.

Della had just got off the phone to Jonas to report she was seriously wounded and not to worry. Everyone, except for Jack, who was a deaf twat and was at the time focused on avoiding questionable teas, could hear Jonas responding in a panicky concerned way. Della then proceeded to expertly mollify her Gypo man, by saying he was not to worry, she will just need some expert stroking and fondling when she got home for tea and tiffin.

Tea and tiffin is posh English code for serious rumpy pumpy and not a beverage with biscuits – and so, Jonas was mollified – and, he is a rufty-tufty, Gypo type – so you see, no man is immune to feminine mollifying guile.

The lopsided poles and the one half in and half out of the neighbouring greenhouse, could be seen from the dining room window. 'A strikingly Mondrian tableau, for those with an autistic bent,' Jack said when he noticed everyone looking, 'not that I'm Stoke-on-Trent am I sweet'art?' Jack hurriedly added, seeking support from his trouble and strife, not realising he minced as he said it.

'No sweetheart, you are not bent,' Mandy responded, stifling her amusement, 'but I think you made an impression on the professor.'

Jack spluttered, his excuse being that his girl grey tea was hot and therefore blamed Aedd, who should have known Jack has his tea blown on by Mandy before she gave it to him, otherwise she would have to blow on his burnt tongue. Mandy preferred the indignity of blowing Jack's tea, to the alternative, as she now blew on his outstretched tongue. He poured his girl grey into the saucer and drank from that, like the Kings of Ireland used to do, which is why they never dunked their ginger nuts, as saucer tea is generally quite shallow.

Della, supping her monkey tea, relishing the warmth, strength and comforting aspects of a Hobnob biscuit, dunked and soggily transferred to her mouth, just before it collapsed into a heap, suggested Jack start while he waited for his tea to cool. She had no time for the Kings of Ireland, which as you can imagine, upset Aedd inordinately and he bounced Della on her head with the tray. It was a testament to the value of a good cuppa and a dunked Hobnob, that Della only crushed a few of Aedd's bones and fortunately, not his ginger nuts.

Jack passed his tea to Mandy, so she could blow on it and he stood and ponced around the room a couple of times, his tongue hanging out.

You have to do something while you wait for your tea to be cooled by a tea cooling Wallah – it's like in China, where they have peasants who cool the

Chinese green tea for their masters and they are called coolies.

Jack returned to his starting point, mentioned he needed to collect two hundred pounds as he had passed GO and that maybe people could have a whip-round, whilst he told the story of the destruction of Frisian Tun. The exception being his and Mandy's house, of course, which may be a dead giveaway if your bent was in criminal investigation, like you were a bent copper and Jack was not, as we have already surmised, he wasn't even gay, though he did on occasion mince. He was a back room Brainiac spook Wallah, so there you have it and, he may also have retired and formed a new detective agency?

He started which surprised everyone who had fallen asleep while he babbled on expressing his thoughts.

'We learned from Weasel that the Banana Boys had come out from lying low and being on the lamb and were hell bent on revenge against me, although, via Weasel, I did send a message back to say that it was all Mandy's fault,' and Jack folded up in pantomime mirth. Nobody else did as they could see Mandy struggled to be amused by Jack's comments (*wise heads prevailed*). Jack saw also, but knew he could mollify her later with some serious stroking, the majority above liberties position.

'You could never mollify me, you tosspot and, you can consider yourself excused liberties for some time to come,' Mandy said.

Jack was not bothered, because he had not mollified her yet, so of course she would say that now.

'Jack, get on with it, please, and even if you mollified me, you will still be sleeping in the spare room tonight,' Mandy said, responding to Jack's outspoken thoughts.

You see, men cannot do mollifying, and worse, will probably have to talk about things before bedtime.

Jack thought he would only sleep with Mandy tonight if she mollified him now, because he was currently a tad upset. It was unfair of her to listen in on his thoughts; they were privately outspoken. Mandy decided not to even rise to that challenge, she would sleep with him anyway because she loved him and, loved being beside him and knew also, she would have to mollify him later; but that was a piece of cake (*told yer*).

'Jack get on with it, please,' it was Cecelia,

who had a placid, note taking Pimple, beside her; she had already mollified him if you recall.

Jack took up his position and started. 'Is my tea cool yet dearest lovely Elisabeth,' he asked of Mandy, knowing his use of *Pride and Prejudice* mollified his wife.

'Not yet, Wickham,' she answered, knowing this would get her man upset, but what the heck, she would be mollifying him later anyway, so in for a penny, knowing Jack didn't even like being Bingham. He was Darcy or nothing and, if Mandy was any good at guessing, and she was, Jack would want to share a bath this evening and he will sit in with her, wearing his shirt, presuming this act would mollify her and, in truth, it did. It was funny; well it was the first time.

'Jack, start and then we can ask everyone to leave, I fancy a bath.'

Jack was galvanised into mollified action, only worried about what shirt to wear as all of his were clean and usually he liked to wear a dirty one into the bath, or if he dived into a lake, so he did not need to wash it after. Then he giggled to himself, he could wear the one he already had on, it had burn marks, blood and some snot, as he had blown his nose on the tails. Mandy, for some strange reason, did not like him getting his handkerchief out in public. He then resolved to bathe in this shirt and maybe he would put his hankie in the top pocket, being a half decent multitasker.

Mandy looked revolted and everyone looked upon her with sincere sympathy.

TWENTY-NINE

JACK, JANE, DICK, MANDY, DUCK, THE ROCKET LAUNCHER (BAZOOKA)

JACK STARTED AFTER HE HAD ADMONISHED Mandy with a stare; his tea had gone cold. She should not have blown so hard he told her, but let her off, realising she was likely excited at the prospect of a bath with him in his shirt and with his hankie.

'So, we expected the Banana Boys,' he said, starting before Mandy could get back at him and maybe nick his hankie, 'and, we expected them also to come up with a diabolically violent plan to wreak havoc on Mandy and I. When we learned they were to be in town on the 6th June, the seventieth anniversary of Der Day...'

Mandy interrupted, 'D, Jack, it's Dee.'

'It's Dick, Duck, and yes I'd love another cup

of Dee, this one's gone cold. Yer dozy mare, you blew too hard.'

Mandy kept her silence, knowing this would scare him more than any retort she could think of, plus she couldn't think of one. She had deliberately blown hard on his girl grey to make it cold, for a laugh.

'So, despite us having people on the lookout, it turned out to be foggy on the morning of the sixth, a right pea-souper in fact. I could hardly see Mandy's bum in front of my face, could I love?' Mandy nodded, remembering him making that joke on Der Day; appropriately; der.

'Mandy and I went for a walk along the seafront and we cut back across the common, where they had the old World War Two paraphernalia, armour, materiel and that, all laid out and I said at the time to Mandy, what a tin barf if Keef Bananas nicked a tank and, how lucky it was I had asked Jimbo to get a bazooka. I remember Mandy laughing.' Everyone looked at Mandy's face and knew she likely didn't laugh. 'So, what with one thing and another, Mandy got all excited cause I had me hand on 'er Aristotle, obviously, as I couldn't see it and didn't want to lose it, it's one of the bits I like about her, her bum,' he looked at his wife adoringly, 'and her fireman's hose, I really like that, don't I luv?'

Mandy confirmed he did like her nose and

her, Aristotle, bottle and glass, arse, bum and suggested he should get on with it. He did.

'And then, after we got home, Mandy decided to sit on the bazooka with no Alan Whickers on, the daft cow. Course we all laughed,' and Jack looked to Jimbo, who nodded, he had laughed too, 'even Jimbo laughed,' recalling he had looked through the letterbox at the time. 'I had excited Mandy so much, she wanted me in the hallway, naturellament,' Jack said, rolling his head while Mandy blushed, so everyone knew it was true. 'Old Abe thought it was funny as well, when he looked through, didn't he love.'

Della interrupted, 'Abe was there? Mossad, what were they doing here?'

'They keep an eye out for me, and now Mandy, as she doesn't want to leave my side, naturellement.' Jack said and Della picked up on the French.

'Custard there?' she asked, referring to Henri Cousteau...

Jack calls Henri Cousteau, Custard, of French intelligence (which Jack thinks is an oxy thing; I think he means an Oxymoron; not unlike Jack, but he doesn't have the Ox, except in appearance) – don't ask; read Ghost and Ragman Roll.

. . .

... And CIA, Bubba?' Della pressed for more information.

Jack looked as though he considered all of this should have been obvious, which confirmed his opinion Della was learning impaired as well as visually impaired, as she frequently called him an ugly tow rag. He wasn't ugly, Jack erroneously thought, just before the packet of hobnobs hit him full on his ugly face. Despite her perceived visual impairment, he had to concede, Della was a good shot with a packet of biscuits.

'Jack,' Mandy said.

The look on her beautiful face said to Jack that he should get on with it, probably wanted to help washing his shirt and hankie, because if he was honest, the shirt was a bit whiffy in the armpit department, not that women found this unattractive in a man, he erroneously thought, again, which is why Della often called him "a smelly tow rag" as well.

'Well, as it happened, it was just as well we had the bazooka.'

'Rocket launcher,' Jimbo corrected.

'That's what I said diddli,' Jack said, 'so I got the bazooka out of Mandy's backside, cleaned it off with my pants, because my Mum always said,

"Never go out with a dirty Bazooka in case you have an accident", or was that don't go out with dirty underpants? Anyway, I cleaned the bazooka with my pants, before I put them back on.' He looked up, wondering why there were retching noises.

Pimple mentioned to Cecelia, looking up from his note taking that Mater had instilled in him to be most particular about having clean underwear and, cleaning his bits and pieces. Cecelia looked pleased about that and nodded to Jack to resume, he did.

'Then we went outside, just in time to hear an inordinately loud and disturbing rumble and, out of the fog, we saw a Sherman tank nose into view, squeaking and clanking, the turret swinging as though searching out a target. A machine gun began firing at my front door. Fortunately, unlike myself, they were shite shots and the first salvo took out some overhanging trees that always brushed on my head as I walked along, so I was quite pleased about that, wasn't I Mandy?'

Mandy nodded yes and mentioned he had banged on a lot about that afterwards, as well as his apparent heroics with a rocket launcher.

'Bazooka darlin',' Jack said and Mandy cursed sharing the bathwater with her husband as she had caught speaking her thoughts; still at least he had clean shirts and may now go out with a clean handkerchief. 'Anyway, I rolled out of the house, a bit like Arnold Thingybob, you now, when he's in Postman Pat and rolls out from the Greendale Post Office. Well, how was I to know the bazooka had one up the spout?'

Jimbo muttered he had warned him, but Jack was a deaf twat and, on this single occasion, this was his chosen defence. It worked well, except he suggested to Cecelia and her Pimple note taker, they omit it was him who had, inadvertently, fired the bazooka that destroyed the patrician villa. They reassured Jack they would skirt around that point.

Mandy interrupted Dick Schwarzenegger, 'Jimbo, you had better say what happened next as the bazooka had hurt Jack's shoulder, when he accidentally blew up the Duchess's villa, because he missed the rest of the fire fight, crying behind the wall of our garden,' Mandy said. She still had her doubts about his claim it was accidental blowing up the Duchess Villa, knowing how much glee Jack had displayed having arranged for the Duchess's garden to be dug up. She had thought, more than once, that it would be just like Jack to blow up the house deliberately, but then of course, had he aimed at the house he would have missed and likely have hit the tank as he was a notoriously bad shot and, this was his defence and, once again it was accepted; naturellament.

Jimbo chuckled and missed his opportunity to speak.

'I didn't hide,' Jack said indignantly, 'I fell over into the big bushes and some of the thorns hurt me and, that is why I cried,' he looked quite smug. Jack could not understand why people laughed.

If you can comprehend Jack considered it manlier to cry because of a few scratches from a thorn bush than the recoil from a bazooka, then you have your answer, and a better picture of Jack, Jane, Dick, Austin you could never have.

Jimbo asserted himself, still amused, but he had known Jack for a very long time and knew also there were many reasons why he was a back room Wallah, a cry baby being just one of them. 'I took the rocket launcher from Jack,' he paused to dare Jack to call it a bazooka, he did, and Jimbo carried on, (*told you he knew Jack*) 'I re-loaded, fired at the Sherman and disabled it. The lid flew open and belched smoke and Bananas, as the gang piled out coughing and firing whereupon Abe and Bubba were able to despatch them quite easily. I rushed after Keef who was making his way to Waitrose...'Jimbo paused again, while Jack said the gangster was going to get some milk, '... and then I tripped on some debris, the tank machine gun recommenced firing and Bubba was hit, thankfully not too bad and, by then Jack had reloaded the rocket launcher...'

'Bazooka.'

'... thank you, Jack, and he fired and this time, missed the tank and hit Keef and, parts of this particular Banana were distributed all over Frisian Tun. It was just after that the tank exploded, shrapnel scattering everywhere, causing the principle damage you see now...' and he waved his hands like a prima-donna MI5 man setting out telegraph poles in a back garden, '... to the surrounding houses, with the exception of Jack blowing up number 13...' he looked at Jack, '... accidentally,' Jimbo finished off.

'So you can see why the Duchess would seek revenge. Jack not only arranged for her precious garden to be dug up, he blew-up her house and then blew-up her favourite nephew.

THIRTY

THE END BIT WHERE ALL IS BRILLIANTLY REVEALED

THERE WAS QUIET AROUND THE TABLE, JUST the sound of Jack slurping cold girl grey and going Yuck. It had been a short telling to the tale, but it was potent, as was the resultant destruction of a middle class decorous idyll.

'Why would the Duchess act that way?' Pimple asked.

'Because it is her way,' Jack said, 'it's the way she grew up, fighting the law with as much violence as possible and accumulating wealth and power, in a local gangster way. She was, the scourge of South London, one Frankie White.'

Jimbo filled in some detail, 'Frankie White was a notorious gangster who disappeared in the early nineties. *He* was presumed to have been killed by rivals and the body made to disappear. Nobody much cared, the streets were well rid.'

Pimple recalled the name, he had a mind for vintage news, 'Was not Frankie White also known as Mad Axe Frankie and, he was a man, not a woman. Are you saying...?'

Jack nodded, 'Yes Pimple, my old son, well remembered. We need to interrogate the Duchess, but I am convinced she is a man and, she is Frankie White. I have sent a massage up the line and we should have feedback any time, not all the salient facts, but I think we can interpret those pretty accurately. I also think a lot of the bodies we found in the garden and the gangster who was dumped when Mandy was kidnapped, all died at the hands of Frankie White after the Duchess had had her, his, way with them. She, he, could not afford the truth of his identity, even that she was a man, to leak out.'

Pimple prodded, growing in stature as a reporter. 'He, she, married Lord Teapot. We know he was reported to have been gay and later presumed to have left with an old school friend, but nobody knows where?' Are we likely to find that one of the bodies in the garden is Lord Teapot?'

'This has already been established,' Jack said. 'We presume he outgrew his usefulness. It was well known that high profile London gangsters attended early days London gay clubs, never official, but they existed and were known. We are still researching, but my guess is that it was at one of these clubs, Frankie White met Lord Teapot. Some MP's and Lords were famed for their dalliances and often cherished the excitement of mixing with known gangsters. I am pretty sure we will see that this was the case. I think also, we will find out that Lord Teapot was not the font of the wealth and the disappearing act of Mad Axe Frankie White, suited both Lord Teapot, as he needed money and, Frankie, who needed to disappear and have a method for laundering his ill gotten gains. All in all, it was quite a plan and would have worked if not for her / he, eejit behaviour, and the love of Frankie for her, his, nephew, Keef Bananas, one Keith White. Familial ties run deep in the old London gang families and the regular appearance of Keef in posh turnip Southsea should have sounded a clarion, but it didn't.'

'Did the Duchess have any involvement in all of the troubles down here and, was she involved in the conspiracy that you were able to unearth?' Pimple probed further and further impressed Cecelia who was taking notes for him now; a true partnership forming.

'No, we don't believe she was involved, other than she was duped and used by either Beth or

Brian Mayhew, who in their turn, used Archie Pointe-Lace and, of course Len (read *Merde and Mandarins*). They likely knew the Duchess's identity and the Bananas were a good and ready source of muscle.'

Pimple was about to enquire further, when Cecelia stayed him with a hand on his wrist. 'We will be getting all of the information from Jack...'

'Dick,' Jack interjected.

'Shut it, Dick,' Cecelia said, and carried on talking to Pimple. 'We will then write the whole article together, linking in the story of Ghost and the Mandarins and it will blow the sides out of the Establishment.'

Mandy looked worried. 'I'm not sure about this. It has Jack Austin shite written all over it,' and Jimbo laughed energetically. 'What Jimbo?'

'It is what is needed Mandy and, if Cecelia and Pimple are brave enough to take this on and, we believe the paper will print it because we have already leaned on Sir Wendy, then it needs to be done. It is what Del Boy and more importantly, Samuels (head of the MI5 branch), wants.' He looked at Cecelia and Pimple, 'The Home office, apart from Amlodd Jones, is not aware by the way. So keep it close to your chest. The responses from the Home Office can come after publication. When this breaks it needs to be nuclear, to have the desired effect. It cannot be diluted or hushed up and, you will have protection.'

'Protection?' Pimple asked with the hint of a returning stutter. Had he been walking, he most certainly would have picked, maybe even minced gingerly.

'Yes,' Jimbo said. 'MI5, and possibly a little help from Mossad, CIA and the French,' and he chuckled some more, then answered his phone, listened. 'Jack, they have confirmed the identity of the Duchess as Frankie White.' There was silence around the room, except for Jimbo, who strolled off, still talking on the phone, a muffled conversation.

'What happens now?' Cecelia asked.

Jack answered, 'You and Pimple stay with us and, over the next few days, we will debrief with you. You will have your story. You will write it here and when it is complete, you can file it electronically to your paper and we will arrange for syndication, in the event Sir Wendy shites himself, or gets nobbled. Okay?'

Cecelia appeared excited, Pimple worried.

'What's your problem Pimple?' Mandy asked. 'It will work out alright, you will see,' she noticeably had her fingers crossed.

'I am sure it will Mandy, but where will I sleep? And, I haven't got any pyjamas.'

Cecelia smiled. 'You will sleep with me

Pimple and you won't need your pyjamas.' She kissed him. Pimple coloured, whether with embarrassment or excitement, it was hard to tell.

'Someone will collect your things,' Jack said, 'and you will be comfortable.'

THE END...

Dear Reader

Thank you for reading, Road Kill – The Duchess of Frisian Tun. Word of mouth is an author's best friend and is much appreciated. If you enjoyed this book or any other of Pete Adams, books, please consider supporting this author:

- Leave a book review on Amazon, Goodreads, BookBub or any other site you follow, to help market and promote this book.
- Tell your friends, family, and colleagues all about this author and his books.
- Share brief posts on your social media platforms and tag the book #RoadKill or #DaDaDeteciveAgency or author, #PeteAdams on Twitter, Facebook, Instagram, Pinterest, Youtube, linked-in and snapchat.
- Suggest the book for book clubs, to bookstores or to ant libraries you know.

Thank you, but... the story moves on in Book 2 of the DaDa Detective Agency series:

Rite Judgement – *Heads Roll - Corpses dance*

*Jack and Amanda Austin, reveal themselves in their private eye colours,
and 1950's fashion of Ooh La Lovelies - the DaDa Detective Agency.
Cecilia and Pimple publish their story and it swamps the world, the Establishment is rocked, the people now awake.
This is a tale, where the DNA of the real and surreal, loop in a spiral of dissembling, as the Establishment crumbles at the threat of an Insurrection of Biblical proportions.
Rite Judgement, sees the Pope, the Archbishop of Canterbury, and the Grand Numpty of Cairo, team up with MI5, VI6 and the DaDa Detective Agency, to take on the might of the Corporate and Religious world; The Illusionati, The Religious orders, and,*

The dastardly, roller skating, Holy Barbaras...

...and in the chaos, a discordant Nightingale sings in Berkeley Square.

A surreal novel where life imitates art in the *Rite of Spring* - A Religious crime mystery thriller, with classical dance, beautiful hair, death and resurrection...*and, the Illussionati*

"Makes the *Da Vinci Code* look like a pin number for an Italian painter and decorator." Pete the painter

To read the first chapter for free, please head to: https://www.nextchapter.pub/books/rite-judgement

Lightning Source UK Ltd.
Milton Keynes UK
UKHW041931200121
377415UK00001B/92